ARI...
TRAVEL

GW00362999

ARIZONA

TRAVEL  SMART®

Tamara Hawkinson

John Muir Publications
Santa Fe, New Mexico

John Muir Publications, P.O. Box 613, Santa Fe, New Mexico 87504

Printed in the United States of America.
First edition. First printing August 1999.

ISSN 1524-0150
ISBN 1-56261-367-7

Editors: Peg Goldstein, Heidi Utz
Graphics Editor: Bunny Wong
Production: Janine Lehmann
Design: Marie J. T. Vigil
Cover design: Janine Lehmann
Typesetting: Melissa Tandysh
Map style development: American Custom Maps—Jemez Springs, New Mexico
Map illustration: Kathy Sparkes
Printing: Publishers Press
Front cover photos: *small*—© Leo de Wys, Inc./William P. Kraus (San Xavier del Bac Mission, Tucson)
                    large—© Photo Network/Henryk T. Kaiser (Canyon de Chelly, Spider Rock)
Back cover photo: © Lake Havasu Tourism Bureau (Lake Havasu)

Distributed to the book trade by
Publishers Group West
Berkeley, California

While every effort has been made to provide accurate, up-to-date information, the author and publisher accept no responsibility for loss, injury, or inconvenience sustained by any person using this book.

ARIZONA TRAVEL·SMART: A GUIDE THAT GUIDES

Most guidebooks are primarily directories, providing information but very little help in making choices—you have to guess how to make the most of your time and money. *Arizona Travel•Smart* is different: By highlighting the very best of the state and offering various planning features, it acts like a personal tour guide rather than a directory.

TAKE THE STRESS OUT OF TRAVEL

Sometimes traveling causes more stress than it relieves. Sorting through information, figuring out the best routes, determining what to see and where to eat and stay, scheduling each day—all of this can make a vacation feel daunting rather than fun. Relax. We've done a lot of the legwork for you. This book will help you plan a trip that suits *you*—whatever your time frame, budget, and interests.

SEE THE BEST OF THE STATE

Author Tamara Hawkinson has lived in Arizona for almost 10 years. She has hand-picked every listing in this book, and she gives you an insider's perspective on what makes each one worthwhile. So while you will find many of the big tourist attractions listed here, you'll also find lots of smaller, lesser known treasures, such as the London Bridge in Lake Havasu City or the Boot Hill Graveyard in Tombstone. And each sight is described so you'll know what's most—and sometimes least—interesting about it.

In selecting the restaurants and accommodations for this book, the author sought out unusual spots with local flavor. While in some areas of the state chains are unavoidable, wherever possible the author directs you to one-of-a-kind places. We also know that you want a range of options: One day you may crave southwestern cuisine while the next day you would be just as happy (as would your wallet) with a bowl of chili. Most of the restaurants and accommodations listed here are moderately priced, but the author also includes budget and splurge options, depending on the destination.

CREATE THE TRIP YOU WANT

We all have different travel styles. Some people like spontaneous weekend jaunts, while others plan longer, more leisurely trips. You may want to cover as much ground as possible, no matter how much time you have. Or maybe you prefer to focus your trip on one part of the state or on some special interest, such as history, nature, or art. We've taken these differences into account.

Though the individual chapters stand on their own, they are organized in a geographically logical sequence, so that you could conceivably fly into Phoenix, drive chapter by chapter to each destination in the book, and end up close to where you started. Of course, you don't have to follow that sequence, but it's there if you want a complete picture of the state.

Each destination chapter offers ways of prioritizing when time is limited: In the Perfect Day section, the author suggests what to do if you have only one day to spend in the area. Also, every Sightseeing Highlight is rated, from one to four stars: ★★★★—or "must see"—sights first, followed by ★★★ sights, then ★★ sights, and finally ★ or "see if you have time"—sights. At the end of each sight listing is a time recommendation in parentheses. User-friendly maps help you locate the sights, restaurants, and lodging of your choice.

And if you're in it for the ride, so to speak, you'll want to check out the Scenic Routes described at the ends of several chapters. They take you through some of the most scenic parts of the state.

In addition to these special features, the appendix has other useful travel tools:

- The Planning Map and Mileage Chart help you determine your own route and calculate travel time.
- The Special Interest Tours show you how to design your trip around any of eight favorite interests.
- The Calendar of Events provides an at-a-glance view of when and where major events occur throughout the state.
- The Resource Guide tells you where to go for more information about national and state parks, individual cities and counties, local bed-and-breakfasts, and more.

HAPPY TRAVELS

With this book, you have many reliable recommendations and travel tools at your fingertips. Use it to make the most of your trip. And have a great time!

WHY VISIT ARIZONA?

From the awe-inspiring Grand Canyon to the Red Rocks of Sedona, from America's largest grove of towering ponderosa pines to the saguaro cactus in the high Sonoran desert, Arizona offers a myriad of unforgettable scenery. From the prehistoric cliff dwellings of a lost civilization to the spas and golf courses of the nation's finest resorts, the Grand Canyon State is a land of visual and cultural contrasts. Experience the Old West in the raucous town of Tombstone or explore the art galleries in sophisticated Scottsdale. History buffs can trace the routes of the old Spanish conquistadors or visit the site of Arizona's only Civil War battle. And rockhounds will find plenty of books on lost gold mines, complete with maps. Visits to the Hopi and Navajo Reservations offer a glimpse of ancient life and culture. The diversity of Arizona's climate makes traveling the state a year-round opportunity. During the winter, you can snow ski in Flagstaff and, within a couple hours, bask beneath the warm glow of the Phoenix sun. And in summer, enjoy the cool mountainous regions for plenty of hiking, camping, rodeos, and art festivals.

LAY OF THE LAND

You undoubtedly know Arizona as "The Grand Canyon State." Considered one of the seven natural wonders of the world, the canyon draws millions of worldwide travelers to its breathtaking edges each year. But you may not realize that Arizona is also home to the largest contiguous ponderosa pine forest in the United States or that it is the only state in which North America's four deserts converge. The unique red rocks of Sedona and the stunning monolith spires of Navajo country have been photographed thousands of times and have served as backdrops for countless Westerns. Because of its constantly changing terrain, Arizona's colorful canyons, blistering deserts, and more than 200 mountain ranges constantly beckon you to drive around that next curve or hike toward that next peak.

This geologic wonderland is comprised of three regions: the Basin and Range Deserts of southern and western Arizona; the mountainous Central Highlands; and the Colorado Plateau, located in the northern region of the state. Humphreys Peak, north of Flagstaff, towers over the state at 12,670 feet above sea level, but by the time you've journeyed to the state's far southwestern corner where the Colorado River flows into Mexico, the elevation has dropped to a mere 70 feet.

At the top of the state, the Colorado Plateau, a giant uplifted landmass towering 4,000 to 9,000 feet above sea level, is dotted with volcanic craters, deep gorges, and twisted canyons. More than 2 billion years of erosion and explosions have created miles of haunting vistas with layers of subtle horizontal hues forming this vast, sometimes lonely land.

The Central Highlands to the south almost bisects the state with its strings of valleys and basins cut through the crumpled, rugged mountain ranges. This area receives the most rainfall, and streams and small lakes abound. Piñon and juniper forests are found here, along with stands of ponderosa pine and Douglas fir.

In Arizona's southern half the sun-baked desert alternates with mountain ranges of smoothly domed summits and precariously perched granite boulders. Thrusting up thousands of vertical feet from the Sonoran and Chihuahua Desert floors, "sky islands" provide unique protective habitats for flora and fauna.

Within Arizona's 113,956 square miles you'll find an extraordinary mix of terrain. From the purple mountains, painted deserts, and red rocks, to the sheer cliffs, windswept mesas, and rambling rivers, the state's ecological and geological diversity continues to lure adventurers back time and again.

FLORA AND FAUNA

Because Arizona's elevation spans over 12,000 feet, it is divided into six life zones, which are inhabited by hundreds of plant and animal varieties.

The Lower Sonoran Zone, covering about one-third of the state, is Arizona's famed desert country. It hosts the stately saguaro, which towers up to 50 feet, can weigh 12 tons, and has a lifespan of 200 years. Young saguaros often mature under the shade of the smooth, green Palo Verde, Arizona's state tree. Other desert shrubs and trees include the spindly ocotillo, creosote, and the aromatic mesquite.

Prickly-pear, cholla, and organ-pipe cacti flourish here. Each variety sports its own distinctive flower and fruit, ranging from pure white to the brightest pink, deepest purple, and brilliant yellow, many blooming continuously throughout spring and summer. The white, funnel-shaped blossoms of the saguaro, designated as the state flower, unfold in May or June, attracting long-nosed bats and white-winged doves migrating from Mexico. Scooting along the desert floor are snakes, scorpions, and the rare Gila monster. Wildlife includes coyotes, javelina, and bighorn sheep. In addition, more than 400 bird varieties, including 15 species of hummingbird, make southeastern Arizona one of the country's most popular birding destinations.

You may be surprised to learn that the towering palm trees that define Phoenix are not native. In fact, many desert communities are starting to ban their use, along with the overuse of grass and other nonnative materials in landscaping.

The Upper Sonoran Zone in central Arizona climbs up to 6,000 feet. While much of the vegetation is the same as in lower altitudes, you may spot deer or black bear. Be cautious—this is rattlesnake country.

The Transition Zone is the mountainous area in which you will see ponderosa pine along with oak, juniper, and fir. Black bears, deer, elk, and mountain lions roam the woods, while fish abound in fresh streams and lakes.

The Douglas fir dominates the cool, wet forests of the Canadian Zone, ranging up to 9,000 feet. Here blue spruce are interspersed with groves of aspen, which blaze yellow and orange during the early fall, while fern and wildflowers blanket the lush mountain meadows.

The Hudsonian Zone occurs only atop Arizona's highest mountains, where blue spruce and bristlecone pine battle the snow, strong winds, and an unusually short growing period. And at 11,500 feet is the Alpine Zone, found only on the San Francisco Peaks north of Flagstaff, where snow can blast the mountain slope even in midsummer. Its hardy denizens encompass 80 plant species, many found in the North American Arctic, including a variety of groundsel and buttercup.

The Nature Conservancy has been active in acquiring pristine ecological lands, and numerous plant and animal preserves are found throughout the state.

HISTORY

Arizona's history is a colorful patchwork of cultures and lifestyles etched over thousands of years. By A.D. 500, the mysterious Anasazi (Ancient Ones) flourished in spectacular cliff dwellings perched along the 1,000-foot sheer rock walls of Canyon de Chelly, along the northern plateaus. Two other prehistoric Indian tribes inhabited the state: the Hohokam, in the low southern deserts, and the Mogollon, in the central mountains. The ruins and relics left by these extinct peoples attest to their high degree of sophistication in dry farming, water management, and astronomy. Their far-flung trade routes indicate the extent of their jewelry, pottery, and textile marketing.

There has never been a single "Indian culture" in the Southwest. By the time of Coronado's first expedition into this territory in 1540, there were 15 different firmly established Native American tribes using 18 distinct languages. The exact reason for the disappearance of these groups is still controversial.

Arizona became a province of Spain in 1542 and remained so until the early 1800s. But by 1853, the United States had taken over all of the land that today defines the state. During the Civil War, Confederates found their way west and one brief skirmish did occur, but after Southern troops retreated the Union regained control over the territory.

While some Native American tribes lived peacefully with the Spanish and, later, the Americans, many fought the destruction of their lands and their lifestyle, as mountain men and prospectors edged west in greater numbers.

In the 1860s, Kit Carson was sent after the warring Navajo, trapping them in wintertime in their own Canyon de Chelly, then slaughtering their sheep and cutting down their 200-year-old peach groves. To the south, the intense hatred between the Apache and the Mexicans spilled into combat with the newly arrived Americans. Mexicans offered bounties on Apache scalps—including children—and American citizens were responsible for more than one massacre. Legendary Apaches Cochise and Geronimo retaliated with continuous outbursts of murder and torture.

During this barrage of Indian warfare, the Wild West kicked into high gear, with Tombstone and other mining boomtowns luring cowboys, gunfighters, and prostitutes. Major gold and silver strikes created millionaires overnight, but a more common story was one of destitution and hard living. As the railroad cut into the territory, Geronimo realized the old ways were gone and he surrendered, ending the Indian Wars in 1886. The gunfight at the O.K. Corral had occurred five years earlier, and the Earps had already moved on. By the late 1880s, the Old West had become modernized. In 1912 Arizona was granted statehood—the last state in the continental United States.

But the Old West has a grip on Arizona, and even today it continues to fascinate Americans and especially visitors from abroad. In fact, much of Tombstone's economy revolves around reliving that relatively short period in history. And while the cowboy remains a beloved American hero, his job, in reality, meant low pay, long hours, and horrendous work conditions. Nevertheless, rodeos, dude ranches, shoot-outs, and cowboy steakhouses have become staples of Arizona culture.

Although the Spanish influence is evident throughout the state, it's most obvious in Tucson and its architecture, foods, and celebrations. Other cultures that have helped shape the area include Asian Americans, who first came to Arizona in the 1880s to work on the railroads, and African Americans, who served as Buffalo Soldiers around the same time.

THE ARTS

Arizona is famous for the fine arts and crafts created by its varied Native American tribes. The Navajo are known for the color and detail of their handwoven rugs; the Hopi are known for their elaborately carved kachinas. Baskets from Apache and Tohono O'odham artists and pottery from various tribes are prized collectibles. Native American jewelry is similarly diverse. The silver overlay style of the Hopi contrasts with the large turquoise nuggets often found in Navajo work and with the fine inlay and small stones favored by Zuni silversmiths.

Cheap overseas imitations have recently flooded the market so it's important to deal only with reputable retail stores and galleries. Look for the artist's "hallmark" or signature and ask for his/her biography. The Heard Museum in Phoenix, the Museum of Northern Arizona in Flagstaff, and the Amerind Museum east of Tucson house extensive Native American collections, and their stores offer fine examples of authentic arts and crafts.

Searching for a fine-art souvenir? Scottsdale is the place, with more galleries than anywhere else in the state. Every Thursday evening its Old Town galleries host the popular Artwalk, which many of the artists often attend. Sedona, another popular art destination, attracts world-famous musicians for its "Jazz on the Rocks" festival each September, while the prestigious Cowboy Artists of America convene at the Phoenix Art Museum for their national show every October. The old ghost town of Jerome and the original Spanish presidio of Tubac are thriving artist colonies, holding festivals throughout the year.

Arizona's rich heritage is evident in the diverse collections housed in local museums. History buffs can check out the Yuma Territorial Prison or the Pioneer Arizona Living History Museum. Rockhounds will be awed at the Arizona Mining and Mineral Museum in Phoenix, where over three thousand minerals are on exhibit. The Desert Botanical Museum and Boyce Thompson Arboretum showcase the state's colorful plantlife, and the Raven Site Ruin and Casa Malpais Pueblo offer hands-on archaeological experiences. Kids love the Arizona Science Museum and the Tucson Children's Museum. And Taliesin West, the winter studio of famed architect Frank Lloyd Wright, is a treat for anyone interested in architecture and design.

Because of Arizona's varied climates, special events occur year round, including cowboy-poetry gatherings, fiddlin' contests, rodeos, Indian markets, wine-tasting, chile cookoffs, and birding festivals. From the Tucson Gem and Mineral show to the Grand Canyon's Music Festival, Arizona has a lot to offer.

CUISINE

Mexican food is definitely an Arizona favorite, although it is different than the heavy Tex-Mex version found in Texas and the Midwest. "Sonoran style" Mexican food is lighter, emphasizing green chile sauces instead of red, although both are usually on the menu. And you're more likely to find shredded beef or pork in your enchilada than ground hamburger.

In keeping with the Mexican tradition of giving tamales during the Christmas season, some of the best Mexican restaurants are besieged with big orders, shipping tamales around the world at that time. Restaurants prepare several varieties, including green corn tamales, a real treat. Always look for a recommended family-owned restaurant instead of one of the "Mexican chains" to get a true taste of Sonoran-style fare.

Cowboy cuisine is another popular choice. Mesquite-flavored steaks and chicken cooked over large outdoor grills, along with cowboy beans and all the fixin's, are often served "family style" on sawdust-covered floors. Deep-fried rattlesnake is a fun appetizer and, although the buffalo is not native to Arizona, buffalo burgers are included on many menus.

"New Age" Sedona and the college town of Flagstaff offer excellent health-food restaurants, while Wickenburg, named after its German founder, Henry Wickenburg, has seen a resurgence in authentic German foods. The Chinese, who came to build the railroads in the 1880s, introduced a variety of Oriental foods that have remained popular.

Both Tucson and the Phoenix area have hundreds of restaurants serving virtually every cuisine imaginable and, because of the high number of resorts, the selection of world-class cuisine is overwhelming. About 15 years ago, a local French chef began combining Southwestern ingredients with classical French cookery, starting what is commonly referred to as Southwest Cuisine. While many local chefs have refined their own styles, don't be mistaken: This is not just fancy Mexican food. Don't be afraid to ask if you're not sure about a particular dish.

Finally, if you're dining out in Arizona, it's important to understand a little about the famous chile. Chiles come in a wide variety, and they all pack different amounts of heat. The Anaheim has a mild, flavorful taste, while the jalapeño can set your mouth ablaze. But beware, the *habañero* is 120 times hotter than the jalapeño—it can send even the toughest cowboy under the table.

OUTDOOR ACTIVITIES

The majority of Arizona's land is either National Forest or part of the vast National State Park or Arizona State Parks system, meaning almost unlimited opportunities for outdoor experiences. With more than 200 mountain ranges and numerous picturesque canyons throughout the state, hiking is a popular sport. The Forest Service and the state and national parks provide good hiking maps noting the length and difficulty of each trail. Probably the most famous hike in Arizona is the trek down to the floor of the Grand Canyon. Some folks train for months and book their hike more than a year in advance, while others are content to take a burro ride down the rocky trail and are thankful to have something to ride on the way back up.

Even in the middle of Phoenix, you can climb Camelback Mountain for a fabulous view of the Valley. Phoenix Mountain Preserve and South Mountain Park, both within the city limits, offer hiking, picnicking, and horseback riding. Jeep tours provide backroad experiences and are a popular way to check out the desert or the red rocks area of Sedona.

Watersports abound, from a thrilling white-water raft ride down the turbulent Colorado River to a milder tubing experience along the Salt River. Lake Powell and Lake Havasu provide plenty of space for ski boats and Jet Skis. If you're looking to relax, renting a houseboat on either lake is a good move. Other large lakes dot the state, offering camping, fishing, and boating. And the cool mountain streams are stocked with plenty of trout.

Because of the vast amount of public lands, campsites are plentiful, although they vary in amenities. Some are nothing more than a fire ring and a small cleared area, while a new campground near Lake Roosevelt boasts the largest solar facilities in the nation, including large bathroom and shower facilities and extensive children's play areas.

You can ski at the Snow Bowl just north of Flagstaff, the Sunrise Ski Resort on the White Mountain Apache Reservation, and Mount Lemmon, just outside of Tucson. Southern Arizona is a birder's paradise, with nature preserves and bird sanctuaries hosting more than 450 species. And dude ranches throughout the state offer a variety of packages, from basic horseback riding to the *City Slicker* experience of a real cattle roundup.

Arizona is also a favorite golf destination, with dozens and dozens of courses. In the Phoenix area alone are more than 40 world-class golf courses, while Tucson and Sedona also contain nationally recognized courses.

PLANNING YOUR TRIP

Arizona offers a multitude of travel experiences, so whether you're going for a glimpse of the Wild West, to soak up some rays at a resort pool, or to peer over the edge of the world's greatest canyon, here are some tips you should know.

Desert summers are blazing hot, but you can still have fun if you respect the heat. Carry water with you everywhere—and drink it. If you're taking a road trip, the rule of thumb is to pack a gallon of water per person per day. Staying hydrated will help you avoid heat exhaustion—and unfortunately, diet soda or beer doesn't count. Schedule your summer tours for morning or evening and never, never, never leave children or animals in a parked car, since fatal heatstroke can occur within a very short time.

Late summer brings monsoons, which can develop into flash floods that will wash away anything in their path, including cars and campsites. During a monsoon, do not try to ford a flooded road unless you can see the bottom. Monsoons also bring fabulous lightning storms that sometimes cause hundreds of ground strikes. Better to end your golf game early than be caught under a tree during a lightning storm. At other times, dust storms can block driving visibility, but since they are usually short-lived it's best to pull off the road and wait until you can see.

Don't wear open-toed shoes if you're exploring the desert. It might take pliers to remove some wicked cactus barbs from your toes. And remember

WHAT TIME IS IT?

Arizona does not observe Daylight Saving Time. However, the Navajo Reservation, within the Arizona borders, does observe Daylight Saving Time, while the Hopi Reservation, within the borders of the Navajo Reservation, does not. Got that?

that digging up cactus is against the law. If you happen upon Indian pottery shards, petroglyphs, or any other antiquities, you may study and photograph them, but leave them where they are. That's also the law.

And finally, whether you're exploring the desert or a mountain wilderness, always apprise another person of your plans.

HOW MUCH WILL IT COST?

Arizona vacations can come with a number of different price tags, depending on your travel time and destination. If you're looking to escape the winter blahs by heading to sunny Phoenix or Tucson between January and May, be prepared for the highest-season rates. Expect to pay $75 to $125 per night for a basic chain motel, although you can find them for less.

Especially in Phoenix, prices plummet from mid-June to September, when a $300 resort room could drop to $125 per night. Many world-class hotels offer summer family packages as well as golf/spa packages for couples, and during the hot months, look for chain and suite motels to hover from $50 to $75 per night or less.

While basic restaurant prices don't change during summer, many do offer summer specials, including early-bird dinners. Three- and four-course meals can sometimes cost less than $20 per person if ordered before 6 p.m. Again, so many restaurants are available in the large metropolitan areas that most any budget can be satisfied. However, if you're planning to dine at a world-renowned restaurant, you could easily spend up to $50 per person. If you'd like the experience without the higher price, consider a long afternoon lunch.

Other areas of the state are exactly the opposite when it comes to the off season. The Grand Canyon, for example, can be cold and snowy during the winter, so accommodations are higher during the summer. However, the towns leading to the Grand Canyon offer good motels from $35 to $75 per night, often including a continental breakfast. A room within the Grand Canyon Park itself runs from $100 to $200 per night, but campgrounds are also available.

Sedona and Oak Creek Canyon, as well as the White Mountains to the east, are other popular summer getaways. Campsites are plentiful at $10 to $20 per day but are often filled by midday Friday, so plan ahead. Phoenicians stream out of the summer heat on weekends, so favorite campgrounds are packed. Mountain-town accommodations range from $40 to over $100 per night, with streamside cabins from $75 to $100. Sedona is filled with high-end resorts as well as wonderful bed-and-breakfasts. An average motel is about $75, and resorts can soar to over $300 per night.

Guest ranches are popular destinations and, while their prices seem high at first ($150 to $300-plus per person), they are generally based on the American plan, including all amenities and three meals per day.

Since many popular Arizona activities, such as hiking and sightseeing, are so inexpensive, with a little planning even the tightest budget can be met.

WHEN TO GO

By late October, "snowbirds" are streaming into Arizona's desert communities, headed to their winter home or favorite RV park. "Snowbird" is the popular term for the retired folks that annually flee the cold of their hometowns, making the population noticeably increase, especially in the smaller areas. The winter months are glorious in central and southern Arizona, with the average high generally approaching 78. It rarely freezes and, with more than 300 days of sunshine a year, most days are clear with deep blue, cloudless skies. Nights are mild, meaning that outside dining is still popular on restaurant patios equipped with heat lamps.

The intense summer heat has subsided by the end of October, and the mercury won't head back up until mid-April. It's a wonderful time to be outdoors hiking, shopping, sightseeing—maybe even taking a dip in a heated pool. Even if a day tops out around 90 degrees, because there is virtually no humidity, the slightest breeze after hopping out of the pool will send shivers down your spine.

Not surprisingly, winter sees the greatest crowds, and hotel prices rise accordingly. Another attraction is that lots of events are scheduled. Tempe hosts the Fiesta Bowl football game each New Year's Day, including the nationally televised parade on December 31. Both the Phoenix Open Golf Tournament and the Barrett-Jackson Auction, the world's largest classic and collectors' car auction, are held each January, luring almost a half-million people to Scottsdale.

In mid-February, Tucson hosts the Gem & Mineral Show, the world's largest gem and rock show. A week later the Scottsdale Arabian Horse Show opens, bringing more than 1,700 of the finest Arabians from all over the globe.

During winter, Arizona's three ski slopes are usually buzzing, but occasionally the snow can be light, so always call ahead. And if you just want a visual experience at the Grand Canyon and don't plan on much hiking, the uncrowded winter months can be perfect—but be sure to check conditions first. Average winter daytime temperatures range in the 40s or 50s, but can plunge to way below freezing at night.

The Grand Canyon is Arizona's greatest tourist destination and is packed during the entire summer. If you want to stay in the park, make reservations a year in advance. If possible, visit during the week.

Summer festivals are held all over Arizona. You can attend two of the nation's oldest rodeos—during the first week in July in Prescott or the third weekend of August in Payson. Avid birders flock to Sierra Vista, the hummingbird capital of the United States, for the Southwest Wings Birding Festival in mid-August. A month-long music festival draws international guests during Flagstaff's Festival of the Arts in July and August.

Dress in Arizona is casual year-round. Men rarely wear ties, and light, comfortable clothing is definitely the style. Winter evenings in the desert will require a sweater or light jacket, although you'll need to dress much warmer for the higher elevations. Bring lots of sunscreen and wear a hat.

ORIENTATION AND TRANSPORTATION

Of the two major airports that serve Arizona, the largest and most accessible is the Phoenix Sky Harbor International Airport. If you're staying in Phoenix or heading north, this is the airport to use. Most airlines fly into Sky Harbor, including price-conscious Southwest Airlines. If southern Arizona or Tucson is your destination, fly directly into Tucson International Airport. Short flights out of Phoenix are available to other Arizona towns, though they can be pricey.

Amtrak makes a limited sweep across the state, stopping in Tucson and Flagstaff. While this isn't the best arrangement for statewide sightseeing, if you enjoy the leisure of train travel, it will get you to a city where you can rent a car and explore further. Greyhound also serves the major towns, but you'll need a car once you're there.

Mass transit is not very developed in Arizona, so even if you're in Phoenix or Tucson, it can be a challenge getting around. Having a car is really the only way to see the great Arizona sights.

Purchasing Native American Arts and Crafts

Many visitors want to purchase Native American arts and crafts during their visit to Arizona. You'll find shops, galleries, and individual artists with items for sale throughout the state. Please beware: A lot of merchandise out there is fake, so be armed with a few facts.

The Hopi are known for their colorful kachinas, which are brightly painted wood carvings. Each design has important religious significance. A quality kachina can cost several hundred dollars, especially if made by a well-known carver.

Recently, with much controversy, the Navajo have begun to carve wooden dolls that are sometimes presented as "Navajo kachinas." Most of these carvings are inexpensive, and they have no tribal significance. Do your homework if you want to invest in an authentic Hopi Kachina.

Both the Navajo and Hopi are well known for their jewelry. The Navajo "squash blossom" is probably the most famous design, and there are many variations. Navajo silversmiths typically use heavy silver with sand-casting or stamping techniques, often with dramatic use of large turquoise stones. You'll also find earrings, bracelets, concho belts, and other items. The Hopi developed a style known as "silver overlay," which uses two fused layers of silver, the top layer cut with a design. Typically, no stones are used. You can find small bracelets, earrings, money clips, and so forth for under $100, but expect to pay several hundred dollars for larger, more detailed pieces made with fine stones. Most Hopi and Navajo artists mark the backs of their pieces with a personalized hallmark or signature.

Apache and Tohono O'odham baskets as well as Hopi and Navajo pottery are also popular collectibles. Handwoven Navajo rugs make a great investment. The best and most expensive are highly detailed and made from hand-dyed yarns. Beware of inexpensive Mexican versions.

"Indian style" arts and crafts flood in from overseas, so always look for proof that a piece is authentic. Ask for the artist's name, and purchase from museum stores or finer galleries, on the reservation, or directly from the artist. Don't be fooled by 50-percent-off claims.

Arizona has several good highways. I-40 cuts east and west from Albuquerque, through Flagstaff, and on to Los Angeles. To the south, I-10 comes from El Paso to Tucson, where it forks north to Phoenix, then west to California. It also connects with Highway I-8, a direct route to San Diego. I-17 is the major north/south highway, linking Flagstaff with Phoenix, where you can pick up I-10 and continue on to Tucson.

The smaller towns are connected by paved two-lane roads, where you often cruise past incredible scenery. Be careful if you decide to take a dirt road. Though many are well marked and traveled regularly, you should ask a local in the closest town about current conditions. If you're looking to explore some out-of-the-way locations or planning to visit the high country during winter, you may want to rent a four-wheel-drive vehicle.

Pay attention to the speed limit because it varies throughout the state. The major highways are 75 m.p.h. but can drop down to 65 in areas with numerous curves. The two-lanes are usually 55 m.p.h., but watch as you approach towns.

Remember to monitor your gas gauge because service stations can be far apart, especially in the west or across the Navajo Reservation. And don't forget to carry water at all times.

I-19, which travels south from Tucson to Nogales, is the state's only metrically signed road.

RECOMMENDED READING

Probably Arizona's most famous publication is the monthly *Arizona Highways*. Started in 1924, this magazine (800/543-5432) is known for its stunning photography. With stories of lost mines, off-road experiences, and the old West, this magazine fascinates both residents and visitors.

If you'd enjoy some interesting reading as you're tooling around the state, try Marshall Trimble's *Roadside History of Arizona* (Mountain Press Publishing, 1986), which includes stories of gunfights, mining boomtowns, and battles with Indians as local communities were established. Another Marshall Trimble favorite is *Arizona, A Cavalcade of History* (Treasure Chest, 1989). If you're planning any back-road trips, check out *Arizona Atlas & Gazetteer* (DeLorme Mapping, 1993), a set of topo maps for the entire state that includes distinctions between primary, improved, and unimproved roads and details hiking trails. If you're into rock and mineral collecting, Gerry Blair has penned the ultimate guide, *Rockhounding Arizona* (Falcon Press, 1992).

One of the most interesting accounts of early Arizona is *Vanished Arizona*, by Martha Summerhayes (University of Nebraska Press, 1911, reprinted in

1979). As an army wife, she and her husband were dispatched to the wild territory in the mid-1850s and saw remarkable changes as the land was settled. Arizona's most famous Indian, Geronimo, recounted his life in 1906, while a prisoner at Fort Sill, Oklahoma, to S. M. Barrett in *Geronimo, His Own Story* (Meridian Press, reprinted in 1996). And in 1989, Penguin reissued the true story of John Wesley Powell's expedition down the Colorado River and through the Grand Canyon, *Exploration of the Colorado River of the West and Its Tributaries.*

Arizona Highways has recently started a new Wild West book series that compiles some of the wildest times in Arizona's early history. It includes *Manhunts & Massacres, Days of Destiny,* featuring some of the state's worst desperadoes and the lawmen who brought them in, and Marshall Trimble's *Law of the Gun.* Books continue to proliferate about Wyatt Earp, Doc Holliday, and the Clantons, as well as the West's most famous shoot-out, the gunfight at the O.K. Corral.

For some good Western fiction, try anything by Zane Grey or contemporary author Tony Hillerman, whose mysteries are set around the Navajo Reservation. And for a truly quirky look at life, try cowboy poet and entertainer Baxter Black's *Coyote Cowboy Poetry* (Coyote Cowboy Company, 1986). An Arizona resident and regular commentator on National Public Radio's *Morning Edition,* Black has a sense of humor enjoyed by cowboys and city folk alike.

Of the numerous books describing Native American arts and crafts, Jerry and Lois Jacka's *Beyond Tradition* (Northland Press, 1988) is especially gorgeous, as is their new book, *The Art of the Hopi* (Northland Press, 1998).

1
PHOENIX

Compared to other cities, the history of Phoenix is fairly short, totaling just over 130 years. Yet more than 1,500 years ago, the Hohokam civilization farmed this parched area of the Salt River Valley, leaving a complex maze of irrigation ditches as a monument to their resourcefulness. After the Hohokam mysteriously disappeared around A.D. 1450, the area was abandoned. Then, as pioneers started moving across the territory in the mid-1800s, a few took advantage of the old irrigation system and began farming again. The name Phoenix was adopted in 1868, when one of the founders declared, "A new city would spring phoenix-like upon the ruins of a former civilization."

Today the greater Phoenix area, home to more than 2.8 million people, comprises numerous cities merging together for miles. With its relatively low cost of living, Phoenix has seen its technology industry especially flourish, with more and more companies opting to relocate here. For years the area has been known as the "Valley of the Sun," with more than 300 days of glorious sunshine and less than eight inches of rain per year. And with winter temperatures hovering in the 70s, the town has become a mecca for retirees and vacationers.

The Phoenix area offers professional sports, numerous museums, excellent performing arts, and, of course, golf. The area has more five-star resorts than anywhere else in the country, yet it blends its Native American, Hispanic, and Anglo cultural heritages to produce a distinct Southwestern casual charm.

DOWNTOWN PHOENIX

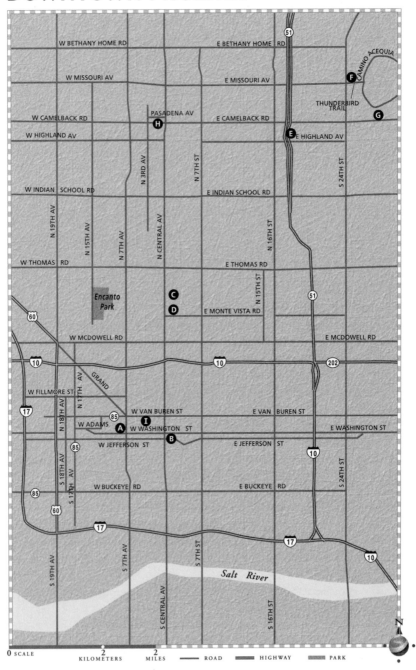

A PERFECT DAY IN PHOENIX

Book an early morning tee time on one of the area's many famous golf courses or explore Native American history at the Heard Museum. Then head over to Old Town Scottsdale for lunch on the patio of the Old Town Tortilla Factory. Spend the afternoon cruising the many Main Street galleries and the varied tourist shops along Fifth Avenue. For a mid-afternoon break, take a horse-drawn carriage ride around Old Town and have ice cream at the Sugar Bowl. To cap off the day, drive north into the McDowell Mountain foothills to Pinnacle Peak Patio for a cowboy-style sizzling steak. Ask for patio seating to enjoy the panoramic sunset views of Phoenix. And remember that if you wear a tie, they'll cut it off!

ORIENTATION

If you're planning to see the sights around the Valley of the Sun, it's best to have a car. While the bus system is efficient in some areas, it won't get you everywhere. If you travel by air, you'll land at Sky Harbor International Airport, which is centrally located and offers easy highway access. This area is very spread out, and it can easily take 30 to 45 minutes to drive from downtown Phoenix to Scottsdale. However, main streets are laid out in mile grids, making it simple to get around. Most area museums are in Phoenix, but most of the shopping, galleries, and five-star, five-diamond resorts are in Scottsdale and Paradise Valley.

I-17 (Black Canyon Highway) cuts through the city north to south and merges with I-10 just west of the airport. U.S. 60 (the Superstition) branches off I-10 and heads east to Apache Junction, while another north-south option is AZ 51 (Squaw Peak Parkway). In the next few years, major road and highway projects are scheduled for northeast Scottsdale, so be sure to consult with your hotel concierge for the best routes to take.

SIGHTS

- **A** Arizona Mining and Mineral Museum
- **B** Arizona Science Center
- **A** Arizona State Capitol Museum
- **C** Heard Museum

SIGHTS *(continued)*

- **B** Heritage Square
- **D** Phoenix Art Museum

FOOD

- **E** Ed Debevic's
- **F** Wright's

LODGING

- **F** Arizona Biltmore Resort and Spa
- **G** Embassy Suites Biltmore
- **H** Maricopa Manor
- **I** San Carlos

Note: Items with the same letter are located in the same place.

SIGHTSEEING HIGHLIGHTS

★★★★ ARIZONA STATE CAPITOL MUSEUM
1700 W. Washington Street, Phoenix; 602/542-4581
Arizona was an official U.S. Territory for more than 30 years before achieving statehood in 1912. Because of local politics, the capitol moved four different times before it finally landed in Phoenix. In 1900, a copper-domed granite building was erected to house the territorial government; when Arizona outgrew the building in 1972, it was restored to its 1912 look. The Senate and House Chambers feature wooden desks, antique lamps, and spittoons while other rooms honor Arizona's Supreme Court Justice Sandra Day O'Connor and the battleship *Arizona*.
Details: *Mon–Fri 8–5; closed state holidays. Free. (1–2 hours)*

★★★★ HEARD MUSEUM
22 E. Monte Vista Road, Phoenix; 602/252-8840 or 602/252-8848 (taped info)
This museum provides a wonderful overview of the history and culture of the Southwest Indians. Housed in a historic Spanish Colonial–style hacienda that has been renovated and expanded over the years, the extensive holdings include pottery, weavings, basketry, paintings, and jewelry from different tribes as well as an impressive collection of Hopi and Zuni kachinas. Prehistoric tools, clothing, and weapons evince the various extinct cultures that originally inhabited these lands. Numerous interpretive displays and an actual Navajo hogan give you a glimpse into "the old ways." Be sure to visit the current special exhibits and don't miss the hands-on gallery designed for kids. The Heard's gift shop is also a great place to purchase authentic Native American arts and crafts.
Details: *Open Mon–Sat 9:30–5:00, Sun 12–5; closed state holidays. $6 adults, $5 seniors, $3 children 4–12. (2–4 hours)*

★★★★ OLD TOWN SCOTTSDALE
Scottsdale Road and Main Street, Scottsdale 480/990-3939 (Scottsdale Gallery Association)
Old Town features a unique combination of world-class galleries and typical tourist shops. Along Main Street east of Scottsdale Road and several blocks north to Fifth Avenue, you'll find boots, Western clothing, Native American arts and crafts, and general southwestern

souvenirs. If you're buying Indian items, note that many stores mix in foreign-made goods. If you're interested in authentic Native American crafts, walk west to the Main Street gallery area or at least ask for information about the artist. The more than 60 galleries along Main and in the Marshall Arts District show a variety of styles, though Scottsdale is world renowned for its Western art galleries.

Details: Store hours vary, with longer hours in winter and shorter hours in summer. Thursday ArtWalk: galleries open until 9. (2–4 hours)

★★★★ PHOENIX ART MUSEUM
1625 N. Central Avenue, Phoenix; 602/257-1222

After a major renovation and expansion in 1996, this museum is now the largest of its kind in the Southwest, so there's lots to see around every corner. The major artistic movements from the Renaissance to the current day are well presented, and the museum also features such modern artists as O'Keeffe, Rousseau, and Picasso. Its permanent galleries encompass Western art, decorative arts, historic fashions, an Asian gallery, and the popular Thorne Miniature Collection. If you're visiting in late October, take in the Cowboy Artists of America exhibit, a preview of their annual show and sale that attracts international collectors. Plan on having lunch at the café, then check out the gift shop.

Details: Tue–Sat 10–5, Thu–Fri 10–9. Closed Mon and major holidays. $6 adults, $4 seniors, $2 children 6–18, Thu free. (2–4 hours)

★★★ DESERT BOTANICAL GARDENS
1201 N. Galvin Parkway, Phoenix; 480/941-1217

If you're interested in learning more about desert plant life, this is the place. In the unique terrain of Papago Park next to the Phoenix Zoo, more than 20,000 plants have been gathered from deserts throughout the world. A three-acre permanent exhibit includes a saguaro forest, a mesquite thicket, a desert stream, and an upland chaparral habitat; historic and prehistoric structures also exist along the trail. March to May is peak blooming season, and during the holidays the trails are lined with Mexican luminarias, making for a festive evening outing. Tours are self-guided, but docents are stationed throughout. The gift shop offers natural-history items and cactus specimens.

Details: East of Galvin Parkway in Papago Park; enter from 6400 E. McDowell Rd. Oct–Apr daily 8–8, May–Sept daily 7–8; closed Dec 25. $7 adults, $6 seniors, $1 children 5–1002. (1–3 hours)

SCOTTSDALE AREA

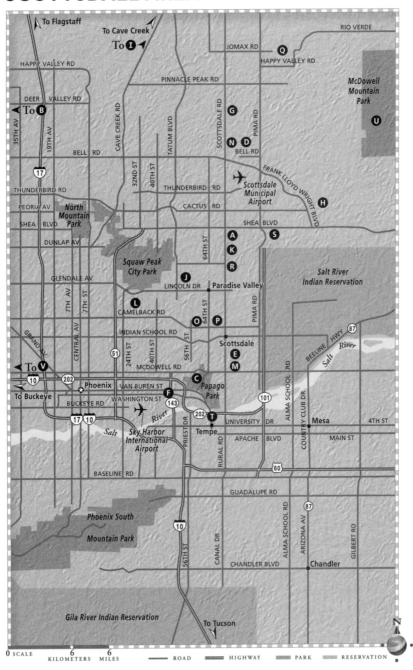

★★★ HERITAGE SQUARE
115 N. Sixth Street, Phoenix; 602/262-5029

Heritage Square showcases some of the few extant buildings from early Phoenix. Visit these eight National Register structures clustered around a garden patio, and you'll feel like you've stepped back in time. Built in 1886, the antique-furnished Rosson House is open for tours. The Teeter House, an 1899 bungalow, is now a Victorian tearoom; and a 1912 schoolhouse now hosts the Arizona Doll and Toy Museum. The 1900 neoclassic revival–style Silva House features historical exhibits, while other homes contain restaurants, a gift shop, and a bakery.

Details: Rosson House: 30-minute guided tours Wed–Sat 10–4, Sun 12–4. $3 adults, $2 seniors, $1 children 6–12. Arizona Doll and Toy Museum: $2 adults, 50 cents children 6–12, all others free. (2–4 hours)

★★★ PHOENIX ZOO
455 N. Galvin Parkway, Phoenix; 602/273-1341

Situated on 125 acres in Papago Park, this zoo is one of the nation's

SIGHTS
- **A** Buffalo Museum of Scottsdale
- **B** Deer Valley Rock Art Center
- **C** Desert Botanical Gardens
- **D** Fleischer Museum
- **E** Old Town Scottsdale
- **C** Phoenix Zoo
- **F** Pueblo Grande Museum
- **G** Rawhide
- **H** Taliesin West

FOOD
- **I** Crazy Ed's Satisfied Frog
- **J** El Chorro Lodge
- **K** The Golden Swan
- **L** Lon's at the Hermosa
- **M** Los Olivios
- **N** Marquesa
- **O** Mary Elaine's
- **E** Old Town Tortilla Factory
- **P** P.F. Chang's China Bistro
- **Q** Pinnacle Peak Patio

FOOD *(continued)*
- **G** Rawhide Steakhouse
- **R** Roy's
- **M** Sugar Bowl

LODGING
- **E** Best Western Papago Inn
- **S** Comfort Inn
- **A** Country Inn & Suites by Carlson
- **E** Days Inn Scottsdale
- **T** Fiesta Inn
- **L** Hermosa Inn
- **O** La Estancia
- **J** Marriott's Camelback Inn
- **D** Resort Suites
- **O** Royal Palms Hotel and Casitas
- **E** Scottsdale's 5th Avenue Inn

CAMPING
- **U** McDowell Mountain
- **V** West Citrus

Note: Items with the same letter are located in the same place.

finest, featuring more than 1,300 animals, many in their natural habitats. Organized into five different trails, the zoo's popular exhibits include a baboon colony and the Southwestern Trail. A Rain Forest exhibit has been recently added. Children love the petting zoo, where they can watch eggs hatch, pet miniature goats, and have their picture taken on a giant tractor. During the holidays the staff creates Zoolights, a popular festive event featuring thousands of colored lights strung throughout the trees along the pathways.

Details: *May 1–Labor Day daily 7–4, Labor Day–Apr 9–5; closed Christmas. $8.50 adults, $7.50 seniors, $4.25 children 3–12. (half-day)*

★★★ **TALIESIN WEST**
Cactus Road and Frank Lloyd Wright Boulevard, Scottsdale; 480/860-2700
Taliesin West was architect Frank Lloyd Wright's wintertime home and "desert camp" from 1937 until his death in 1959. This is a fascinating glimpse into the life of a man who changed the course of architecture. During his long career, Wright conceived innovations we now take for granted, such as skylights, breezeways, and carports. He even developed the first drive-up banking window. The complex sits on 600 acres of pristine desert at the base of the McDowell Mountains, offering sweeping views of the Valley.

Although the site is a National Historic Landmark, Taliesin West remains a working educational facility, housing the Wright Archives, the Wright School of Architecture, and Taliesin Architects, who continue the architectural practice Wright started in 1893. A variety of tours are offered, from a one-hour Panorama Tour to the three-hour Behind the Scenes tour, which offers a glimpse into the living quarters of Wright and his wife.

Details: *Enter at the intersection of Cactus Road and Frank Lloyd Wright Boulevard (114th Street) in northeast Scottsdale. Open 9–4; closed major holidays. Tours $14–$35, with senior and student discounts and reduced summer rates. Reservations recommended.*

★★ **ARIZONA MINING AND MINERAL MUSEUM**
1502 W. Washington Street, Phoenix; 602/255-3791
The Spanish first explored this area searching for the Lost Cities of Gold; two centuries later, Americans succumbed to a similar fever, spilling into the territory lured by stories of silver and gold. The mining industry has played an important role in Arizona's development,

and while this museum displays some old mining implements, it is better known for its awesome display of Arizona minerals. Giant specimens of azurite, chrysocolla, and malachite sit among the many richly colored samples. You can even view fluorescent minerals in a specially black-lit room. Kids and adults alike enjoy this museum, and its gift shop is packed with affordable rocks, minerals, and maps on where to pan for gold.

Details: Mon–Fri 8–5, Sat 1–5. Free. (1–2 hours)

★★ ARIZONA SCIENCE CENTER
600 E. Washington, Phoenix; 602/716-2000

This recently opened state-of-the-art building features more than 350 hands-on exhibits, such as a giant bubble-making machine, huge telephones, and an area where you can make and launch exotic paper airplanes. Kids love this place, which is generally packed with school tours, but adults also enjoy the interactive exhibits. The Science Center features a large-screen theater and planetarium.

Details: Daily 10–5; closed Thanksgiving and Christmas. $6.50–$11 adults, $4.50–$9 seniors and children 4–12. Prices vary depending on extra shows. (2–4 hours)

★★ PUEBLO GRANDE MUSEUM
4619 E. Washington Street, Phoenix; 602/495-0901

Although there's not much left of this prehistoric Hohokam settlement, it's interesting to explore the lifestyle of Arizona's first inhabitants, who occupied the area from around A.D. 1 until their cultural collapse in the mid-1400s. The Hohokam engineered hundreds of miles of irrigation canals to grow beans, squash, and cotton in the desert. Today the museum serves as a repository for all materials discovered in local archaeological projects. It can also arrange tours of other Salt River Valley archaeological sites.

Details: Mon–Sat 9–4:45, Sun 1–4:45; closed major holidays. $2 adults, $1.50 seniors, $1 children 6–17. (1–2 hours)

★★ RAWHIDE
23023 N. Scottsdale Road, Scottsdale; 480/563-5600

If you came to Arizona for a taste of the West, then head on over to Rawhide, pardner. In this stretch of undeveloped desert, you'll find a replica of an Old West town, with gunfights, wooden sidewalks, and even a jail. Here you can take a ride on a stagecoach, train, or even a camel. (An army experiment brought camels to Arizona in the 1800s.) A Native American village and museum teaches about native culture. Kids delight in panning for gold and feeding miniature goats. Themed shops sell Civil War– and Old West–replica guns, Western clothing, chile peppers, and more. This is a great place to watch fireworks on July 4.

Details: Oct–May Mon–Thu 5–10, Fri–Sun 11–10; June–Sept daily 5–10. Free admission, but rides and shows $2–$3 each. (1–3 hours)

★ BUFFALO MUSEUM OF AMERICA
10261 N. Scottsdale Road, Scottsdale; 480/951-1022

If you're in Scottsdale, stop by this unusual museum, especially if you have kids. This is one man's tribute to the American bison, and the building is packed with hundreds of items made with the buffalo image. You'll find mementos from Buffalo Bill and his Wild West Show as well as a buffalo prop from *Dances With Wolves*. Kids can sit on a buffalo (stuffed, of course) for photos, hear a buffalo family sing (a little hokey but still fun), and watch an informative video.

Details: Located on the southeast corner of Scottsdale Rd. and Shea Blvd. Mon–Fri 9–5; closed major holidays. $3 adults, $2.50 seniors, $2 children 6–17. (1–2 hours)

★ DEER VALLEY ROCK ART CENTER
3711 Deer Valley Road, Phoenix; 623/582-8007

This is the valley's largest collection of petroglyphs, which are thousand of years old. The 47-acre desert site in the Hedgpeth Hills is operated by Arizona State University's Department of Anthropology. An easy, quarter-mile trail leads to more than 1,500 different petroglyphs, which range from simple spirals to deer herds etched in the base of volcanic rock. The interpretive center features a 45-minute film on petroglyphs and offers information about the images.

Details: Late Sept–mid-May Tue–Sat 9–5, Sun 12–5; mid-May to late Sept Tue–Fri 8–2, Sat 9–5, Sun 12–5; closed major holidays. $3 adults, $2 seniors, $1 children 6–12. (1–3 hours)

★ FLEISCHER MUSEUM
17207 N. Perimeter Drive, Scottsdale; 480/585-3108

This is a small but worthwhile museum if you enjoy fine art. It's the first of its kind to feature primarily artists from the California School of American Impressionism. Exhibited paintings, mainly oils, focus primarily on the expansive scenery and seascapes of the West. A courtyard displays numerous bronze sculptures. This collection is housed in the office headquarters of Franchise Corporation of America, which has sought to integrate a work environment with an artistic setting.

Details: *Daily 10–4; closed major holidays. Free, contributions accepted. (1–2 hours)*

FITNESS AND RECREATION

Although there's no shortage of outdoor activities in the Valley of the Sun, golf is undoubtedly the most popular. Even though Phoenix boasts more than 180 golf courses, winter tee times can still be at a premium. So if you're staying in a golf resort, remember to book a time with your reservation. For further information, call Resort Tee Times, 800/468-7918. Or stay at Scottsdale's Resort Suites, known as a "golfer's hotel," where guests receive preferred tee times at the valley's top resorts. If you're looking for the ultimate golfing experience, try Heli-Golf, where the hotel will fly you by helicopter to play at one of Arizona's most scenic courses, including those in Sedona and Tucson (800/541-5203 or www.resortsuites.com).

DOWNTOWN PHOENIX

© Jessen Associates, Inc.

Hiking is especially popular, with several good locations in the middle of the Valley. **Camelback Mountain**, East McDonald Dr. at Tatum Blvd., 602/256-3220, is a hiker's favorite, offering a variety of trails and steep 200-foot cliffs leading to the top. **South Mountain Park**, 602/495-0222, is a 16,000-acre wilderness containing 40-plus miles of hiking trails. Drive or hike to the highest peak, Dobbins Lookout, for impressive views of the Valley. You'll also find riding stables just outside the park. Located eight miles south on Central Avenue, South Mountain is open daily from 5:30 a.m. to 10:00 p.m.; admission is free.

Jeep excursions are a fun way to see the Sonoran Desert; call Wild West Jeep Tours at 800/282-6826. Or for an ecotour, call Walk Softly Tours, 480/473-1148. Biking Desert, 888/249-BIKE, offers two-, three-, and four-hour bikeseeing tours of the desert.

For horseback riding, call Fort McDowell Adventures, 480/816-1513, or MacDonalds Ranch, 480/585-0239. Both offer one-hour to all-day rides with cookout and camp-out options.

Feeling a little more adventurous? Book a sunrise hot-air balloon ride with Unicorn Balloon Company of Arizona, 800/468-2478; or call Ascend Guide Service, 800/227-2363, for the ultimate in rock-climbing and rappelling adventures.

DINING

Since Phoenix is a popular resort destination, restaurants run the gamut from world-class to down-home. If your budget allows, try to have a least one meal at a resort restaurant. The service is impeccable, the food is sumptuous, and it's fun to wander through the resort. But plan on dropping some cash, especially if you add wine. Reserve ahead and be sure to ask about dress code, since some resorts require jackets.

With its stunning architectural decor, **Wright's**, at the historic Arizona Biltmore, Missouri and 24th St., Phoenix, 602/954-2507, serves innovative American fare complemented by an award-winning wine list. **Mary Elaine's**, on the top floor of The Phoenician, 6000 E. Camelback Rd., Scottsdale, 480/423-2530, is one of the city's most elegant and sophisticated restaurants and boasts sweeping views of the Valley. Its contemporary French cuisine is prepared with North African and Asian accents.

The **Golden Swan** at the Hyatt Regency, 7500 E. Doubletree Ranch Rd., Scottsdale, 480/991-3388, provides a rich Southwestern cuisine in a classic resort atmosphere, with dramatically lighted royal palms and jazz accompanying the soft splash of fountains in the background. This is also a favorite for Sunday brunch, featuring an incredible Bloody Mary bar.

To dine in the romantic ambiance of an eighteenth-century Spanish villa, try the **Marquesa** at the Scottsdale Princess resort, 7575 E. Princess Dr., Scottsdale, 480/585-4848. The cuisine is Spanish/Catalonian, complemented by one of the country's greatest selections of Spanish wines. Sunday brunch on the patio accompanied by Spanish guitar music is also outstanding.

Other options for memorable fine dining include the casually elegant **Lon's at the Hermosa**, 5532 N. Palo Cristi Rd., Paradise Valley, 602/955-7878. This 1930s hacienda offers contemporary American cuisine with classic Arizona charm. Try the tortilla-crusted salmon and crab cakes or Lon's famous white-chocolate cheesecake swimming in a blueberry pond. **Tarbell's**, 3213 E. Camelback Rd., Phoenix, 602/955-8100, has a decidedly New York feel. Popular chef Mark Tarbell's American bistro café uses only locally grown organic greens and serves free-range chicken and chops from humanely raised veal.

P. F. Chang's China Bistro, 7014 E. Camelback Rd., Scottsdale, 480/949-2610, is the popular spot for upscale Chinese fare at which you're likely to run into a few famous locals. The Bistro doesn't take reservations and the wait can get lengthy at peak times, but it's well worth it! For Pacific Rim cuisine in a simple, sophisticated atmosphere, **Roy's**, 7001 N. Scottsdale Rd., 480/905-1155, is the place. You'll forget you're in the desert when you see the fresh seafood on the menu.

If it's steak you crave, there's no shortage of excellent choices. **El Chorro Lodge**, 5550 E. Lincoln Dr., Scottsdale, 480/948-5170, has been a local favorite for more than 50 years. Set at the base of Camelback Mountain, this old adobe structure decorated with a Western flair was once a girls' school. If the weather is nice, request the patio.

After a visit to Rawhide, consider dining at the rustic Old West **Rawhide Steakhouse**, 23023 N. Scottsdale Rd., Scottsdale, 480/502-5600, where you can munch on fried rattlesnake appetizers and select from mesquite-broiled steaks, ribs, and chicken. Live bands play in the restaurant and adjoining saloon, and a roving magician entertains the kids.

Pinnacle Peak Patio, 10426 E. Jomax, Scottsdale, 480/585-1599, Arizona's original Western steak house, is nestled in the foothills of the McDowell Mountains, meaning incredible views of the Valley. This casual, relaxing place has a strict "no-tie" policy—waitresses waste no time cutting off ties and hanging them from the rafters. At last count, there were about a million. Get there at sunset and request patio seating. You'll be entertained with gunfighters and singing cowboys.

The metropolitan Phoenix area is also loaded with quality restaurants for lunch or a less expensive dinner. The kids will love '50s-style **Ed Debevic's**, 2102 E. Highland, Phoenix, 602/956-2760, serving hamburgers and fries. Or try the rustic and lively dining at **Crazy Ed's Satisfied Frog**, 6245 E. Cave Creek Rd. (in Frontier Town), Cave Creek, 602/253-6293, for barbecue or Mexican food.

For Sonoran-style Mexican fare, head to **Los Olivos**, 7328 E. Second St., Scottsdale, 480/946-2256, owned by the Corral family for more than 40 years. Tortillas are homemade daily, and the green corn tamales melt in your mouth. This was one of Barry Goldwater's favorite restaurants.

If you're shopping in Scottsdale's Old Town, consider a relaxing southwestern lunch on the patio at the **Old Town Tortilla Factory**, 6910 E. Main, Scottsdale, 480/945-4567 (kids probably won't appreciate the sophisticated menu). The whole family will enjoy the **Sugar Bowl**, 4005 N. Scottsdale Rd., Scottsdale, 480/946-0051, for burgers, sandwiches, or one of their famous ice cream concoctions. This valley landmark is a favorite of *Family Circus* author Bill Keene, who used it as a setting for several of his cartoons.

LODGING

A couple of nights at one of the valley's resorts could undoubtedly wipe out most of the average traveler's entire vacation fund. However, if you happen to be in Phoenix during summer, these resorts offer incredible bargains and lots of packages.

For the most part, Phoenix-area lodging is expensive. During season, one night's stay at a resort can set you back $250 to $600, and the basic chain motels range from $75 to $125. While you can cut costs by staying farther away from the resort areas, you'll sacrifice the convenience of being close to most of the action. Because of the valley's growth, new motels are sprouting up everywhere, especially along the highway corridors, so finding a place to stay should be fairly easy.

Phoenix boasts many top resorts. One valley favorite is the historic **Arizona Biltmore Resort and Spa**, 24th St. and Missouri, 602/954-2550, which brought Frank Lloyd Wright to Phoenix in 1929. The lobby is filled with memorabilia about famous guests, who include Clark Gable and Elizabeth Taylor, and the pool area is simply incredible. **Marriott's Camelback Inn**, 5402 E. Lincoln Dr., Scottsdale, 800/242-2635, is another historic resort. Recently renovated, it has a 27,000-square-foot spa, a health club with massage studio, and 36 holes of golf.

Two other higher-priced options bear mentioning because of their classic Arizona charm. The **Hermosa Inn**, 5532, N. Palo Cristi Rd., Paradise Valley, 800/241-1210, was built in 1930 by Lon Megaree, best known for his painting found inside Stetson cowboy hats. Most of the 35 rooms in this classic hacienda have fireplaces and patios. The 50-year-old **Royal Palms Hotel and Casitas**, 5200 E. Camelback Rd., Phoenix, 800/672-6011, is furnished with European antiques, while its gardens are filled with exotic plants. The casitas were recently renovated as part of a Designer's Showcase and are exquisitely decorated and furnished.

La Estancia, 4979 E. Camelback Rd., Phoenix, 602/808-9924, is a luxurious bed-and-breakfast. Offering five rooms, it was built in 1930 and is situated on two acres among citrus tree groves. Freshly squeezed lemonade is always on hand, and wine and cheese are set out each afternoon. **Maricopa Manor**, 15 W. Pasadena Ave., Phoenix, 602/274-6302, is a renovated 1920s Spanish-style house with five one-bedroom suites. Prices are reasonable because of its location, but among its excellent amenities is a continental breakfast delivered to your door each morning.

Embassy Suites Biltmore, 2630 E. Camelback Rd., Phoenix, 800/EMBASSY, was renovated to Southwestern style in 1996. It's conveniently located near upscale shopping and plenty of restaurants, making it one of the higher priced hotels in this chain. The **Country Inn & Suites by Carlson**, 10801 N. 89th Place, Scottsdale, 800/456-4000, a new facility in north Scottsdale, is conveniently located yet reasonable. Not far away is a new **Comfort Inn**, 7350 E. Gold Dust Ave., Scottsdale, 480/596-6559, featuring Southwest decor and plenty of amenities. Another option is **Resort Suites**, 7677 E. Princess Blvd., Scottsdale, 800/997-5277, www.resortsuites.com, next to the luxurious Princess. It offers reasonably priced one-, two-, and four-bedroom condo-style suites, and guests receive preferred tee times on more than 40 golf courses.

Surprisingly, several value-priced motels do exist in downtown Scottsdale. **Scottsdale's 5th Avenue Inn**, 6935 Fifth Ave., 800/528-7396, with its typical motor inn design, is ample for sightseers seeking a convenient location

SHOPPING DESTINATIONS

If you love to shop, then Phoenix has plenty to offer you—from discount malls to high-end boutiques. The big malls are open until 9. Smaller boutiques and specialty shops often close earlier, especially during summer.

Arizona Mills, I-10 and Superstition Freeway, 480/491-9700. High-end discount mall with over 175 stores, including Off 5th-Saks Fifth Avenue Outlet, Off Rodeo Dr., Beverly Hills, Virgin Megastore, and Rainforest Cafe.

Biltmore Fashion Park, Camelback and 24th St., 602/955-8400. Over 60 unique shops and restaurants including Macy's, Laura Ashley, and Planet Hollywood

Borgata of Scottsdale, 6166 N. Scottsdale Rd., Scottsdale, 602/998-1822. High-end specialty shops and galleries in an outdoor European setting

El Pedregal, Scottsdale Rd. and Carefree Hwy., Carefree, 480/488-1072. High-end shops and galleries, including the Heard Museum North, in a stunning outdoor setting next to the Boulders Resort

Glendale, west of I-17 on Glendale Ave., 623/930-2957. One of the top 15 antiquing spots in the nation.

Scottsdale Fashion Mall, 7014-590 E. Camelback Rd., Scottsdale, 480/941-2140. Large, upscale, enclosed shopping mall with over 200 stores, including standard mall anchors but also high-end retailers such as Saks Fifth Avenue, Tiffany's, Neiman Marcus, and the only Nordstrom in Arizona

without a fancy room. Or try the **Days Inn Scottsdale**, 4710 N. Scottsdale Rd. (next to Scottsdale's Fashion Square Mall), 480/947-5411. Nearby, the **Best Western Papago Inn**, 7017 E. McDowell Rd., 800/528-1234, offers 56 rooms and two suites.

Farther south is the **Fiesta Inn**, 2100 S. Priest Drive, Tempe, 800/528-6481. This older, casual resort includes lots of recreational facilities. Located near Arizona State University and convenient to the airport, it's a great value. Downtown Phoenix's **San Carlos**, 202 N. Central Ave. 800/528-5446, is a small, European-style hotel built in 1928 and listed on the National Register of

Historic Places. Rooms are small, but they're renovated, reasonably priced, and right downtown.

CAMPING

The most convenient campsite is **McDowell Mountain Park**, 480/471-0173, about five miles north of Fountain Hills. It accommodates campers and RVs, and from the hilltop location you get incredible views across the Sonoran Desert to Four Peaks, a rugged mountain range. Rates are $3 per vehicle for day use and $15 for camping with full hookups. RVers will like the **West Citrus Grove KOA**, 1440 N. Citrus, Buckeye, 800/KOA-1225. About 15 miles west of Phoenix, this nice park has RV hookups and tent sites. It offers a laundry, snack bar, rec room, pool, and playground.

NIGHTLIFE

The greater Phoenix area can supply just about any type of entertainment you can think of. The best source for current happenings is *The Rep*, an *Arizona Republic* supplement that comes out every Thursday. Its extensive listings include movie theaters. For concert updates, call 602/271-5656 and enter 9562. For movie information, call 602/444-4444. You can also access complete current information on the Internet at www.azcentral.com/ent.

For country, try **the Rockin' Horse**, 7316 E. Stetson Dr., Scottsdale, 480/949-0992, a popular hot spot for years. And if you're looking to kick up your heels, **Toolies Country**, 4231 W. Thomas Rd., Phoenix, 602/272-3100, brings in a variety of local and name bands, and there's always a lot of action of the dance floor. ASU presents a Western variety show at the **Red River Opry**, 730 N. Mill Ave., Tempe, 602/829-OPRY. Phoenix also hosts frequent jazz, rock, and country concerts.

Jazz fans will want to check out the **Cajun House**, 7117 E. Third Ave., Scottsdale, 602/945-5150, for a lively evening. An intimate club with jazz piano and an outdoor patio is **J. Chew & Co.**, 7320 Scottsdale Mall, Scottsdale, 602/946-2733. Or call the Jazz in AZ Hotline, 602/254-4545, for a statewide schedule of performances.

To enjoy a classy evening, head to one of the resort lounges for a cocktail. Or if you need something a little wilder, try **America's Original Sports Bar**, 455 N. Third St., Phoenix, 602/252-2112, a huge sports bar with 60 TVs, 10 big-screen TVs, and a sand volleyball court.

The valley boasts an excellent variety of performing arts. For more information, call the **Arizona Opera**, 602/226-SING, the **Phoenix Symphony**,

800/AT-CIVIC, the **Gammage Center for Performing Arts**, 602/965-3434, the **Scottsdale Center for the Arts**, 602/944-ARTS, or the **Herberger Theater**, 602/252-8497.

SPORTS

Phoenix offers professional sports year-round. America West Arena, 201 E. Jefferson, Phoenix, 602/379-7836, www.americawestarena.com, is home to the NBA's **Phoenix Suns**, AFL's **Arizona Rattlers**, WNBA's **Phoenix Mercury**, NHL's **Phoenix Coyotes**, and a variety of family entertainment. For ticket information on the NFL's **Arizona Cardinals**, call 800/999-1402. Phoenix's new Bank One Ballpark is probably the finest in the nation, with its retractable roof and swimming pool. It's home to the **Arizona Diamondbacks**, 602/514-8400, www.azdiamondbacks.com.

During March and April, seven Major League Baseball teams hold spring training camps throughout the Valley, including the **California Angels**, **Chicago Cubs**, **Colorado Rockies**, **Milwaukee Brewers**, **Oakland A's**, **San Diego Padres**, **San Francisco Giants**, and the **Seattle Mariners**. A schedule of games is available through the Greater Phoenix Convention and Visitor's Bureau, 602/254-6500 or 877/CALLPHX.

The dogs race nightly at the **Phoenix Greyhound Park**, 3801 E. Washington St., Phoenix, 602/379-2800, www.phxgp.com. And from October through May, thoroughbreds race at **Turf Paradise**, 1501 W. Bell Rd., Phoenix, 602/942-1101.

For amateur drag racing and NHRA races, head to **Firebird International Raceway Park**, 20000 Maricopa Rd., Chandler, 602/268-9200. The **Phoenix International Raceway**, 7602 115th Ave., Avondale, 602/252-2227, sponsors NASCAR and Indy car racing on the world's fastest one-mile oval.

Phoenix hosts three major golf tournaments annually. In January, the **Phoenix Open Golf Tournament**, 602/870-0163, happens at the Tournament Players Club in Scottsdale. In March, the **Standard Register PING LPGA Tournament**, 602/495-4653, is held as a charity event at Moon Valley Country Club. **The Tradition**, a Senior PGA Tour, is held each April at Desert Mountain golf course. For tickets to most sporting events, call Dillard's Box Office, 800/638-4253.

2
SEDONA AND
OAK CREEK CANYON

Sedona and Oak Creek Canyon draw millions of visitors each year to gaze at their world-famous red rocks and take one of the most scenic drives in America. This was Apache country until the Army took over in the mid-1800s. In 1876, J. J. Thompson decided to build a cabin near the Indians' deserted gardens and natural spring. By 1902, about 20 families had ventured into the region, including Carl and Sedona Schnebly. Carl chose his wife's name for the town after the post office deemed "Oak Creek Crossing" and "Schnebly Station" too long.

Hollywood soon discovered the area Zane Grey once fished and hunted, and used the fire-red buttes and red-rock landmarks in several John Wayne and Jimmy Stewart Westerns. As its fame grew, artists, inspired by its resplendent scenery, flocked to the area. The Cowboy Artists of America started here in 1965. Today Sedona is considered one of the top five arts communities in the nation.

A PERFECT DAY IN SEDONA AND OAK CREEK CANYON

Wake up to the smells of a homemade breakfast at one of the many bed-and-breakfasts in Sedona. Then spend the morning exploring the most spectacular geological formations and other popular sites in a hair-raising jeep tour. Be

SEDONA

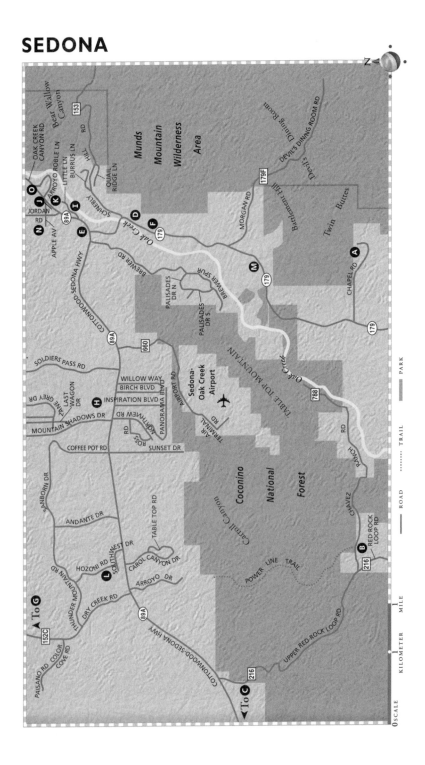

sure it includes a drive through Oak Creek Canyon. Relax for lunch at the Terrace at L'Auberge de Sedona Resort, idyllically set under towering oaks next to the soft bubbling of Oak Creek. Spend the afternoon browsing through Tlaquepaque, one of the most unique shopping centers in the country, then stroll through uptown Sedona's galleries and boutiques.

SIGHTSEEING HIGHLIGHTS

★★★★ RED ROCK CROSSING
Chavez Ranch Road, Sedona

This is visitors' favorite local photo spot. It's appeared on countless postcards and in lots of Sedona promo pieces. Part of a National Forest Recreation Area that contains hiking trails leading to Cathedral Rock, it gets very busy in the summer. You may have to park on the road and hike in. You'll find picnic tables, but overnight camping is not allowed.

    Details: Take 89A west and turn south onto Upper Red Rock Loop Road, then turn left onto Chavez Ranch Road. $3 parking. (1–3 hours)

★★★★ SLIDE ROCK STATE PARK
Highway 89A, Oak Creek Canyon; 520/282-3034

This park contains a unique swimming hole that is loads of fun for kids and kids at heart. It's part of a 43-acre historic apple farm dating from 1912. Antique farm implements, a fruit-packing barn, and the old Pendley Homestead line the walk to Slide Rock, named after the slippery creek bottom just below the old house. Over the years,

---

SIGHTS
- **Ⓐ** Chapel of the Holy Cross
- **Ⓑ** Red Rock Crossing
- **Ⓒ** Red Rock State Park
- **Ⓓ** Tlaquepaque Arts & Crafts Village

FOOD
- **Ⓔ** Cowboy Club
- **Ⓕ** El Rincon
- **Ⓖ** Enchantment Yavapai Dining Room
- **Ⓗ** Heartline Cafe
- **Ⓘ** L'Augerge de Sedona
- **Ⓙ** Sedona Coffee House & Bakery
- **Ⓣ** Terrace at L'Augerge de Sedona Resort
- **Ⓚ** WenDeli's Delicatessen

LODGING
- **Ⓛ** Boots & Saddles Bed & Breakfast
- **Ⓜ** Poco Diablo Resort
- **Ⓝ** Matterhorn Lodge

CAMPING
- **Ⓞ** Hawkeye/Red Rock RV Park

Note: Items with the same letter are located in the same place.

---

water has created a slick natural chute that twists and turns you down the creek. Steep banks next to deep clear pools make great jumping-off spots. Just below Slide Rock is a cliff area where brave teenagers gather their courage to leap into the cold water below. Wear old denim shorts and sneakers. You can also enjoy a 3/8-mile nature trail, plenty of picnic tables, and a snack bar. Pick up a bird-sighting checklist at the Ranger's Office.

At Slide Rock, you're halfway through Oak Creek Canyon, so be sure and continue the drive to the top, then turn around for another fabulous view on the way down.

Details: *Seven miles north of Sedona. Daily 8–6. $5 per vehicle. (2–4 hours)*

★★★ TLAQUEPAQUE ARTS & CRAFTS VILLAGE
AZ 179, Sedona; 520/282-4838

More than 40 galleries and shops line the maze of narrow alleys and overlook the flower-laden balconies in this unique shopping center built to resemble an old Mexican village. Even if you're not in a buying mood, explore Tlaquepaque's courtyards, fountains, chapel, and bell tower, and watch artists working in their gallery studios.

Details: *At the Oak Creek bridge on the south side of town. Daily 10–5. (2–4 hours)*

★★★ VERDE CANYON RAILROAD
300 N. Broadway, Clarkdale; 800/293-7245
www.verdecanyonrr.com

Everyone will enjoy leisurely clicking along the Verde River in these 1940s Pullman cars. A fancy first-class coach and open-air gondolas can also carry you over the 20-mile trek. You'll ride past dramatic rocky canyon walls, cliff dwellings, and inaccessible desert to the ghost town of Perkinsville. Although the daytime views are stunning, check out the summer schedule of starlight rides, which are also popular.

Details: *Take Highway 89A 20 miles west of Sedona to Clarkdale. Usually Wed–Sat departures at 1 p.m. $34.95 adults, $30.95 seniors, $19.95 children under 13, $52.95 first-class. Schedule varies through-out the year; call ahead. Reservations suggested. (4 hours)*

★★ MONTEZUMA CASTLE NATIONAL MONUMENT
I-17, Camp Verde; 520/567-3322

Because of its overwhelming size, the U.S. Army scouts that hap-

BELL ROCK

© Bob Clemenz

pened upon this site in 1864 assumed that it must have been built by Montezuma. In fact, the Aztecs were nowhere near these parts. The prehistoric Sinaguas constructed these dwellings around A.D. 1100 and occupied them for the next 300 years, until the group mysteriously disappeared. You'll find two structures: a remarkably preserved five-story cliff dwelling wedged high into an alcove and a six-story "castle" that is badly deteriorated. You can't climb into the structures, but the self-guided nature trail is impressive, and the visitor center offers excellent info on local geology and the history of the Sinagua and Hohokam Indians.

Eleven miles northeast of Montezuma Castle (follow the signs) is the monument's other part, Montezuma's Well, a giant limestone sinkhole rimmed by several pueblo ruins.

Details: 35 miles south of Sedona on I-17, exit 289. Memorial Day–Labor Day daily 7–7, Labor Day–Memorial Day daily 8–5. $2 adults, under 17 free. Free admission to the Well.(1–2 hours)

★★ **RED ROCK STATE PARK**
Highway 89, Sedona; 520/282-6907
Environmental education is the focus of this park. Start at the visi-

GREATER SEDONA

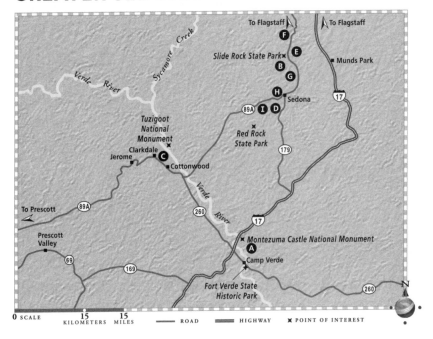

SIGHTS
A Montezuma Castle National Monument
B Slide Rock State Park
C Verde Canyon Railroad

LODGING
D Canyon Villa Bed & Breadfast Inn
E Don Hoel's Cabins
F Enchantment Resort
E Garland's Oak Creek Lodge
G Holiday Inn Express

CAMPING
H Cave Springs
I Sedona Pines Resort

Note: Items with the same letter are located in the same place.

tor center, which is packed with hands-on exhibits about Oak Creek's diverse riparian habitat and its plants and wildlife. A variety of special tours includes nature walks to learn about park ecology, guided bird walks, and hikes to Eagles Nest Overlook. Jack Frye, president of TWA Airlines, built his vacation retreat, House of Apache Fire, overlooking the land in 1946. The house is now part of the park and available for touring. Although you can't swim or camp, its 10 developed trails mean plenty of hiking with spectacular red rock views.

Details: Take Highway 89 west out of Sedona and turn left on Lower Red Rock Loop Road to the park. Daily 8–6. $5 per vehicle. Earth Day is free. Call for specific tour times. Pets are prohibited. (2–4 hours)

★ **CHAPEL OF THE HOLY CROSS**
Chapel Road, Sedona; 520/282-4069

This architectural landmark was designed by Marguerite Brunswig Staude, a devout Catholic painter, sculptor, and designer. Although she was inspired with the design in 1932, the chapel was not built until 1957. Rising from two redstone pinnacles, the cross and the chapel seem to sprout directly from the rock. Regular services are not held here, but it is a peaceful place for meditation.

Details: Just south of Sedona, east of Highway 179. Daily 9–5. Free. (1 hour)

ART GALLERIES

Sedona is considered one of the top arts destinations in the country, and for good reason. More than 40 galleries exhibit works from Western to contemporary arts. In addition, the **Sedona Arts Center**, in uptown Sedona on 89A, has ongoing exhibits and regularly scheduled performing arts. Call 520/282-3809 for current information.

The prestigious Cowboy Artists of America was started in Sedona by Western art legends Joe Beeler, Charlie Dye, John Hampton, and Jim Reynolds. Many galleries lure collectors from throughout the world with their excellent Western art selections. Two such Tlaquepaque shops are **El Prado**, 800/498-3300, and **Mountain Trails Galleries**, 800/527-6556, www.fine art@mountaintrails.com, where renowned sculptor Susan Kliewer maintains a working studio. Fine-art photography featuring Western scenes is available at **Exposures Gallery of the West**, Hillside Shops, 671 Highway 179, 800/526-7668.

For authentic Native American arts and crafts, try **Garland's Navajo Rugs**, 411 Highway 179, 520/282-4070, and the **Turquoise Tortoise** at Hozho Center, 431 Highway 179, 520/282-2262. Also in Hozho Center, you'll find contemporary art at **Lanning Gallery**, 520/282-6865.

Exploring Sedona's numerous galleries and boutiques is an adventure. You'll find handcrafted kaleidoscopes, handwoven clothing, and custom pottery, as well as Southwestern antiques, gift items, and T-shirts. Depending on how comfortable your shoes are, this is definitely a town in which you can shop 'til you drop.

FITNESS AND RECREATION

One of the best ways to experience the spectacular scenery around Sedona is to see it up close, perhaps by taking a hike. Stop by the **Coconino National Forest/Sedona Ranger Station**, 425 Brewer Rd., 520/282-4119, open weekdays from 7:30 to 4:30, for trail information. Rangers can provide hiking maps marked with hike length and difficulty.

For some striking views, head west on Highway 89A to Dry Creek Road and turn right. Take the left branch to **Boynton Canyon** trailhead, just outside the Enchantment Resort gates. The red rock scenery on this three-mile hike is awesome, but don't expect solitude on this heavily used trail (try to go midweek). Just south of town on Highway 179, you'll see one of nature's striking formations, **Bell Rock,** on the east side of the road. Park at the base of the rock and take one of the trailheads leading to the top. Oak Creek Canyon offers several hikes, but the most popular is the six-mile round-trip walk up the **West Fork of Oak Creek**, where sheer walls rise over 200 feet in areas sometimes only 20 feet wide.

Jeep tours are also a popular way to see the sights. Try Pink Jeep Tours, 800/8SEDONA, www.pinkjeep.com, for 1 1/2-hour to all-day tours, seven days a week. If you're into New Age, check out a Vortex tour from Sedona Red Rock Jeep Tours, 800/848-7728, www.redrockjeep.com., who also offers helicopter tours and horseback riding. For an aerial view, book a hot-air-balloon ride from Northern Light Balloon Expeditions, 800/230-6222, www.sedona.net/fun/balloon.

Before you visit **Sedona Red Rock Pathways**, an elaborate system of biking trails, rent bikes at Sedona Bike and Bean, 376 Jordan Rd., 520/282-3515, a fun bike shop with a coffee bar. Golfing opportunities include the 18-hole course at **Oak Creek Country Club**, 690 Bell Rock Road Boulevard, 520/284-1660, and Arizona's number-two-rated course at the **Sedona Golf Resort**, 7260 Highway 179, 520/284-9355.

The local streams are stocked with trout (you'll need a license), but if you want to guarantee that your kids will catch a fish, head to the **Rainbow Trout Farm**, 3500 N. Highway 89A, Oak Creek Canyon, 520/282-3379, www. troutfarmaz.com, where you won't need a license and the ponds are loaded. You pay by the pound, and while it's not the cheapest way to fish, kids love it.

FOOD

French, Italian, Thai, Mexican, health food, or cowboy steak, Sedona has it all. In addition, the resorts here mean that your selection of fine dining is extensive. The red rocks of Boynton Canyon serve as a dramatic backdrop for dinner or lunch at the **Enchantment Yavapai Restaurant** in the Enchantment Resort, 525 Boynton Canyon Rd., 520/204-6000. This is one of the more expensive restaurants, but the food and atmosphere are worth it. For French cuisine, **L'Auberge**, 301 Little Lane, 520/282-1667, is considered the most elegant restaurant in Sedona. It sits on the edge of Oak Creek and offers a six-course fixed-price dinner. Sunday brunch is also popular, and it won't set you back as much.

For cowboy steak and cowboy atmosphere, dine amid the steer horns at the **Cowboy Club**, 241 N. Highway 89A, 520/282-4200. **El Rincon**, in Tlaquepaque, 520/282-4648, combines Mexican and regional Navajo for what they've dubbed "Arizona Style" Mexican food. Be sure and try one of the famous Margaritas Magnifica.

The **Heartline Cafe**, 1610 W. Highway 89A, 520/282-0785, serves tasty Southwestern lunches and dinners, which you can enjoy inside or on an outdoor courtyard. Sedona's only creekside restaurant is **Terrace on the Creek**, at L'Auberge de Sedona Resort, 520/282-1667, where you can relax along Oak Creek for breakfast, lunch, or dinner.

WenDeli's Delicatessen, 276 N. Highway 89A, 520/282-7313, in uptown Sedona, is a great place to grab a sandwich in between browsing the shops. And for gourmet coffee and mouthwatering pastries, stop by the **Sedona Coffee House & Bakery**, 293 N. Highway 89A, 520/282-2241. You'll also find healthy sandwiches, soups, and salads. Sedona is busy year-round, and reservations are recommended even for lunch at most restaurants.

LODGING

Set at the base of some of the country's most spectacular scenery are some equally spectacular resorts. In secluded Boynton Canyon, you'll find 56 casitas at the **Enchantment Resort**, 525 Boynton Canyon, 800/826-4180. Here, you can relax on your own patio in the shadows of the towering vermilion cliffs.

Or, for a family resort vacation, **Poco Diablo Resort**, 1752 S. Highway 179, 800/528-4275, offers family-sized rooms and even has a video arcade for the kids. While you can expect all the amenities from golf and tennis to health spas at these resorts, the average stay will run from $200 to $400 per night.

Equally popular in Sedona are the numerous idyllic and cozy bed-and-breakfasts. The more than 30 choices range from $75 to over $200 per night but include breakfast and lots of personal attention. For a romantic hideaway, try **Canyon Villa Bed & Breakfast Inn**, 125 Canyon Circle Dr., 800/453-1166, where you'll be pampered with delectable homemade cinnamon rolls for breakfast and afternoon hors d'oeuvres. For some Old West hospitality, mosey over to the **Boots & Saddles Bed & Breakfast**, 2900 Hopi Dr., 800/201-1944, http://bb.sedona.net.

Both families and couples will appreciate the 18 country cottages at **Don Hoel's Cabins**, 9440 N. Highway 89A, 800/202-4635, situated on the banks of Oak Creek 15 minutes north of Sedona. Also in Oak Creek Canyon, **Garland's Oak Creek Lodge**, 520/282-3343, charges $160 to $170 a night and has a great restaurant.

You'll find plenty of quality chain and suite motels throughout town, but the rates are higher than chains in other cities. For easy access to shopping, try **Sedona's Matterhorn Lodge**, 230 Apple Ave., in uptown, 520/282-7176. Otherwise, you can always count on the **Holiday Inn Express**, 6176 Highway 179, 520/284-0711, in the Village of Oak Creek.

CAMPING

Six Forest Service campgrounds lie along Oak Creek Canyon, most staying open from Memorial Day through Labor Day. The bathrooms are kept clean, but there are no showers or electrical hookups. **Cave Springs**, 12 miles into the canyon, is a family favorite. This campground is under the pines and further off the road next to Oak Creek, which is great for wading or fishing. A short walk down the trail brings you to a clear, cool swimming hole at the base of a canyon wall. Take a lawn chair and a good book, and the kids will have a blast. Eleven sites can be reserved by calling 800-280-CAMP. Otherwise, be aware that all of these campgrounds fill early during summer. Check at the ranger's station for a complete list of other local campgrounds.

Hawkeye/Red Rock RV Park, 40 Art Barn Rd., 800/229-2822, is located near Oak Creek but within walking distance of uptown. **Sedona Pines Resort**, 6701 W. Highway 89A, 800/547-8727, has RV and tent sites, along with a pool, spa, horseshoe pits, and children's playground, and restaurant.

NIGHTLIFE AND SPECIAL EVENTS

After a full day of hiking and shopping, you may just want to relax under the stars in a hot tub. But if you're ready for some two-steppin', the historic **Rainbow's End Steakhouse & Saloon**, 3235 W. Highway 89A, 520/282-1593, keeps a lively country band playing throughout the evening. Most of the resorts offer luxurious settings for an evening cocktail or appetizer. Adjacent to Tlaquepaque, at Los Abrigados Resort and Spa, a billiards club opens at 11 a.m. at **Steak & Sticks**, 160 Portal Lane, 520/204-STIX. Next door, **On the Rocks Bar and Grill,** 520/282-1777, boasts Sedona's only 10-foot TV screen, which is usually broadcasting a sports channel.

Sedona hosts numerous special events throughout the year. Some favorites are the **Sedona Chamber Music Festival** in early June, 520/526-2256, and **Sedona's Jazz on the Rocks** in late September, 520/282-1985, followed by the **Sedona Arts Festival** in mid-October, 520/204-9456.

Schnebly Hill Road

If you're heading to I-17, either south to Phoenix or north to Flagstaff, consider the old wagon trail carved out almost 100 years ago by Carl Schnebly. You'll find **Schnebly Hill Road** off Highway 179, north of the village of Oak Creek but just before the "Y" in Sedona. Turn east and be prepared for some unpaved bumpy areas, smoothed out by breathtaking views. One has to wonder what Sedona Schnebly must have thought as she first came across this canyon in a covered wagon. It doesn't require a four-wheel-drive vehicle, but always check for road conditions, 520/282-4119, especially in the winter and after a rain. Several turnouts and hiking trails exist along the drive. Five miles up you'll see Schnebly Hill Vista, where you'll want to have your camera ready. From there it's another six miles until you reach Mund Park and I-17.

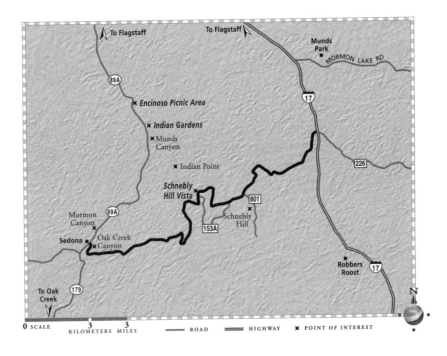

3
GATEWAY TO THE
GRAND CANYON

The southern region of the Colorado Plateau around Flagstaff and Williams is a mixed land of pine forests, volcanic peaks, canyons, and alpine lakes. The dramatic San Francisco Peaks thrust over 12,000 feet into the air and are dotted with aspens, wildflowers, and ponderosa pines. In the shadow of the peaks, hundreds of volcanic cones and miles of hardened lava flow share the area with thousands of prehistoric sites left by the Sinagua, Anasazi, and Cohonina Indians who settled in the area almost 1,000 years ago. And at the base of the mountains is Flagstaff, a charming small town with the culture and attractions of a big city.

It's home to Northern Arizona University, which helps maintain a forward-thinking cultural environment, yet the townsfolk also struggle to preserve their pioneer heritage. At this gateway to the Grand Canyon you'll find quality museums and scenic national monuments. One of Arizona's premier winter playgrounds, Flagstaff also attracts many Phoenicians for cool summer getaways.

A PERFECT DAY IN FLAGSTAFF
Linger over an espresso at one of the many coffeehouses in historic downtown. Then head to the Museum of Northern Arizona and browse through its numerous exhibits to learn about local history and geology. Pack a picnic and

FLAGSTAFF

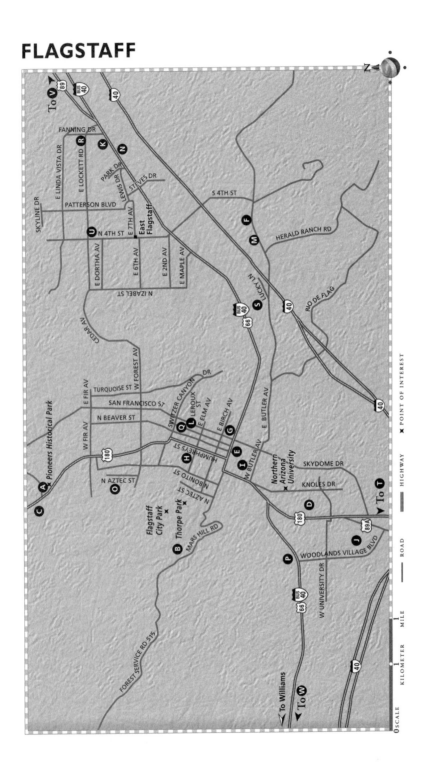

take the scenic drive to the Arizona Snowbowl, then catch the chairlift to the top of the San Francisco Peaks for some awesome views. Traverse some of the hiking and cross-country trails by foot or on horseback or mountain bike. Have dinner at a historic house restaurant, then check out the music scene back in the historic district. Finally, settle in at one of Flagstaff's charming bed-and-breakfasts.

SIGHTSEEING HIGHLIGHTS

★★★★ ARIZONA SNOWBOWL
Highway 180, Flagstaff, 520/779-1951
No matter what time of year you visit, the Snowbowl offers spectacular scenery and lots of outdoor action. From mid-December to mid-April, skiers can choose from four chairlifts and 32 trails with 2,300 feet of vertical drop.

If you're not into vertical, ask about the **Flagstaff Nordic Center**'s 40 kilometers of groomed cross-country trails. Occasionally, the snow comes late or melts early, so check ski conditions before planning your trip.

In the summer and fall, ride a chairlift to the Mount Aggassi summit and enjoy views all the way to the Grand Canyon. Late

SIGHTS
Ⓐ Arizona Historical Society's Pioneer Museum
Ⓑ Lowell Observatory
Ⓒ Museum of Northern Arizona
Ⓓ Riordan State Historic Park

FOOD
Ⓔ Beaver Street Brewery & Whistle Stop Cafe
Ⓕ Black Bart's Steakhouse
Ⓖ Cafe Espress
Ⓗ Chez Marc

FOOD (continued)
Ⓘ Cottage Place
Ⓙ Crown Restaurant & Railroad Cafe West
Ⓚ Crown Restaurant & Railroad Cafe East
Ⓛ Down Under New Zealand Restaurant
Ⓜ Little America Grand Ballroom

LODGING
Ⓝ Best Western Pony Soldier
Ⓞ Comfi Cottages of Flagstaff
Ⓟ Days Inn Route 66

LODGING (continued)
Ⓠ Inn at 410
Ⓡ Jeanette's B&B
Ⓜ Little America Hotel
Ⓢ Red Roof Inn
Ⓣ Sled Dog Inn

CAMPING
Ⓕ Black Bart's RV Park
Ⓤ Coconino National Forest District Office
Ⓥ Flagstaff/Grand Canyon KOA
Ⓦ Woody Mountain Campground and RV Park

Note: Items with the same letter are located in the same place.

spring brings valleys of wildflowers, while during fall, the mountains are blanketed with blazing yellow and orange aspens. Call the Flagstaff Visitors Center or Coconino Forest Service for snow, or leaf, information.

Details: Skiing, $19–$31. Shuttle from Highway 180 turnoff, $4 round trip. Round-trip summer/fall lift, $9 adults, $6.50 seniors, $5 ages 6–12, under 6 free. The Nordic Center is 8 miles past Snowbowl. All-day passes, $12 adults, $7 seniors and ages 8–12. Rentals, guided tours, and lessons available. (half to full day)

★★★★ LOWELL OBSERVATORY
1400 W. Mars Hill Road, Flagstaff; 520/774-2096

Founded by Boston businessman Percival Lowell in 1894, this observatory is one of the oldest in the Southwest. Lowell, an amateur astronomer, spent years studying Mars. The planet Pluto was discovered here in 1930, and the Theory of the Expanding Universe was formed. A new visitor center offers several interactive exhibits, plus telescopes for daytime viewing. But nighttime visits are particularly fascinating. The observation domes aren't heated, so be sure to bring a coat.

Details: Open daily Apr–Oct 9–5, Nov–Mar 12–5. $3 adults, $1 ages 5–17. Call for special programs and nighttime schedules. (1–2 hours)

★★★★ MUSEUM OF NORTHERN ARIZONA
3101 N. Fort Valley Road, Flagstaff; 520/774-5213

This excellent museum is a great way to familiarize yourself with the history, anthropology, and geology of the Colorado Plateau. The charming stone building sits among a stand of ponderosa pines and houses one of the finest collections in the Southwest. Besides archaeology exhibits and thousands of fossil, rock, and mineral specimens, you'll see wonderful examples of prehistoric and current Native American arts and crafts, including painting and sculpture. The gift shop is an excellent source for authentic Native American arts and crafts. There's also a self-guided nature trail.

Details: Open daily 9–5. $5 adults, $4 seniors, $3 students, $2 ages 7–17. (2–4 hours)

★★★ GRAND CANYON RAILWAY
Grand Canyon Boulevard and Railroad Avenue, Williams; 800/843-8724

For a leisurely view of the Grand Canyon and surrounding country-side, take the historic steam train into the Grand Canyon Village. Vintage steam and diesel engines pull 1920s passenger cars along the tracks. You'll depart from the **Williams Depot**, housed in a reno-vated 1908 hotel, which contains a railroad museum, gift shop, and restaurant. On board, you'll be entertained by Western characters and strolling musicians. You'll disembark at the 1910 log terminal in front of El Tovar on the South Rim. Choose among five travel classes, from basic coach to a luxury parlor car with chairs and sofas. When you re-serve the train trip, consider also booking a Grand Canyon bus tour, which will allow you to see more sites.

Details: Departs daily. $49.95–$119.95 adults, $24.95–$94.95 ages 3–17, plus $6 per person Grand Canyon entrance fee. Eight-hour trip, with 3¹/₂ hours at the Canyon.

★★★ METEOR CRATER
I-40 Exit 233; 520/289-2362

You may think this sounds like a Hollywood movie, but a few thou-sand years ago, a gigantic meteor of around 100 feet in diameter blasted into Earth at 45,000 miles per hour. After the dust settled, trees were flattened and every living thing for miles around was dead. This best-preserved impact crater on Earth extends almost a mile wide and 550 feet deep. It so resembles moon craters that NASA trained Apollo astronauts here in the 1960s. On its rim, a visitor cen-ter features fascinating space exploration and astrogeology exhibits, including a ³/₄-ton meteorite. To protect it, visitors cannot hike into the giant crater, but trails explore the rim.

Details: 35 miles east of Flagstaff. Open daily. Summer 6–6, winter 8–5. $8 adults, $7 seniors, $2 ages 6–17, under 6 free. (1–2 hours)

★★★ WALNUT CANYON NATIONAL MONUMENT
I-40 exit 204, Flagstaff; 520/526-3367

During the thirteenth century, the prehistoric Sinagua discovered this tranquil, pristine, stream-cut gorge and decided to make it home. Today you can hike along a half-mile rim trail and peer into the ravine, or head down the Island Trail for a closer view of these ancient cliff dwellings. Keep in mind that it's a steep climb back up from the bottom.

Details: Daily 8–5, Island Trail closes at 4. $3 adults. (1–3 hours)

★★ RIORDAN STATE HISTORIC PARK
1300 Riordan Ranch Street, Flagstaff
520/779-4395
Brothers Timothy and Michael Riordan were successful business partners and decided to live together as well—sort of. They built this 13,000-square-foot, 40-room structure in 1904 as two separate houses with a common central area under one roof. You can tour this richly furnished home filled with handcrafted furniture and personal mementos, stop at the visitor center, or have a picnic. During December, the house is festively decorated with old-fashioned ornaments, and guides share holiday and folklore traditions.

Details: Daily May–Sept 8–5, Oct–Apr 11–5. $4 adults, $2.50 ages 7–13, under 7 free. Guided tours on the hour. Reservations suggested. (1–2 hours)

★★ SUNSET CRATER VOLCANO NATIONAL MONUMENT
Highway 89, 520/526-0502
This 1,000-foot-tall red-and-orange cinder cone is the result of a volcano that started erupting in 1064, spewing black rivers of lava over 800 square miles. It's actually just one of more than 500 volcanic cinder cones near Flagstaff, but certainly the most spectacular. At the crater's base are a mile-long interpretive trail and a visitor center where you can learn more about volcanoes and Sunset Crater. Ranger programs and hikes happen throughout the summer.

Details: 18 miles north of Flagstaff. Open daily 8–5. $4 per vehicle. (1–3 hours)

★★ WUPATKI NATIONAL MONUMENT
Highway 89, 520/679-2365
Along these sage-covered mesas and lava plains you'll discover more than 800 ancient Indian ruins, including a rare "ball-court." They're remnants of three prehistoric cultures—Kayenta Anasazi, Sinagua, and Cohonina—that inhabited the area nearly 1,000 years ago. The largest pueblo is the three-story Wupatki, containing nearly 100 rooms. Numerous others are within walking distance of the visitor center, which features exhibits about the ancient peoples. Check for ranger-guided tours in summer.

Details: 36 miles north of Flagstaff. Open daily 8–5. $4 per vehicle, payable at Sunset Crater. (1–3 hours)

★ **ARIZONA HISTORICAL SOCIETY'S PIONEER MUSEUM**
2340 Fort Valley Road, 520/774-6272
This interesting collection of pioneer memorabilia from the area includes photos from Grand Canyon photographer Emery Kolb. You can't miss the building. It was built in 1906 of volcanic tuff, and a 1929 Baldwin logging train and Santa Fe caboose are parked out front.
Details: Mon–Sat 9–5. Free. (1 hour)

FITNESS AND RECREATION

You'll find lots of hiking trails around Flagstaff. Probably the most popular and challenging trail leads to the top of **Humphreys Peak**, at 12,633 feet the highest point in Arizona. Plan on spending all day on this grueling nine-mile round-trip trek. **Veit Spring** is a short, family-friendly hike in the San Francisco Peaks that takes you through lush vegetation to an old cabin site.

For some spectacular views, head north of Flagstaff to **Kendrick Peak**. Check with **Coconino National Forest** headquarters, 2323 E. Greenlaw Way, 520/527-3600, for hiking maps and campground lists.

The **Flagstaff Urban Trail System** (FUTS) is an extensive network of walking and bike trails that allows passage to city parks, cultural centers, national monuments, and small canyons. The cross-country trails at the **Flagstaff Nordic Center** are open for mountain biking in the summer.

Stop by Mountain Sports, 1800 S. Milton Rd., 520/779-5156, www.mountainsport.com, for mountain bike, ski, snowboard, and hiking rentals. If you want to see the forest or Walnut Canyon by horseback, call Hitchin' Post Stables, 4848 Lake Mary Rd., 520/774-1130. Ask about their winter sleigh rides. Peaks 'N' Places, 2532 N. Fourth St., 520/779-8028, provides a unique excursion through the Coconino National Forest to a private ranch homesteaded in the 1800s. Winter tours are by Snowcat; summer tours, by four-wheel-drive vehicle.

The **Arboretum at Flagstaff**, 520/779-1951, is on Woody Mountain Road, south of Route 66. It encompasses 200 acres of ponderosa pine forest with a visitor center; wildflower, herb, and children's gardens; a nature trail; and picnic tables. Call for hours and tour schedule. Nearby, **Lake Mary** provides great fishing, hiking, and boating. It's home to lots of waterfowl as well as elk, deer, and antelope herds. If you'd like to learn more about the area's prehistoric tribes, the **Elden Pueblo Archaeological Project**, on Highway 89, 520/527-3475, is open to the public for hands-on excavation projects.

GREATER FLAGSTAFF

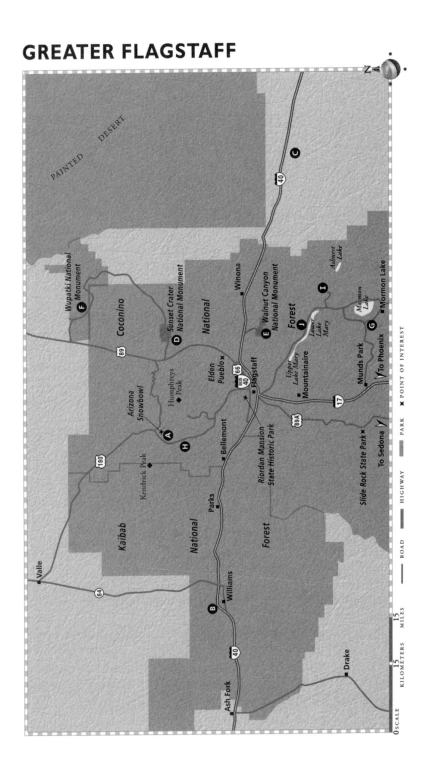

N

PAINTED DESERT

Wupatki National Monument **F**

Coconino

Sunset Crater National Monument **D**

National

Winona

Walnut Canyon National Monument **E**

Ashurst Lake

Forest

I

Mormon Lake

C

40

89

Humphreys Peak

Elden Pueblo

Flagstaff

66

BUS 40

Upper Lake Mary

Lower Lake Mary

Mormon Lake

G

Mountainaire

Munds Park

To Phoenix

Arizona Snowbowl

A

H

Bellemont

Riordan Mansion State Historic Park

89A

17

180

Kendrick Peak

Slide Rock State Park

To Sedona

Valle

Kaibab

National

Parks

Forest

64

Williams

B

40

Drake

Ash Fork

0 SCALE   15 KILOMETERS   15 MILES

— ROAD   ═ HIGHWAY   PARK   ✖ POINT OF INTEREST

FOOD

Part of Flagstaff's charm is the array of choices among quaint coffeehouses, pubs, and cafés in the town's historic district. One of the favorite local hangouts is the **Cafe Espress**, 16 N. San Francisco St., 520/774-0541. It's a friendly place with great breakfasts and the largest full-service vegetarian restaurant in town. Try the garden burger. Nearby, the **Beaver Street Brewery & Whistle Stop Cafe**, 11 S. Beaver St., 520/779-0079, makes for a fun lunch or dinner. Wood-fired pizzas and specialty sandwiches nicely complement its local brew and near-nightly entertainment.

For unusual fine dining, try the **Down Under New Zealand Restaurant**, 413 N. San Francisco, 520/774-6677, located in a 1910 carriage house. Besides lamb and venison concoctions, vegetarian entrees and delectable homemade pastries are served at lunch and dinner. Choose from a selection of Down Under wines. During the summer, ask for patio seating. Closed Sunday.

Chez Marc, 503 N. Humphreys St., 520/774-2557, is located in a historic house and serves country-French lunches and dinners, including original ostrich and buffalo entrees. Another fine-dining option is the **Cottage Place Restaurant**, 126 W. Cottage Ave., 520/774-8431, offering an intimate setting in an old house and continental cuisine. Its four-course meals are enhanced by an excellent wine list. Dinner is served Tuesday through Sunday.

For less expensive, down-home cooking, try the **Crown Restaurant & Railroad Cafe East**, 3300 E. Route 66, 520/522-9237; or **West**, 2700 S. Woodlands Village Blvd., 520/774-6775. Both are open daily for all three meals. You'll find huge electric train displays at each location.

For an authentic cowboy steak and beans, try **Black Bart's Steakhouse**, 2760 E. Butler Ave., 800/574-4718, at which local college students provide

---

SIGHTS

- Ⓐ Arizona Snowbowl
- Ⓑ Grand Canyon Railway
- Ⓒ Meteor Crater
- Ⓓ Sunset Crater Volcano National Monument
- Ⓔ Walnut Canyon National Monument
- Ⓕ Wupatki National Monument

LODGING

- Ⓖ Montezuma Lodge at Mormon Lake
- Ⓗ Ski Lift Lodge

CAMPING

- Ⓘ Lake Ashurst Campsites
- Ⓙ Lake Mary Campsites
- Ⓒ Meteor Crater RV Park
- Ⓖ Mormon Lake Campsites

Note: Items with the same letter are located in the same place.

nightly Western musical entertainment. On Sunday from 10 to 2, the **Little America Grand Ballroom**, 2515 E. Butler Ave., 800/865-1399, has a fabulous champagne brunch.

LODGING

Of the more than 20 bed-and-breakfasts in Flagstaff, the premier choice is the **Inn at 410**, 410 N. Leroux St., 800/774-2008, a charming 1907 home with nine luxurious guest rooms, some with fireplaces, and whirlpools. Rates range from $110 to $155. **Jeanette's B&B**, 3380 E. Lockett Rd., 800/782-1912, is a new Victorian-style home furnished with antiques.

Close to downtown, **Comfi Cottages of Flagstaff**, 1612 N. Aztec St., 888/774-0731, rents six charming cottages, each with a fireplace, kitchen, picnic table with barbecue, and bicycles. The **Sled Dog Inn**, 10155 Mountainaire Rd., 800/754-0664, nestled in the pines south of town, offers year-round guided adventures or simple relaxation in a sauna or spa.

If you're looking for a blazing bonfire and marshmallow roast, stay in one of the cabins at **Montezuma Lodge at Mormon Lake**, 30 miles southeast of Flagstaff, 520/354-2220. The **Ski Lift Lodge**, seven miles north of Flagstaff on highway 89, 520/774-0729, at the base of the San Francisco Peaks, features cozy cabins with wood stoves, and a restaurant. During summer, guided horseback rides are available. Ask about lodging/ski packages.

A good selection of chain motels exists along I-40 and Route 66. **Little America Hotel**, 2515 E. Butler Ave., 880/865-1399, is a full-service establishment with good restaurants, a pool, and an exercise room. Or try the **Best Western Pony Soldier**, 3030 E. Route 66, 800/356-4143; **Days Inn Route 66**, 1000 W. Route 66, 520/774-5221; or **Red Roof Inn**, 2520 E. Lucky Lane, 800/545-5525.

CAMPING

The **Flagstaff/Grand Canyon KOA**, 5803 N. Highway 89, 800/KOA-FLAG, supplies RV and tent sites, plus a few cabins, year-round. It has lots of amenities, including groceries, planned summer activities, a playground, and hiking trails. The **Woody Mountain Campground and RV Park**, 2727 W. Route 66, 800/732-7986, is open April through October and also offers full amenities including a heated outdoor pool. Another fun option is **Black Bart's RV Park**, 2760 E. Butler Ave., 520/774-1912, which rents RV and tent sites year round. It sits next to Black Bart's Steakhouse and an antique store.

The Coconino National Forest District Office, 520/527-3600, has maps and info on Forest Service campsites in the surrounding mountains. You'll also find a great selection of scenic sites around **Lake Mary** and the nearby **Mormon Lake** and **Lake Ashurst**. Call the Mormon Lake Ranger District, 520/526-0866, for details. If you want to stay a few miles out of town, stop at **Meteor Crater RV Park**, Meteor Crater Road and I-40 exit 233, 800/478-4002, which also rents a few tent sites. Open year-round, it has a gas station, showers, and laundry.

NIGHTLIFE AND SPECIAL EVENTS

Flagstaff's historic downtown railroad district, www.flagguide.com/mainstreet, is filled with boutiques, antique shops, and galleries. At night, you'll find live entertainment at many of the coffeehouses and pubs, where you can hear anything from jazz and country to rock, alternative, and maybe even some bagpipes. For some cowboy two-stepping, head to the **Museum Club**, 3404 E. Route 66, 520/526-9434. A Route 66 fixture since 1931, it's hosted such country greats as Bob Wills and Willie Nelson. A huge collection of mounted animals adorns the walls of this classic cowboy bar. The **Flagstaff Symphony Orchestra**, 113A E. Aspen, 520/774-5107, features "Great Classics" and "Best of Pops" concerts. Call for schedules and celebrity guests.

Flagstaff **Winterfest**, held each February, comprises more than 100 events, including sled-dog races, skiing competitions, stargazing, concerts, and cultural events. The **Flagstaff Festival of the Arts** and **Grand Canyon Shakespeare Festival** occur annually in July and August. The summer months also bring arts and crafts festivals, chili cookoffs, and rodeos. Call the Flagstaff Visitors Center, 800/217-2367, for details.

4
GRAND CANYON

Even though you may have seen hundreds of pictures of the Grand Canyon, there's no way to describe the feeling of awe when it suddenly appears in front of you. The bottom of the canyon contains some rocks that are more than 2 billion years old. The result of erosion that's taken 5 to 6 million years to occur, the canyon runs one vertical mile from rim to river and 18 miles wide in certain areas. The Colorado River in the Grand Canyon runs about 277 miles from Lee's Ferry to Grand Wash Cliffs.

Evidence of humans in this area dates to more than 8,000 years ago. Ancestors of today's Navajo people migrated to the area around A.D. 1300. The Hopi, Navajo, Hualapai, Paiute, and Zuni Indians all currently inhabit lands near the canyon and have strong beliefs about their Grand Canyon connections. The Havasupai people still live in a remote inner canyon region west of Grand Canyon Village.

In 1869, a one-armed Civil War veteran pioneered a small party in four wooden boats and charted the turbulent Colorado River for the first time. Major John Wesley Powell's famous journey drew other adventurers to the area. Initially, mining brought the first American pioneers. But after the first settlements appeared along the rim in the 1880s, residents realized that more money could be made from tourism than mining. By 1901 the railroad ran to the South Rim, and by 1905 the historic El Tovar Hotel had been constructed.

SOUTH RIM

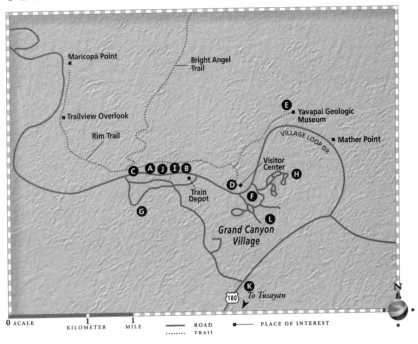

SIGHTS
A Fred Harvey History Museum
B Hopi House
C Kolb Studio
D Visitor's Center
E Yavapai Observation Station

FOOD
F Babbitt's General Store
A Bright Angel Dining Room
G Maswik Cafeteria
H Yavapai Cafeteria
I El Tovar Dining Room
J Arizona Steakhouse

LODGING
A Bright Angel Lodge
I El Tovar
J Kachina Lodge
G Maswik Lodge
J Thunderbird
H Yavapai Lodge

CAMPING
K Grand Canyon Camper Village
L Mather Campground

Note: Items with the same letter are located in the same place.

The 1,905-square-mile Grand Canyon received National Park status in 1919, and today, more than 5 million visitors view this natural wonder each year.

A PERFECT DAY AT THE GRAND CANYON

Start the day early by watching the pink and orange hues change as the sun rises, then stop by the Visitor's Center for park maps and information. Head east along the rim drive, stopping at the different overlooks. Climb the Watchtower at Desert View for some unbelievable panoramic views, then have a picnic along the way back to Grand Canyon Village. After lunch, head to the Hopi House for an excellent selection of Grand Canyon souvenirs as well as authentic Native American crafts. Walk along the rim and browse through Kolb and Lookout Studios before catching the shuttle for the West Rim Drive. Be sure and make it to the edge of the canyon to watch a spectacular sunset. After dark, have a sumptuous dinner at the El Tovar Dining Room.

SIGHTSEEING HIGHLIGHTS

★★★★ EAST RIM DRIVE

This is the most popular section of the Grand Canyon. A 26-mile two-lane road winds along the edge, offering spectacular views around each bend. Several lookouts deserve a stop. After leaving Grand Canyon Village, you'll come to **Yaki Point**, near the trailhead for the South Kaibab trail leading to Phantom Ranch. Then there's **Grandview Point** and **Moran Point**, each providing dramatically different views. The **Tusayan Museum** (see page 63) is the next stop, followed by **Lipan Point**, containing an incredible combination of geological formations. The drive ends (or begins) at **Desert View** (see next page), with the park's east entrance just beyond.

Details: Open to private vehicles year-round. Expect heavy congestion during summer; snow and ice in winter. (2–4 hours)

★★★★ WEST RIM DRIVE

This scenic drive heads west out of Grand Canyon Village and dead-ends eight miles later at Hermits Rest. Along the way, you'll find eight different lookouts, including the **Trailview Overlook** and **Maricopa Point**, which offer views of the Bright Angel Trail descending into the canyon. The **Powell Memorial** offers interesting information about the canyon's first American explorer, John Wesley Powell; and at **The**

Abyss you'll see one of the most awesome views in the park, with a 3,000 foot drop-off created by the Great Mojave Wall. The drive ends at **Hermits Rest**, where you'll find rest rooms, snacks, and a gift shop. This 1914 structure, designed by Mary E. J. Colter, is listed on the National Register of Historic Places.

Details: Closed to private vehicles from mid-May to mid-October. Free guided shuttle buses, stopping at most overlooks, run every 15 minutes. Hermit's Rest is open 9–5 in winter, 8–7 the rest of the year. (2–4 hours)

★★★ DESERT VIEW AND WATCHTOWER
AZ 64; 520/638-7893

At this upper end of the canyon, the Colorado River is dramatically close. Every view is spectacular, but you'll want to climb the Desert View Watchtower for a look through the coin-operated binoculars that provide close-up canyon views. Look northeast to see the Painted Desert, north to see Marble Canyon, and south to see the San Francisco Peaks. Perched at canyon's edge, the Watchtower looks like it's been there for centuries, with petroglyph reproductions and pictographs covering the walls. Actually, it was designed less than 75 years ago for the Fred Harvey Company by Mary E. J. Colter. A gift shop is on the first floor. The adjacent Desert View Trading Post offers a service station, restaurant, general store, and visitor information.

Details: Just inside the park's entrance. Daily 9–5. (1 hour)

★★★ GRAND CANYON VISITORS CENTER
Village Loop Drive, Grand Canyon Village; 520/638-7888

If you're a first-time visitor, you'll definitely want to stop by. This excellent resource traces human history in the canyon, provides geological exhibits, and displays examples of indigenous plant and animal life. A continuous slide show and lots of guidebooks, maps, and brochures are available. Rangers answer questions and lead hikes and star-watches. Trail conditions, hikes, and bus schedules are also posted in the center.

Details: Daily 8–5. Free. (30 minutes)

★★★ HOPI HOUSE
Grand Canyon Village

Inspired by the ancient dwellings on the Hopi Reservation, Hopi House is another example of Mary E. J. Colter's historic designs. Frequently the site of ceremonial dances and artists at work, it was completed by Hopi craftsmen in 1905. Be sure and visit the second floor, where the Fred Harvey/Waddell Trading Gallery features a wonderful variety of authentic Native American arts and crafts.

Details: *Across from El Tovar. Daily May–Oct 8–8, Nov–Apr 9–5. Free. (30 minutes)*

★★ KOLB STUDIO
Bright Angel Trailhead, Grand Canyon Village

This is an intriguing building perched on the edge of the canyon near the trailhead of the park's most popular hike, Bright Angel Trail. It was built in 1904 by brothers Emery and Ellsworth Kolb, photographers who created the first motion pictures of the Colorado River. It's fun looking at their old photos, and the canyon views are fabulous.

Details: *Daily May–Oct 8–7, Nov–Apr 9–5. Free. (30 minutes)*

★★ TUSAYAN MUSEUM AND RUIN
East Rim Drive

This small but interesting museum hosts exhibits on the prehistoric Anasazi culture as well as contemporary Native American cultures. It's the site of an Anasazi dwelling probably occupied by about 30 people around A.D. 1185. You can take a self-guided tour through the ruins.

Details: *23 miles from Grand Canyon Village along East Rim Drive. Open daily 8–6 in summer, 9–5 the rest of the year. Free. (1–2 hours)*

★★ YAVAPAI OBSERVATION STATION
East Rim Drive near Yavapai Point

You can see all the way to the canyon floor, and views of the Phantom Ranch and Colorado River are enhanced with polarized glass. There is a great bookstore, and rangers are on-site during peak season.

Details: *Daily 8–8 summer, 9–5 off season. Free. (1 hour)*

★ FRED HARVEY HISTORY MUSEUM
Bright Angel Lodge, Grand Canyon Village

In this large room off the Bright Angel Lodge lobby, you'll find a fascinating overview of the man and the company who brought hospitality to the West. Fred Harvey built a string of restaurants and hotels along the Santa Fe Railroad. When the railroad line into the Grand Canyon was completed in 1901, this entrepreneur started planning many of the hotels and gift shops still used today.

Details: *Daily 9–5. Free. (30 minutes)*

FITNESS AND RECREATION

The best way to see the canyon is by getting out of your car. National Park Service rangers offer free guided walks that you'll find listed in the park newspaper, *The Guide*. If you prefer to explore the canyon on your own, several good hiking trails do exist, but don't start out unless you're prepared. Understand the difficulty of the trail you're about to attempt and make sure you have sturdy shoes and plenty of food and water. Several people are killed each year hiking the canyon. If in doubt, take a ranger-guided tour.

Day hikes don't require a permit and are a popular way to experience the canyon. The easiest is the **South Rim Trail**, a 2.7-mile paved trail from Yavapai Observation Station. The **West Rim Trail** then continues on another six miles to Hermit's Rest. This dirt trail offers an easy stroll with fabulous views. In the summer, you can catch a shuttle back to Grand Canyon Village.

If you want to hike partially down into the canyon, there are several trails. Remember to pace yourself, since you'll have to turn around and hike back out. Carry at least two quarts of water per person for short hikes and a gallon per person for full days. **Bright Angel**, the most popular and best-maintained trail, is the main route to Phantom Ranch, 9.6 miles away. It's not an easy trail, and even the other, shorter three- and six-mile round-trip day hikes are considered strenuous. The **South Kaibab Trail**, starting near Yaki Point, contains a steep descent and strenuous climb out, but the views are dramatic. For a nice day trip, you can hike 1.5 miles to Cedar Ridge before turning around. It's 7.1 miles down to the Colorado River. The **Grandview** and **Hermit Trails** are steep and not regularly maintained; only experienced, well-prepared hikers should attempt them.

If you plan on backpacking into the canyon, you'll need a Backcountry Use Permit to camp overnight. The non-refundable fee is $20 per permit, plus $4 per person per night. There is often a waiting list for popular spring and fall dates, so start planning early. Call or write to the Backcountry Office, P.O. Box 129, Grand Canyon, AZ 86023, (520/638-7875), for a free *Backcountry Trip Planner*, which includes permit forms and schedules of hikes and seminars offered by the Grand Canyon Field Institute, which can be reached at P.O. Box 399, Grand Canyon, AZ 86023, 520/638-2485. Permit requests can be mailed, faxed to 520/638-2125, or made on the Web at www.thecanyon .com/nps (no phone reservations). You can stay at Phantom Ranch without a permit; reserve by calling 303/297-2757.

If you're not up for hiking, take a two- or three-day round-trip mule ride. It will take you the canyon floor and includes a stay at Phantom Ranch. The one-day (seven-hour) ride is the most popular, descending over 3,000 feet into the canyon, just 1,300 feet above the Colorado River. Make arrangements through

AmFac Parks & Resorts, 303/297-2757. Mule trips are often sold out and can be booked 11 months in advance. You must be over 4 feet, 7 inches, weigh less than 200 pounds, and able to understand English. Trips run $100 to $400 per person.

Horseback rides are available along the rim, but they do not descend into the canyon. Rides range from one to four hours and include campfire trail rides and wagon rides. Contact Apache Stables, P.O. Box 158, Grand Canyon, AZ 86023; 520/638-2891.

Since the turbulent rapids and waterfalls of the Colorado River were first explored by John Wesley Powell in the 1800s, river runners have flocked to the Grand Canyon seeking their own wild adventure. Currently, 17 approved river concessionaires provide a variety of white-water rafting trips, ranging from three days to three weeks. All operators are listed in the park's *Trip Planner*. Most trips start at Lees Ferry near Page. Transportation from the South Rim to Page is available through AmFac, 303/297-2757. Some companies also offer trips starting at Phantom Ranch and one-day smooth-water rafting trips starting near Glen Canyon Dam.

If you don't have a lot of time and want to avoid park traffic, consider a trip on the **Grand Canyon Railway** (800/843-8724), which runs from Williams to Grand Canyon Village. It takes eight hours round trip, including 3 1/2 hours to explore the South Rim. To pack in a lot in a short amount of time, consider one of the guided bus tours offered by Grand Canyon National Park Lodges, P.O. Box 699, Grand Canyon, AZ 86023; 520/638-2631. Tours range from two hours to all day; options include a breathtaking Sunset Tour including Yaki Point.

For an unusual view of the canyon, consider an airplane or helicopter flight. Call Grand Canyon Airlines, 800/528-2413, or Kenai Helicopters, 800/541-4537, for information.

FOOD

If your budget allows, have dinner at the legendary **El Tovar Dining Room**, 520/638-2401. After being outdoors all day, you'll enjoy the service, and the food is award-winning cuisine. Huge windows overlook the canyon, nicely enhancing your lunch or early dinner. Make reservations when you book your stay, or you may not get in.

The **Arizona Steakhouse** in Bright Angel Lodge, 520/638-2401, with its Western atmosphere and sizzling steaks, is another popular dinner choice. It doesn't take reservations, and the line gets long in the summer, but a fabulous Grand Canyon sunset will ease the wait. Bright Angel Lodge also has a coffee

GRAND CANYON AREA

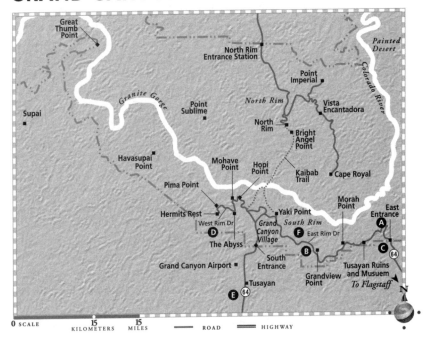

SIGHTS
- **Ⓐ** Desert View and Watchtower
- **Ⓑ** East Rim Drive
- **Ⓒ** Tusayan Musum and Ruins
- **Ⓓ** West Rim Drive

FOOD
- **Ⓐ** Desert View Trading Post Cafeteria

LODGING
- **Ⓔ** Best Western Grand Canyon Squire Inn
- **Ⓔ** Holiday Inn Express-Grand Canyon
- **Ⓕ** Phantom Ranch

CAMPING
- **Ⓐ** Desert View Campground
- **Ⓔ** Ten-X Campground

Note: Items with the same letter are located in the same place.

shop, which is a great place for breakfast or lunch. Ask for a booth, and you can gaze over the canyon during your meal.

For inexpensive, casual dining, try the cafeterias at the Yavapai and Maswik Lodges and the Desert View Trading Post. You'll find a deli at **Babbitt's General Store** (pick up picnic supplies here) and a snack bar at Hermit's Rest. A few miles away, in Tusayan, are several restaurants, including the standard fast-food joints.

LODGING

To experience the fabulous sunsets and sunrises, be sure to stay in the park. Unless you plan on driving back to Flagstaff or Williams, the hotels in Tusayan won't save you much money. Many rooms are booked a year in advance, but last-minute cancellations sometimes occur.

Perched right on the edge of the canyon, **El Tovar** is one of America's great historic hotels. It was built in 1905 in the style of a Swiss chalet, to rival the posh European resorts. The large front porch filled with comfy chairs is a great place to sip a drink and experience a Grand Canyon sunset. Rates range from $112 for a single to $290 for a suite. The rustic **Bright Angel Lodge** is another Mary E. J. Colter design, built in 1935. It sits just west of El Tovar on the canyon rim and has a choice of log cabins or comfortable rooms from $58 to $114.

For more modern accommodations on the rim, try **Thunderbird** or **Kachina Lodge**, at less than $120 per night. A short distance from the rim is **Maswik Lodge**, with rustic cabins or modern rooms from $59 to $112. The **Yavapai Lodges** are just minutes from the rim, nestled in the pine and juniper woodlands. Rates range from $85 to $100.

Phantom Ranch, built in 1922, provides the only lodging at the bottom of the canyon. You can bunk in its dormitories for $21 or stay in a rustic stone cabin for $58. Book at least a year in advance, then reconfirm four days in advance at 520/638-3283. Make all park lodge reservations through AmFac Parks and Resorts, 303/297-2757, or visit their Web site at www.amfac.com. For more information, write to Grand Canyon National Park Lodges, P.O. Box 699, Grand Canyon, AZ 86023; 520/638-2631.

If you can't get a park room, Tusayan is seven miles south of the park entrance. Here you'll find a new **Holiday Inn Express-Grand Canyon**, Highway 64, 800/HOLIDAY, with rates from $58 to $168. (The hotel has no restaurant or pool.) The **Best Western Grand Canyon Squire Inn**, intersection of U.S. 180 and Highway 64, 800/528-1234, offers a pool, tennis courts, whirlpool, bowling alley, and video arcade. There's also a coffee shop and the nicer Coronado Dining Room. Rates are $100 to $200 per night, lower in the off season.

The recently opened **Grand Hotel**, Highway 64, 888/63GRAND, has an indoor swimming pool and the Canyon Star Restaurant. Nationally renowned Navajo medicine man and teacher James Peshlakai offers entertainment and educational workshops at the hotel. Rates run around $140.

CAMPING

Inside the park on the South Rim, you have two choices. **Mather Campground** has year-round tent sites for $15. **Trailer Village** has RV hookup sites. Both are conveniently located near Babbitt's General Store and feature such amenities as coin-op showers and laundry. **Desert View Campground**, 26 miles east, also has $10 tent and RV sites. This May-to-October campground supplies water but no showers. Book sites months in advance by calling BIOSPHERICS, 800/365-2267. If you're going to camp at the bottom of the canyon, obtain a permit from the Backcountry Office, 520/638-7875.

The Forest Service operates **Ten-X Campground**, with $10 RV and tent sites from May to September on a first-come, first-served basis. You'll find water, pit toilets, and barbecues. Primitive camping is allowed in some areas of the **Kaibab National Forest**. Call 520/638-2443, or write the Tusayan Ranger District, Kaibab National Forest, P.O. Box 3088, Grand Canyon, AZ 86023. **Grand Canyon Camper Village**, in Tusayan, 520/638-2887, is open year-round. Mainly an RV park, it has water and electric hookups and charges $19 to $23. It also has a nice tent-camping area and teepees, at $15 and $19 per night, respectively.

NIGHTLIFE

If you're looking for some evening action, head to the sports bar at Maswik Lodge. Enjoy the lounges at El Tovar and Bright Angel or cozy up to a blazing fire in the El Tovar lobby. The massive fireplace in the Bright Angel lobby is also a favorite place to hang out, have a drink, and reminisce about your day. One of the most popular special events is September's **Grand Canyon Chamber Music Festival**, 520/638-9215.

5
ARIZONA
CANYONLANDS

This remote area in northern Arizona contains the Grand Canyon's North Rim and some of the most beautiful scenery and spectacular vistas in the nation. Yet, until a few years ago, it was rarely visited by tourists. The North Rim is almost 1,000 feet higher than the South Rim, with ponderosa pines, fir, and aspens surrounding large meadows. Snow makes winter access impossible, and although it's only 10 miles directly across from the South Rim, the North Rim is 200 miles away by car.

When the Colorado River first cut through the land north of the canyon, it formed impressive gorges and canyons. In 1964 the river was dammed, and scenic Glen Canyon filled with water. Today Lake Powell lures visitors from around the world to its rugged landscape and colorful canyon walls surrounding clear blue-green waters. From the glossy granite walls of Marble Canyon to the spectacular sandstone arch of Rainbow Bridge, the Canyonlands have become a favorite outdoor playground.

THE PERFECT DAY IN THE CANYONLANDS

Hike around the colorful Vermilion Cliffs and explore the historic Lees Ferry site. Be sure to walk across the Navajo Bridge and view the Colorado River from dizzying heights. Spend the afternoon swimming, fishing, or boating on Lake Powell, where you can enjoy a spectacular sunset.

NORTH RIM

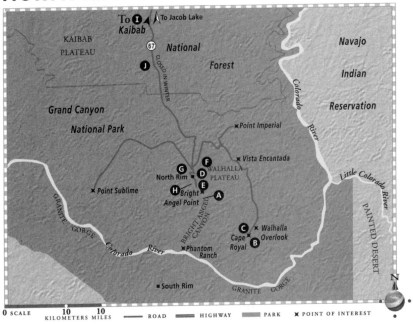

SIGHTS

Ⓐ Bright Angel Point Trail
Ⓑ Cape Royal Trail
Ⓒ Cliff Springs Trail
Ⓓ North Kaibab Trail
Ⓔ Roaring Springs
Ⓕ Uncle Jim Trail
Ⓖ Widforss Trail

FOOD

Ⓗ Grand Canyon Lodge
Ⓘ Jacob Lake Inn
Ⓙ Kaibab Lodge

LODGING

Ⓗ Grand Canyon Lodge
Ⓘ Jacob Lake Inn
Ⓙ Kaibab Lodge

CAMPING

Ⓘ Kaibab Camper Village
Ⓙ Kaibab National Forest

Note: Items with the same letter are located in the same place.

SIGHTSEEING HIGHLIGHTS

★★★★ GLEN CANYON RECREATION AREA
520/608-6405

Construction on the Glen Canyon Dam was completed in 1964, despite protest that it would destroy an area many felt was as beautiful as the Grand Canyon. It took almost 15 years to fill Lake Powell, which now boasts 1,960 miles of shoreline, much of it colorful rock canyon walls jutting above the water. The lake extends 186 miles upstream and has become one of the most popular recreation areas in the nation, drawing almost 4 million visitors each year.

> *Details: Open year-round. Admission is $5 per car, good for one week. Boat fee is $5 per day or $10 per week. (half to full day)*

★★★★ GRAND CANYON'S NORTH RIM
Highway 67; 520/638-7888

If you want to experience the Grand Canyon without the crowds, head to the North Rim, the "undiscovered" part of Grand Canyon National Park. You'll be rewarded with awesome vistas and challenging hikes, and will avoid the noise and overcrowding of the South Rim. As you drive into the park on Highway 67, continue to Bright Angel Point Area, where you'll find the Visitor Center just north lobby of the Grand Canyon Lodge. Park rangers can answer your questions, or you can pick up a copy of *The Guide* for details on park trails and activities.

Rangers offer a variety of daily programs including a 1¹/₂-hour nature walk, archeology tour, geology and night walks, and a Cliff Springs guided hike. There's also a children's program, and kids under 14 can participate in a Junior Ranger program at the Visitor Center. Grand Canyon Trail Rides, 520/638-9875, offers one-hour horseback rides for $15 and half- to full-day rides for $45 to $95.

The **Bright Angel Point Trail** is an easy half-mile hike along a paved path to a spectacular canyon view. Another easy walk is the **Cape Royal Trail**, a .6-mile, 30-minute walk along paved terrain that offers views of the canyon and Colorado River. Markers along the trail provide information about the area's natural history.

Cliff Springs Trail meanders for one mile down a forested ravine and past a small Indian ruin. The **Uncle Jim Trail** is a three-hour, five-mile path (round trip) that winds through the Kaibab Forest to a point overlooking the canyon. The 10-mile, six-hour (round-trip)

Widforss Trail hike blends forest and canyon scenery. Self-guided trail brochures are available at the trailhead.

The **North Kaibab Trail** is the only maintained trail into the canyon from the North Rim. A favorite stop 4.7 miles into the trail, **Roaring Springs** lies 3,000 feet below the rim. North Kaibab descends almost 6,000 feet, continuing on 28.4 miles to the Colorado River. You'll need a Backcountry Permit for overnight hikes. A $5 shuttle from the Grand Canyon Lodge to the North Kaibab trailhead is available at 5:30 a.m. and 7:45 a.m. daily.

Details: Visitor facilities open May 15–Oct 15, with Visitor Center open daily 8–8. Inaccessible because of snow during winter. For recorded weather information, call 520/638-7888. (half–full day)

★★★★ RAINBOW BRIDGE NATIONAL MONUMENT
50 miles up Lake Powell from Glen Canyon Dam

You can see the world's largest natural bridge only by boat or by foot. This spectacular bridge spans 275 feet and arches to over 290 feet. The top is 42 feet thick and 33 feet wide. Most people choose to see it via the water route, since the shortest hike is 13 miles one way. Two unmaintained foot trails traverse the Navajo Nation land, crossing rough canyon country.

Details: Lake Powell Resorts and Marinas, 800/528-6154, offers an all-day boat ride with lunch for $87 or a half-day for $63, with discounted children's rates. Hikers must obtain a permit from the Navajo Nation Parks and Recreation Department, 520/871-6647. (Six-hour boat ride from Wahweap)

★★★★ SLOT CANYONS
Highway 98 Milepost 299, near Page

Antelope Canyon, Corkscrew Canyon, the Windcaves, and the Crack are known as "slot canyons," the geological phenomenon created by wind and water. Such canyons are narrow and deep, sometimes measuring less than a yard across at the top but dropping more than 100 feet from rim to floor. The sandstone striations become almost incandescent as colors bounce from wall to wall, turning red to purple to deep gray. You will need a guide to explore the narrow twists and turns of Antelope Canyon.

Details: Call Scenic Tours, 520/645-5594, Lake Powell Jeep Adventures, 520/645-5501, or Antelope Photographic Tours, 801/645-5501, for guided tours at around $30 per person. At the trailhead, a

CANYONLANDS

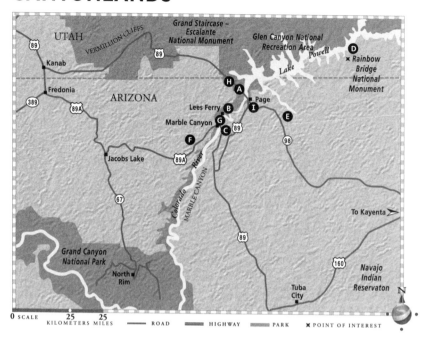

SIGHTS

- **A** Carl Hayden Visitor Center
- **B** Lees Ferry
- **C** Navajo Bridge
- **D** Rainbow National Monument
- **E** Slot Canyons

FOOD

- **F** Cliff Dwellers Lodge
- **G** Marble Canyon Lodge
- **H** Rainbow Room of Wahweap Lodge

LODGING

- **F** Cliff Dwellers Lodge
- **I** Courtyard by Marriott
- **I** Days Inn & Suites
- **B** Lees Ferry Lodge
- **G** Marble Canyon Lodge
- **I** Motel 6
- **I** Super Eight
- **H** Wahweap Lodge

CAMPING

- **B** Lees Ferry Campground
- **H** Wahweap Campground
- **H** Wahweap RV Park

Note: Items with the same letter are located in the same place.

guide will take you to the canyon for $10 plus a $5 visitor's fee. (half-to full day)

★★★ LEES FERRY
North of U.S. 89A at Marble Canyon

For years, Lees Ferry was the last place to cross the Colorado River before it plunged into the Grand Canyon. The site was originally a Mormon outpost operated by John Doyle Lee. Lee was sent to the remote area in 1872, after he was involved in a Mormon-led massacre of a California-bound wagon train in southwest Utah. Although the attack was originally blamed on the Paiute Indians, 20 years after the Mountain Meadows Massacre Lee was taken to the site of the killings and executed by firing squad. You can see some of the remnants of the outpost, Lonely Dell, on a self-guided trail. Nearby are parking areas for river-runners—this is the most put-in spot for Grand Canyon white-water expeditions. Its trophy trout fishing is also legendary.

Details: Open year round. Free. (1–2 hours)

★★ NAVAJO BRIDGE
U.S. 89A

Downstream from Lees Ferry, this graceful steel bridge carries Highway 89A across Marble Canyon. A new bridge was opened a few years ago, and the original crossing, built in 1927, is now a pedestrian walk. From the bridge you can look down almost 500 feet to the bottom of the canyon. You'll find Navajo artists selling jewelry, rugs, and other handmade items on the Navajo Reservation side of the bridge.

Details: Open year-round. Free. About a mile north on 89A is the Navajo Bridge Interpretive Center, plus a restaurant and service station. Open daily Apr–Oct 9–5. Free. (1 hour)

★★ NAVAJOLANDS ACADEMY
Navajo Reservation near Page; 520/645-2741

Spend a fascinating evening with the Navajo. You'll ride a horse-drawn wagon to a Navajo village, where you'll dine on traditional Native American foods, see Navajo dances, and hear songs and stories around the campfire. You'll watch a silversmith and weaver at work, plus see a hogan and a sweat lodge.

Details: Daily 4:30–8 p.m. $40 adults, $30 children. Reserve through the Page Chamber of Commerce, 644 N. Navajo, Suite C,

520/645-2741, or the Visitor Information Bureau, 888/261-PAGE. Living Museum open daily from 9–3. $10 per person. (4 hours)

★ **CARL HAYDEN VISITOR CENTER**
U.S. 89 north of Page; 520/608-6404
At 710 feet, the Glen Canyon Dam is the world's fourth-highest, containing almost 5 million yards of concrete. Here you can learn about its construction and take an elevator ride into its depths for a guided tour.
    Details: *Open daily 8–7 in summer, 8–5 the rest of the year. Tours from 8:30 to 3:30 on the half hour. Free. (1 hour)*

★ **JOHN WESLEY POWELL MEMORIAL MUSEUM**
6 N. Lake Powell Boulevard, Page; 520/645-9496
Lake Powell was named after John Wesley Powell, a one-armed Civil War hero who navigated the white-water rapids of the Green and Colorado Rivers in 1869. This small museum houses historic photographs and memorabilia from Powell's expedition, along with local geology exhibits and videos on the dam's construction. The museum also serves as an information center for Page and Lake Powell, and you can book tours here.
    Details: *Apr–Oct Mon–Sat 8–6, Sun 10–6. Nov–Feb weekdays only 9–5. Closed Dec 15–Feb 15. Free. (30 minutes)*

FITNESS AND RECREATION

You'll find plenty of fun on **Lake Powell.** Wahweap Marina, six miles north of Page, 800/528-6154, offers a variety of rentals to help you explore the lake. Choices range from fishing and speed boats to water skis and personal watercraft. Summer rental rates can run as high as $275 per day for a 20-foot craft.

You can also book sightseeing tours at Wahweap. The paddlewheeler *Canyon King* has one-hour tours ($10 adults, $7 children) as well as sunset and dinner cruises from $22 to $45. If you want to explore the lake's maze of canyons in a quieter fashion, rent a sea kayak from Red Rock Cyclery, 819 N. Navajo Dr., 520/654-1479, for $45 per day. The cyclery also rents mountain bikes and offers a variety of land and lake tours. Another relaxing option is an all-day or half-day float trip down the Colorado, from Glen Canyon Dam to Lees Ferry, provided by Wilderness River Adventures, 520/645-3279, or Lake Powell Resorts & Marinas, 520/645-2433. Tours run between March and October, and adult rates range from $44 to $65. Reserve early in peak summer months.

Fishing is popular, but remember that the lake is in two different states and you'll need appropriate licenses. You can arrange to fish the entire lake at the Wahweap Marina, which also sells bait and tackle. If you want to fish for trout downstream, be sure to get a trout stamp. To obtain a fishing guide, contact Arizona Reel Time, 520/355-2222, or Colorado River Guide Service, 520/355-2247. Lees Ferry Anglers, 800/962-9755, is the fishing headquarters for the region. You can buy tackle and rent waders and boats. For a scenic flight over Lake Powell, call Sunrise Airlines at the Page Airport, 238 10th Ave., 800/245-8668. Or for a picturesque round of golf, book a tee time at the Lake Powell National Golf Course, 400 Clubhouse Dr., 520/645-2023, named one of Arizona's top ten courses by *Golf Digest*.

You can explore the canyons around the lake on plenty of good hiking trails. **Horseshoe Bend** is a popular trail loop with a fabulous viewpoint hundreds of feet above the water on the edge of a sheer cliff. The steep 1.5-mile **Spencer Trail** was built in 1910 to transport coal by pack mule from Wahweap Mine to Lees Ferry. From the top of **Vermilion Cliffs**, you'll glimpse a fantastic view of the Colorado River and Lees Ferry. The 1.25-mile **Cathedral Canyon Trail** leads you to the **Cathedral Rapids** on the Colorado. For backpacking enthusiasts, the **Paria Canyon Trail** follows the Paria River from the trailhead at **Paria Canyon Wilderness Area**. After 34 miles of rugged hiking (three days one way), you'll end up at Lees Ferry. The **Lees Ferry Ranger Station**, Hwy. 89 at Lees Ferry, 520/355-2234, has maps and information. The **Carl Hayden Visitor Center**, 520/608-6404, also has brochures with area day hikes.

FOOD AND LODGING

Between the North Rim and Lake Powell are several historical lodges. You won't find a lot of other options until you get to Page, so make reservations as early as possible to stay in these popular lodges. The classic stone and log **Grand Canyon Lodge**, 303/297-2757, on the edge of the canyon rim, is listed on the National Register of Historic Places. It offers both rooms and cabins for $65 to $90 per night. The lodge's dining hall is open daily for all three meals, and a saloon and snack bar are outside the lodge's front entrance

Kaibab Lodge, 800/525-0924, is five miles north of the North Rim entrance. Built in 1926, the lodge's small rooms ($69 to $95 in summer) are in cozy, rustic cabins. The dining room serves all meals. **Jacob Lake Inn**, at the intersection of Highways 67 and 89A, 520/643-7232, has 11 rooms and 33 rustic cabins. At $66 to $95 in summer and $55 in winter, it's a popular base for cross-country skiers. The inn offers a coffee shop, dining room, and general store.

RAINBOW BRIDGE NATIONAL MONUMENT

Cliff Dwellers Lodge is in a remote area 11 miles from Lees Ferry off U.S. 89A, 800/433-2543. A basic motel has replaced the historic lodge, but the views are still impressive. The restaurant is decorated with old license plates and serves all three meals. **Lees Ferry Lodge**, a stone and log lodge built in 1929, is situated at the foot of the Vermilion Cliffs, 520/355-2231. Its rustic accommodations are popular with river rafters and those fishing along the Colorado. The adjacent Vermilion Cliffs Bar and Grille will cook your freshly caught trout.

Marble Canyon Lodge, U.S. 89A at the Navajo Bridge, 800/726-1789, is a nicely restored 1920s resort with great views, just four miles from Lees Ferry. The restaurant serves Western-style American fare and some vegetarian dishes. **Wahweap Lodge** is on the shore of Lake Powell, 100 Lakeshore Dr., 800/528-6154. It has nearly 400 rooms, most with either a balcony or patio, some with lake views. The lodge features two outdoor pools and access to all sorts of boat and equipment rental. Its popular **Rainbow Room**, 520/645-2433, boasts stunning Lake Powell views. Open 6 a.m. to 10 p.m. (shorter hours in winter), it serves a nightly buffet dinner with entertainment. It will also pack carryout meals for a day on the lake.

Page offers several good chain motels, including **Courtyard by Marriott**, 600 Clubhouse Dr., 800/321-2211, **Days Inn & Suites**, 961 N. Hwy. 89, 520/645-2800, **Motel 6**, 637 S. Lake Powell, 520/645-5888, and **Super Eight**, 115 Eighth St., 520/645-2858.

By far the lake's most popular accommodations are houseboats. They range from 35 to 60 feet, and many can sleep up to 12 people. You'll get plenty of instruction on how to operate your floating vacation home. They are furnished and have fully equipped kitchens—just bring the food. From May to mid-October, Lake Powell Resorts and Marinas, 800/528-6154, rents houseboats for $1,500 to $4,300 per week. Check for reduced winter rates and for three- to six-day packages.

CAMPING

You can reserve 82 different campsites on the North Rim, 800/365-2267. Both open camping and developed campgrounds exist in **Kaibab National Forest**, 520/635-2681. At **Kaibab Camper Village**, on Jacob Lake, 520/643-7804, you'll find RV and tent sites. **Lees Ferry Campground**, Hwy. 89, 520/645-2511, also has scenic tent and RV sites. More info is available at the ranger station, 520/355-2234. **Wahweap RV Park**, 100 Lakeshore Dr., 800/528-6154, offers full marina facilities for $20.50 per night. Nearby **Wahweap Campground**, 100 Lakeshore Dr., 520/645-2471, is $8.50 per night.

6
INDIAN COUNTRY

The Navajo Nation and Hopi Reservation in northeast Arizona are a combination of vast isolation punctuated by spectacular scenery. The Navajo land is the largest Indian reservation in the nation, while the Hopi Reservation sits like a small island in the middle. Their boundaries were defined in the 1800s by the U.S. government, and to this day the two tribes continue to have legal disputes and argue over the land. The Hopi claim the Anasazi as their ancestors and have lived peacefully along these mesas for centuries.

The Navajo migrated into the area later, and their culture was greatly influenced by the invading Spanish explorers in the mid-1500s. They started peach groves from seedlings brought by the Spanish and raised sheep that were not native to the area. Canyon de Chelly was their sacred land, and even during war they retreated to this canyon undefeated. However, the U.S. Army sent Kit Carson in after them in 1863. He trapped the warring tribe in the dead of winter and proceeded to starve them out. After they surrendered, he cut down the fruit trees and slaughtered the sheep. The Navajos were then marched off to a desolate area of New Mexico, where more than one-third of them died. Finally the government let them return to their homeland and established the Navajo Nation.

Throughout the ages, pottery, weavings, baskets, and Hopi kachinas had utilitarian or religious significance. But the jewelry style we know today was started in the late 1800s to sell to American tourists. Many Hopi and Navajo are straddling two worlds, trying to make a living and exist in today's society while clinging to their culture and language. As you enter the special world of the Hopi and Navajo, slow down, catch your breath, and enjoy the scenery and these remarkable people.

A PERFECT DAY IN INDIAN COUNTRY

Spend the night at the Hopi Cultural Center so you can be at the ceremonial dances at dawn. Then try some blue-corn pancakes at the Cultural Center restaurant. Tour Walpi before heading to Navajo country and Canyon de Chelly. Check out the visitor center and book an afternoon jeep tour into the canyon, or drive to the south rim on your own. Cap off the day by sleeping in a hogan at a Navajo bed-and-breakfast. Of course, you really can't see enough of this country in a day, so plan on staying a few more.

SIGHTSEEING HIGHLIGHTS

★★★★ CANYON DE CHELLY
Three miles east of Chinle on Highway 191; 520/674-5500

This 26-mile complex of red-hued canyons provides a spectacular backdrop for hundreds of Anasazi ruins, including multistoried apartments, perched within huge recesses in the vertical sandstone walls soaring 1,000 feet above the canyon floor. The dwellings were built during five periods of Indian culture dating from A.D. 350 to 1300.

Check in at the visitor center for schedules of ranger-guided hikes during the summer. They also have a list of authorized Navajo guides who will share firsthand knowledge of their homeland. If you provide the wheels, they'll take you on a hike or four-wheel drive into the canyon. Thunderbird Lodge, 800/679-2473, can also book you on a half- or full-day "shake-and-bake" jeep tour, on bone-jarring trails that can be quite hot in the summer. But it's worth it to see ancient petroglyphs and ruins up close, with lots of stops for photographs. Horseback tours including overnight trips are available from three authorized operators. Call Justin's Horse Rentals, 520/674-5678, Twin Trail Tours, 520/674-8425, or Totsonii Ranch, 520/755-6209.

The **White House Ruins Trail** is your only chance to enter the canyon without a ranger or guide. You'll descend 600 feet to the canyon floor, where you can see (but not enter) the 80-room ruin. Take lots of water on this two-hour hike. You can also motor along

STAY IN A WIGWAM

If you're looking for a funky place to spend the night, stop at the Wigwam Motel, 811 W. Hopi Dr. in Holbrook, 520/524-3048. The concrete wigwams were built in the 1940s along historic Route 66. They've been renovated but still offer a rustic overnight experience. You'll also find a small museum at the motel.

Holbrook, the closest town to the Petrified Forest, is a rock-hound paradise. You'll find shops all through downtown packed with petrified wood, fossils, and all kinds of collectable minerals.

the north and south rim drives, each providing stunning overlooks and sheer-drop cliffs.

Spider Rock Overlook, on the south rim drive, is probably the most spectacular vista. You'll see the junction of Canyon de Chelly and Monument Canyon, where the twin towers of Spider Rock jut more than 800 feet out of the canyon floor. Each rim drive will take about two hours. Guidebooks are available at the visitor center.

Details: Open daily 8–5, 8–6 in summer. Canyon entrance is free. Navajo guides charge $10 per hour, three hours minimum. Jeep tours run from $35–$55 per person. Horseback tours range from $8 per hour–$70 per full day per person. (half- to full day)

★★★★ **HOPILAND**
Highway 264

The Hopi live in and around several villages scattered on top and below three fingerlike mesas. Many dwell without electricity and plumbing in the same stone homes of their ancestors. First, stop at the **Hopi Cultural Center** on Second Mesa, 520/734-6650. The museum houses historic Hopi weavings, pottery, kachinas, and jewelry, as well as antique photographs and interpretive displays. You can visit the nearby Second Mesa villages or book a 40-minute guided tour of First Mesa at Walpi. Besides learning about Hopi history and culture, you may get to visit inside old stone dwellings. Just drive to the top of First Mesa and look for the information office, 520/737-2262. **Old Oraibi**, the oldest village, is a few miles to the west on Third Mesa.

If you want to shop for Hopi crafts, several excellent galleries and plenty of small shops exist in the villages. At the **Hopi Arts and Crafts Guild** on Second Mesa, 520/734-2463, more than 200 artists sell their work cooperatively. You'll also see tables and stands with pottery, kachinas, and jewelry for sale along the dusty, winding paths, and many stone homes have art for sale.

To see a Hopi ceremonial dance, check with the **Hopi Tribal Council,** 520/734-2441, for details. These are sacred Hopi rituals, and viewing them requires specific codes of conduct. Each village is autonomous, and dances are scheduled according to their own customs and traditions. Look for policy signs posted at each entrance. They request the same reverence due any sacred event: neat attire and respectful, quiet behavior. Shorts are not allowed. Dances usually begin shortly after sunrise on Saturday and Sunday and continue intermittently throughout the day, ending at dusk.

Details: *Hopi Cultural Center Museum: Open Mon–Fri 8–5, Sat–Sun 9–3. $3 adults, $1 children. Photography, sketching, tape-recording, and videotaping the villages or ceremonies is strictly prohibited. All materials and equipment will be confiscated. (2–4 hours)*

★★★★ **MONUMENT VALLEY NAVAJO TRIBAL PARK**
U.S. Highway 163, 23 miles north of Kayenta
435/727-3353 or 727-3287
If you've ever watched a John Wayne Western, you've probably seen the stunning red-earth landscapes and gravity-defying rock formations of Monument Valley. After director John Ford filmed *Stagecoach* here in 1938, it became a popular production location. Movies filmed here include *How the West Was Won, My Darling Clementine, Back to the Future III,* and *Thelma and Louise.*

While you can see some of the red-rock monuments from the highway, you'll need to drive into the park to view such celebrated formations as the **Totem Pole**, a miraculously thin spire rising 470 feet, or the **Sun's Eye** arch. This is a self-guided driving tour along marked valley roads only. No off-road hiking is allowed unless you are with an approved tour guide.

Some of the more remote areas can be seen only with a Navajo guide, who can be booked at the visitor center. Jeep tours (1 1/2 hours to all day) can take you past petroglyphs and rock formations to a traditional Navajo hogan (house). Options include sunrise and sunset tours, cookouts, overnight camping, and photography tours.

Check with Roland's Navajoland Tours, 800/368-2785, or Totem Pole Guided Tours, 800/345-TOUR. If you want to feel like John Wayne riding through the valley, book a horseback tour from Ed Black's Monument Valley Trail Rides, 800/551-4039, or Bigman's Horseback Riding, 520/677-3219. You can also book tours from Goulding's Tours, 801/727-3231.

Goulding's Museum and Trading Post are just a few miles from the park entrance. The trading post is set up as it was in the '20s and '30s, when it was the Gouldings' home. The museum contains lots of displays about movies filmed here.

Details: Open daily 8–5, summer 7–7. $2.50 adults, $1 seniors, free under age 8. Tours cost $20 per person for 1 1/2 hours, $60 for all day, and $100 for overnight. Goulding's Trading Post is open daily 7:30 a.m.–9 p.m. Admission is by donation. (2–4 hours)

★★★★ PETRIFIED FOREST NATIONAL PARK
I-40; 520/524-6228

While this park is best known for its abundance of colorful petrified wood, along the 28-mile park road you'll also find stunning views of the **Painted Desert**, extensive deposits of Triassic-age fossils, and remnants of ancient Pueblo Indian cultures. Three visitor centers each contain varied exhibits and information. The Painted Desert Visitor Center runs an informative film every half-hour. The **Painted Desert Inn National Historic Landmark** was built by the Civilian Conservation Corps (CCC) in the 1930s. Along with exhibits on the inn's history, you'll find demonstrations by Native American craftspeople. The **Rainbow Forest Museum** displays exhibits on the park's archeological and paleontological resources. At an easy half-mile hiking trail along the rim's north end, you can catch desert views and see typical plants and wildlife.

Details: Open daily 8–5. Extended summer hours. $10 per vehicle. (1–3 hours)

★★★ NAVAJO NATIONAL MONUMENT
AZ Highway 564; 520/672-2367

You'll find remarkably preserved 700-year-old Anasazi cliff ruins, but getting to them takes some work. If you're not up for a strenuous hike, take the self-guided **Sandal Trail**, about one mile round trip, which leads you to a breathtaking view of the **Betatakin Ruin** from a scenic overlook. Take binoculars if you have them, or use

INDIAN COUNTRY

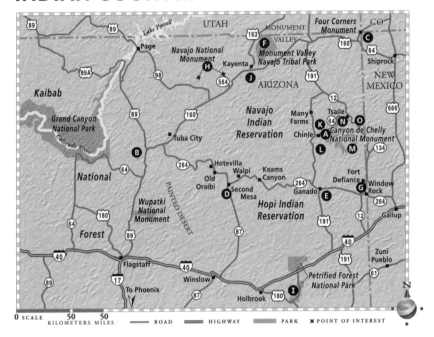

SIGHTS

- **A** Canyon de Chelly National Monument
- **B** Dinosaur Tracks
- **C** Four Corners Navajo Tribal Park
- **D** Hopiland
- **E** Hubbell Trading Post
- **F** Monument Valley Navajo Tribal Park
- **G** Navajo Nation Museum
- **H** Navajo National Monument
- **I** Petrified Forest National Park

FOOD

- **J** Burger King
- **F** Gouldings Lodge and Trading Post
- **K** Holiday Inn-Canyon de Chelly
- **J** Holiday Inn-Kayenta
- **D** Hopi Cultural Center Motel
- **L** Thunderbird Lodge

LODGING

- **F** Country of Many Hogan Bed & Breakfast
- **F** Gouldings Lodge and Trading Post
- **K** Holiday Inn-Canyon de Chelly
- **J** Holiday Inn-Kayenta
- **D** Hopi Cultural Center Motel
- **L** Thunderbird Lodge

CAMPING

- **A** Cottonwood Campground
- **F** Country of Many Hogan B&B
- **F** Goulding's KOA Campground
- **F** Mitten View Campground
- **M** Spider Rock RV Park & Camping
- **N** Tsaile Lake Campgrounds
- **O** Wheatfields Lake Campgrounds

Note: Items with the same letter are located in the same place.

the on-site telescope. The **Aspen Forest Trail** will lead you about 300 feet down into Betatakin Canyon for a stunning view of the forest, but you won't see any ruins along this trail. For a close-up view of the ruins, take the five-mile (round trip) ranger-guided hiking tour 700 feet into the canyon. It takes five to six hours and is as strenuous as hiking in the Grand Canyon. Carry at least a quart of water. The 160-room **Keet Seel** cliff dwelling is located 8¹/₂ miles one way from the visitor center. It's accessible only by hiking or on horseback trips with an NPS backcountry permit. The visitor center has prehistoric artifacts and interpretive exhibits on the Pueblo culture. You'll also find authentic Native American arts and crafts in the center's gift shop, and you can meet individual artists selling their crafts on the patio.

Details: Open daily 8–5, 8–6 in summer. Betatakin Ruin Tours are limited to 25 people. Tour times vary but always begin in the morning. No reservations. Arrive early for a free tour ticket. Backcountry hiking permits to Keet Seel are free but limited to 20 per day. Two months' advance reservations are available. Consider a daylong horseback tour provided by a local Navajo family, $55 per person. (1 hour)

★★ HUBBELL TRADING POST
Highway 264 near Ganado; 520/755-3475
Twenty-three-year-old John Lorenzo Hubbell arrived in the area in 1876 and opened a trading post two years later. In 1883 he started construction on this post, the oldest continuously operated trading post in the country. The trading post was and still is a crossroads of Navajo and Anglo cultures. Start at the visitor center, where rangers can answer your questions. Spend some time watching Navajo rug weavers and silversmiths demonstrating their crafts. Then take a guided tour of the **Hubbell Home**. And finally, explore the Trading Post, which continues to sell handcrafted rugs, pottery, and jewelry. You'll also notice groceries and dry goods for sale because many Navajos still trade here.

Details: Open daily 8–5, 8–6 in summer. Free. Picnic tables available. (1 hour)

★★ NAVAJO NATION MUSEUM
Highway 264, Window Rock; 520/871-6436
This new facility is the country's largest Native American museum, encompassing a research library, gallery, museum, and children's in-

PHOTOGRAPHY ON THE RESERVATION

You can take photographs on the Navajo Reservation, but if you want to include any of the Navajo residents in your picture, always ask permission and plan on tipping at least $1 per person.

Photography is not permitted on the Hopi Reservation. You are also prohibited from sketching or recording any of the ceremonies or any of the Hopi villages. Equipment, including cameras, will be confiscated if used.

terpretive area. Native American music and dance performances are scheduled in the large outdoor amphitheater and indoor theater.

Details: Mon–Fri 8–5. Call about weekend events. Free. (1 hour)

★ DINOSAUR TRACKS
Five miles east of Highway 89, near Tuba City

This is another fun one with the kids. It's hard to believe this area was ever under water, but more than 200 million years ago, a dinosaur roamed across what was then a muddy shoreline. The tracks are visible at about 100 feet from the unpaved road.

Details: You'll usually find some enterprising locals waiting to give you the grand tour. It makes the stop interesting. Expect to tip. Arts and crafts vendors often set up along the road. (30 minutes)

★ FOUR CORNERS NAVAJO TRIBAL PARK
U.S. Highway 160 and AZ Highway 40; 520/871-6647

This is a fun stop, especially for the kids. It's the only place in the United States where the corners of four states—Arizona, Colorado, New Mexico, and Utah—converge. If you're willing to look like you're playing leapfrog, you can position each hand and foot in a different state. There's a nice visitor center, and along the road you will find Navajo artists selling rugs, sandpaintings, art, pottery, and jewelry.

Details: Open daily 8–5, 8–8 in summer. $2.50 per person. Picnic tables. (30 minutes)

FITNESS AND RECREATION

Off-trail hiking and rock climbing are prohibited. Always stay on designated trails or established routes unless you have a permit from the Navajo Parks & Recreation Department, P.O. Box 9000, Window Rock, AZ 86515, 520/871-6637. Trout and bass fishing are available at several lakes in the high pine meadows on the state's eastern edge. Check for license requirements with Navajo Fish and Wildlife, P.O. Box 1480, Window Rock, AZ 86515, 520/871-6451. **Wheatfields Lake**, Highway 191 near the New Mexico border, is the best spot for trout. **Many Hands Lake**, north of Chinle, has largemouth bass and catfish; it's one of two lakes on the reservation with no motor restrictions. If you're visiting during August, stop at the all-Indian rodeos and exciting powwows of **Navajo Nation Fair** in Window Rock.

FOOD AND LODGING

Because the population is sparse throughout Indian Country, most restaurants and lodges are combined. If you're staying in Monument Valley, check out **Goulding's Lodge and Trading Post**, six miles from the park entrance, 801/727-3231. The lodge's guest-room balconies offer superb views, and its restaurant serves American and Navajo fare. Room rates range from $80 to $125, with cabins starting at $130.

For a truly unique experience, stay at the **Country of Many Hogan Bed & Breakfast**, 888/291-4397 (pin 4617) or e-mail nezfoster@prodigy.com, at Boot Mesa in Monument Valley. You'll stay in a hand-constructed hogan with no electricity or running water and dine on Native foods prepared over a juniper-wood fire. Enjoy their feature specialty, the traditional sweat lodge, or arrange hiking and horseback trail rides. The **Holiday Inn-Kayenta**, at the junction of highway 160 and Highway 163, 800/HOLIDAY, has a restaurant that's open from 6 a.m. to 10 p.m. If you're hungry for fast food, the Kayenta **Burger King** has the only display about the Navajo Code Talkers in the Southwest. The **Holiday Inn-Canyon de Chelly**, just outside of Chinle, 800/23-HOTEL, is close to the canyon's entrance and has a restaurant. Native American dances are often held on summer evenings. Rates at both Holiday Inns range from $100 to $130.

The **Thunderbird Lodge**, 800/679-BIRD, is the most historic spot to stay when visiting Canyon de Chelly. Housed in an old adobe building, its guest rooms have rustic furniture and interesting Navajo sandpaintings on the walls. It's built on the site of an early trading post which is now the lodge cafeteria, open from 6:30 a.m. to 8:30 p.m. Rates are under $100. The **Hopi Cultural Center Motel**, on Second Mesa, 520/734-2401, is the only place to stay on

ROCK ART CANYON RANCH

You can see hundreds of Anasazi petroglyphs and visit the site of the last U.S. Army and Apache battle at this remote working cattle ranch located between Holbrook and Winslow. The ranch offers old-time cattle roundups, trail rides, swimming in Chevelon Canyon surrounded by petroglyphs, horseback rides, hayrides into the sunset, and horseshoe pitchin'. You'll also see a pioneer and cowboy museum and the last remaining bunkhouse of the Hashknife Outfit, one of the largest nineteenth-century ranching operations in Arizona. For details, call 520/288-3260.

the Hopi Reservation. It's simple but clean, with rates from $60 to $80. A restaurant, open from 7 a.m. to 9 p.m., serves both American and Hopi dishes. You'll find numerous chain budget motels in Winslow, 70 miles south of Hopi, and also in Holbrook, close to the Petrified Forest. Both are on I-40, and familiar motels line both sides of the highway.

Several bed-and-breakfasts on the Navajo Reservation provide a variety of traditional experiences. Call the Navajo Tourism Department, 520/871-6436, or visit their Web site at www.atin.com/navajoland for a complete list.

CAMPING

At Monument Valley, camp at **Mitten View Campground**, 801/727-3353, for $10 per night plus $2.50 per car; or **Goulding's KOA Campground**, 801/727-3231, for $14 to $22 per night. The latter is near a restaurant and service station. You can also park your RV or camp at the **Country of Many Hogan B&B** (see Lodging). **Cottonwood Campground** has tent sites and RV parking next to Thunderbird Lodge, near Chinle, but water and restrooms are shut down in winter. Also scenic is the **Spider Rock RV Park & Camping**, near Canyon de Chelly, 520/674-8261. Tent and RV sites can be found at **Wheatfields Lake Campgrounds** on Indian Route 12. You can camp at **Tsaile Lake Campgrounds**, but RVs are not recommended.

7
THE WHITE MOUNTAINS AND APACHE COUNTRY

The White Mountains have been inhabited for thousands of years. You'll find examples of petroglyphs from 10,000 B.C. to dwellings from A.D. 1400. The Apache have roamed the mountains for the last few centuries. To protect trade routes and encourage settlement, the U.S. Army established an outpost in the territory in 1870. The post was eventually named Fort Apache. Cattlemen and sheep owners started ranching on the open range, and soon the logging industry moved in. At the end of the Apache wars, the area was settled. Today you'll find an idyllic year-round recreation area full of historic cabins, streams, trout-filled lakes, and miles of hiking trails. It makes for a great family vacation or romantic weekend getaway.

A PERFECT DAY IN THE WHITE MOUNTAINS

Spend the morning exploring the region. Hike along the Trail System or to the top of Mt. Baldy. Be sure and pack a picnic lunch so you can leisurely enjoy the views. Spend the afternoon touring Fort Apache or Raven Site Ruin. Have a steak dinner at a cowboy restaurant, then head back to your cozy cabin for a relaxing evening in front of the fireplace.

WHITE MOUNTAINS REGION

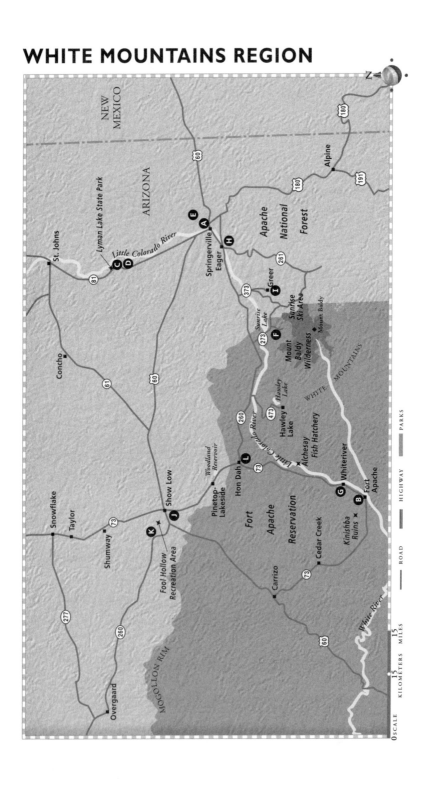

SIGHTSEEING HIGHLIGHTS

★★★★ **FORT APACHE HISTORIC PARK**
Highway 73, Apache Reservation; 520/338-1392
Home to the renowned Apache Scouts, this is the famous 1870 fort where the U.S. Army tangled with Apache warrior Geronimo. General Crook's Headquarters has been turned into a small museum housing artifacts and old photos. The 300-plus acres contain 20 historic buildings, prehistoric ruins, and petroglyphs. At the old cemetery where Indians and soldiers lie buried side-by-side you'll find lots of interesting headstones. Pick up a walking-tour guide at the **Apache Cultural Center**, 520/338-4625, which features rotating exhibits on Apache history, culture, and arts.
Details: Cultural Center open Mon–Fri 8–5. $3 adults, $2 students over 5, under 6 free. Park open daily. Free. (1–2 hours)

★★★★ **RAVEN SITE RUIN**
Route 191/180; 520/333-5857
This prehistoric pueblo ruin, occupied from around 1000 to 1450, contains two kivas and more than 800 rooms. Visit the on-site White Mountain Archeological Center, where you can join a hands-on archaeological excavation. After excavating, you will learn laboratory techniques in curating, restoration, reconstruction, and preservation. You can also take a horseback ride along the petroglyph trail, where you'll see thousands of examples of this ancient rock art. Or hike the

SIGHTS
Ⓐ Casa Malpais Archaeological Park
Ⓑ Fort Apache Historic Park
Ⓒ Lyman Lake State Park
Ⓓ Raven Site Ruin
Ⓔ Springerville Volcanic Field
Ⓕ Sunrise Park Resort
Ⓖ White Mountain Apache Reservation

FOOD
Ⓗ Ms. Elle's of South Fork
Ⓐ Red Bandanna Steak House

LODGING
Ⓘ Greer Lodge
Ⓘ Red Setter Inn B&B
Ⓗ South Fork Guest Ranch
Ⓕ Sunrise Park Resort
Ⓐ Super 8
Ⓙ Holiday Inn Express

CAMPING
Ⓐ Casa Malpais Campground
Ⓚ Fool Hollow Lake Recreation Area
Ⓛ Hon Dah RV Park
Ⓒ Lyman Lake State Park
Ⓖ White Mountain Wildlife and Outdoor Recreation Division

Note: Items with the same letter are located in the same place.

trails into the fossil beds and rockhound in the wilderness. Tent campers and RVs are welcome.

Details: *Visitor Center open daily May 1–Oct 15, 10–5. Free. Guided one-hour site tour $4 adults, $3 seniors and ages 12–17, under 12 free. Three-hour petroglyph tour $18 adults, $15 under 18. Day excavation program $59 adults, $39 ages 9–17.*

★★★★ SUNRISE PARK RESORT
Off AZ 260 on AZ 273, Greer; 520/735-7600

This great winter and summer recreation area is operated by the White Mountain Apache Tribe. It encompasses more than 65 trails on three mountains, for downhill skiing with lots of beginning and intermediate slopes. This is a family-oriented resort with a ski school, 520/735-7518. At the top of 11,000-foot Apache Peak is a day lodge with good food and fabulous views. You'll even find lights for the thrill of nighttime skiing on the weekends. Cross-country skiing, snowmobiling, and ice fishing are also popular winter sports.

After the snow melts, you can fish at **Hawley Lake** or **Sunrise Lake,** where the boat rentals include small sailboats. Hiking, biking, and riding the ski lifts are just a few ways to enjoy the White Mountains' wilderness during summer.

Details: *Ski season starts in November. For snow report, call 888/804-2779. Lift tickets $32 adults, $18 children. (half- to full day)*

★★★ CASA MALPAIS ARCHAEOLOGICAL PARK
318 Main Street, Springerville; 520/333-5375

This is one of the few Mogollon ruins open to the public. The 16-acre pueblo complex is known to archaeologists worldwide for prehistoric qualities never before seen in this part of the world. The site features a Great Kiva made of volcanic rock, an astronomical observatory, a hidden staircase, a ceremonial plaza, and petroglyphs. You can visit the museum and field laboratory and schedule guided tours of the ruins.

Details: *Museum and gift shop open daily 9–4. Guided tours at 9, 11, and 2:30, subject to weather. $4 adults, $3 students and seniors, $1 children under 12. (2–4 hours)*

★★★ WHITE MOUNTAIN APACHE RESERVATION
520/338-1230

The Apache tribe loves to share their rich history and culture with visitors. **Whiteriver**, on Highway 73, serves as headquarters for the Apache Nation. You may see Apache women in colorful native dress, and during summer months you'll find many artists selling their hand-crafted goods. **White Mountain Apache Enterprise**, 520/338-4417, displays full mounts of various wildlife.

One mile past Fort Apache, turn off on a dirt road; in two miles you'll come to the **Kinishba Ruins**. These 200-plus rooms are more than 1,000 years old and were visited by Coronado's expedition in his quest for the Seven Cities of Cibola. While the walls are in good shape, the roof is not, so do not enter. Many additional ruins are on the other side of the canyon.

Fifteen miles south of the Hon-Dah Casino, 520/369-0299, on Highway 73 turn east and proceed five miles on a paved road to the **Alchesay National Fish Hatchery**. It's a nice drive along the North Fork of the White River and a beautiful canyon setting for the hatchery. By the river are good picnic facilities, a display, theater presentations, and fish ponds. The hatchery is open weekdays 7 to 3:30.

Also on the reservation, you'll find more than 25 mountain lakes and nearly 800 miles of clear streams, perfect for camping, hiking, fishing, and white-water rafting. In addition, there are several attractions, motels, restaurants, shops, and seasonal cultural events.

Details: For permit information, call the Fort Apache Office of Tourism, 520/338-1230, or the Wildlife and Outdoor Division, 520/338-4385. A recreation permit is $5 per day, including fishing and picnicking. (half to full day)

★★ AUTO SIGHTSEEING TOURS
Highway 260, Lakeside; 520/368-5111

Two tours are available: The **Lake Mountain Tour** takes four hours to cover 45 miles through pine, fir, and aspen forests. You should see plenty of wildlife and can walk up the Lake Mountain lookout tower. The **Porter Mountain Tour** takes two hours to travel 33 miles. It covers local history, forest management, and timber harvesting.

Details: Check in at the Lakeside Ranger Station, which provides a tape player, cassette tape, and map at no charge.

★★ LYMAN LAKE STATE PARK
Highway 191, 10 miles south of St. Johns; 520/337-4441

If you'd like to combine recreation and history, this is the spot. This relatively unknown lake remains uncrowded, and its calm waters provide great swimming and fishing. You'll find one of the few permanent waterskiing slalom courses in the state here. Take a pontoon boat ride to **Rattlesnake Point Pueblo Ruin**, a 700-year-old ruin, from which you can take a moderate half-mile hike along **Petroglyph Trail**, dating back to 10,000 B.C. You might even see a few buffalo grazing.

Details: Park admission is $4 per vehicle. Daily tours $2 per person. (1–3 hours)

★ **SPRINGERVILLE VOLCANIC FIELD**
Highways 60, 180, and 260; 520/333-2123
More than 1,158 miles of volcanoes exist in this area, which is one of the largest young volcanic fields in the United States. You'll find cinder cones, lava tubes, and more than 405 vents. Just outside Springerville is the shield volcano of Coyote Knoll—this is the same type of volcano responsible for the Hawaiian Islands' formation.

Details: Call the Round Valley Chamber of Commerce, 520-333-2123, for a free map of this self-guided tour. (1–2 hours)

FITNESS AND RECREATION

The White Mountains offer four seasons of family fun and outdoor activities. The White Mountain Trail System is a series of 180-plus miles of interconnecting loops and trails for hiking, mountain biking, horseback riding, and cross-country skiing. **Woodland Lake Park,** a popular fishing spot, is at the center of the system and features a four-mile loop trail. This loop connects with another trail leading to the scenic **Big Springs Environmental Study Area**.

The **Mogollon Rim Overlook** is a one-mile hike with signs describing local vegetation and history. Separating Arizona's northern plateau region from the lower deserts of central and southern Arizona, the rim offers breathtaking views. During fire season (end of May to September, depending on rain), you can climb the Springer Mountain and Lake Mountain Fire Lookout Towers from 8 to 4:30. You'll find other towers at Greens Peak and Big Lake. Inquire at the Lakeside Ranger Station, 520/368-5111, for exact dates.

About six miles past Sunrise Ski area is a beautiful trail along the West Fork of Little Colorado that takes you to the top of **Mt. Baldy**, the second-highest peak in Arizona. Three miles past Sheep's Crossing is another trail that follows the East Fork to the top of Mt. Baldy. Both of these great hikes are part of the **Sheep's Crossing & Mt. Baldy Wilderness Area**.

The **South Fork Trail** follows the South Fork of the Little Colorado River, a stocked trout stream. This is a popular and easy six-mile round-trip

ALONG THE CORONADO TRAIL

This is a remote, winding road that is named for the Spanish explorer Coronado who, in 1540, explored this area looking for the Seven Cities of Gold. Geronimo roamed this same area in the 1800s. Leave Springerville and drive south on Highway 191 to Alpine. This picturesque valley, known as the Alps of Arizona, is surrounded by the **Apache-Sitgreaves National Forest**. This more remote area is a great place to explore trout streams and hiking trails. The aspens are stunning in the fall, and wildflowers blanket the region in spring.

One of the most interesting places to stay is the **Sprucedale Ranch**, 520/333-4984, a working cattle/horse ranch. This is a great family-oriented guest ranch, with rustic cabins, home-cooked meals, and terrific trail rides. Kids can even milk the cows. Most folks stay for a week, but you can always check in for shorter stays.

Highway 191 continues its scenic trail until it intersects with Highway 70.

hike. **Butler Canyon Nature Trail**, outside Greer, is an easy one-mile walk lined with signage describing the flora and geological features along the trail. Trail maps are available at the ranger stations.

You can fish for trout, bass, catfish, walleye, bluegill, and green sunfish in hundreds of miles of clear streams and more than 40 pristine mountain lakes. You'll also encounter the native Apache trout, unique to Arizona, in this popular fly-fishing area. **Lee Valley Reservoir** and the upper west fork of the **Black River** are managed for unique species and are regulated for artificial lure and fly fishing only.

For aspiring fly fishers, Greer Lodge, 888/475-4643, offers private and school instruction from spring to fall. Two-day instruction runs $190 per person; private lessons are $25 per hour. The X Diamond Ranch, west of Eagar, 520/333-2286, has a fly-fishing catch-and-release program. Only five people per day are permitted to fish the two-mile stretch of river, which is known for rainbows and German browns. It's $25 for a half-day, $35 for a full day. Two Phoenix-based fly-fishing schools work with the X Diamond Ranch. For information, call Arizona Fly-Fishing School, 480/730-6808, or Tinnon's Complete Fishery, 602/371-0674.

Rainbow Lake, near Lakeside, is known for trout and bass and offers

PINETOP/LAKESIDE

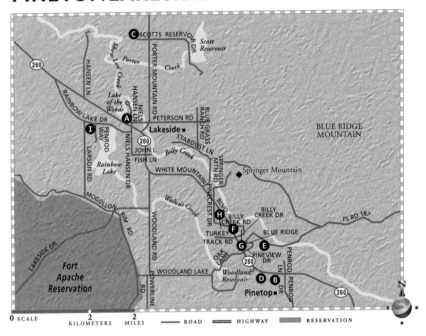

SIGHTS
Ⓐ Auto Sightseeing Tours

FOOD
Ⓑ Charlie Clark's Steakhouse
Ⓒ Chuck Wagon Steak House and 1890 Saloon
Ⓓ Johnny Mocha's Gourmet Coffee House
Ⓔ Lotus Garden
Ⓕ Pinetop Cafe

LODGING
Ⓖ Best Western Inn of Pinetop
Ⓗ Whispering Pines Resort
Ⓘ Rainbow's End Resort

boat rentals, as do **Big Lake,** near Springerville, and **Hawley Lake,** on the Apache Reservation. Call Arizona Game and Fish, 520/367-4281, for fishing reports and license info. For fishing permits on the Apache Reservation, contact the Wildlife and Outdoor Recreation Division, 520/338-4385.

No license is required at **Fred's Lake,** near Pinetop, where you pay by the pound. You can rent equipment and have your fish cleaned mid-May through September. Check with the Pinetop-Lakeside Chamber of Commerce, 520/367-4290 or www.pinetop.com, for maps and information on specific trails and a complete listing of the White Mountains' lakes and streams.

Horseback riding is another popular pastime, especially on the Trail System. Call Lee Valley Outfitters, 520/735-7454, who also offer winter sleigh rides. Pinetop Lakes Equestrian Center, 520/369-1000, features a variety of rides and rents snowmobiles in winter. Porter Mountain Stables, 520/368-5306, has summer horse rides. For golf, call the Pinetop Lakes Golf & Country Club, 520/369-4531, one of six scenic public courses. Check with the Round Valley Chamber of Commerce, 520/333-2123, for fall foliage tours and photo safaris.

FOOD

On Highway 260, between Show Low, Lakeside, and Pinetop, a string of restaurants includes some chain and fast-food establishments. For breakfast, try **Johnny Mocha's Gourmet Coffee House**, 476 W. White Mountain Blvd., Lakeside, 520/367-0586, where you can also grab a gourmet sandwich and homemade soup for lunch. Just down the street, **Pinetop Cafe**, 436 W. White Mountain Blvd., 520/367-2517, is a casual stop for breakfast, lunch, or dinner.

Charlie Clark's Steakhouse, 1701 White Mountain Blvd., 520/367-4900, has been a Pinetop tradition for almost 60 years and specializes in prime rib, steaks, and seafood. Reservations are suggested. Another good steak place is the **Chuck Wagon Steak House and 1890 Saloon**, 4048 Porter Mountain Rd., Lakeside, 520/368-5800.

The **Lotus Garden**, 984 E. White Mountain Blvd., Pinetop, 520/367-2568, serves great Oriental food. In Springerville, the **Red Bandanna Steak House** is a fun Western-style café featuring steaks, burgers, and Mexican entrees. Live bands play on Friday and Saturday. At South Fork Guest Ranch near Eagar, you'll find an interesting restaurant named after the long-suffering mother on TV's *Dallas*. **Ms. Elle's of South Fork**, 520/333-4455, offers a continental cuisine with such dishes as smoked salmon and pesto ravioli. Be sure to check out the dessert tray.

LODGING

One of the fun things about going to the White Mountains is staying in a rustic, streamside log cabin, a charming bed-and-breakfast, or a historic old lodge. This area contains plenty of choices. You can walk to Woodland Lake and Walnut Creek from **Whispering Pines Resort**, in Pinetop, 800/840-3867. Rates are $60 to $124. The **Rainbow's End Resort**, just off Rainbow Lake Road in Lakeside, 520/368-9004, is a year-round spot on Rainbow Lake. The resort offers fully equipped basic cabins and access to pontoon, fishing, and paddleboats, plus tackle and bait. Rates are $65 to $95.

Greer Lodge, in Greer, 520/735-7216, is known for its cozy cabins ($75 to $280) and private fishing ponds. Also near Greer is **Red Setter Inn B&B**, 888-99-GREER, a romantic getaway right on the river. Some rooms have fireplaces and Jacuzzi tubs. Rates are from $120 to $160. The **South Fork Guest Ranch**, outside Springerville, 520/333-4455, is a popular family getaway, with creekside cabins ($35 to $115) and plenty of fishing. If you want to be near the ski slopes, check out **Sunrise Park Resort**, 800/55-HOTEL. Rates from $65 to $95.

From Show Low to Pinetop, you'll find good chain motels like **Holiday Inn Express**, in Show Low, 800/HOLIDAY; **Best Western Inn of Pinetop**, 800/528-1234; and **Super 8**, Springerville, 520/333-2655. All have rooms from $50 to $100.

CAMPING

Lots of scenic campsites exist throughout the area. Check out **Fool Hollow Lake Recreation Area**, near Show Low, 520/537-3680. **Casa Malpais Campground,** on Highway 60 near Springerville, has RV and tent sites for $10 to $16. **Lyman Lake State Park**, on Highway 180/191, 17 miles north of Springerville, 520/337-4441, has water-view campsites. For camping on the Apache Reservation, contact the **White Mountain Wildlife and Outdoor Recreation Division**, 520/338-4385. **Hon Dah RV Park**, next to the casino, 520/360-7400, is a popular spot with lots of amenities.

8
THE MINING MIDDLE

If you're looking for outdoor adventure and unique destinations, discover the people and lands of Middle Arizona. This charming part of the state is steeped in history yet remains an unhurried place to visit. For a great contrast, you can see evidence of prehistoric Indian dwellings from hundreds of years ago, then visit the most ultramodern controlled environment in the world, Biosphere 2. Historic buildings from the wild 1800s mining days sit alongside current open-pit mining operations. You'll hear stories of lost gold mines and tales of Apache and U.S. Cavalry combat. Nature lovers will appreciate the fishing—choose from more than 100 lakes and ponds on the San Carlos Apache Reservation—then sleeping under the stars in the Pinal Mountains.

A PERFECT DAY IN MIDDLE ARIZONA

Start the day at the Boyce Thompson Arboretum. Spend the morning wandering along its scenic nature trails, where the frantic pace of the world fades to the songs of birds. Catch a lecture or tour Colonel Thompson's imposing mansion, then find a shady grove for a picnic lunch. Spend the afternoon exploring the region by car. Take the Highway 177/77 loop to Globe before driving northeast on Highway 60 to the spectacular Salt River Canyon, often referred to as the "mini-Grand Canyon."

MINING MIDDLE AREA

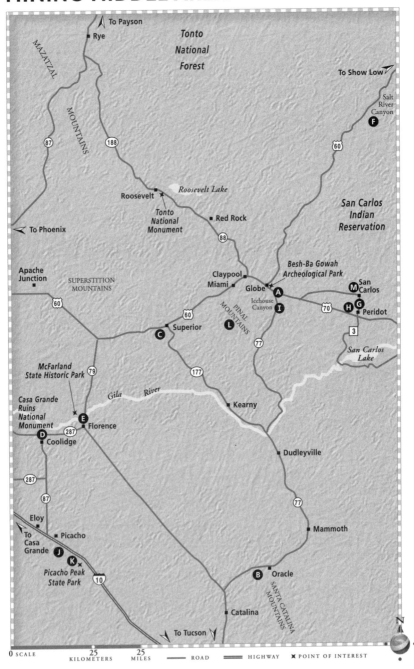

MAZATZAL MOUNTAINS

To Payson

Rye

Tonto
National
Forest

To Show Low

Salt
River
Canyon

F

87

188

60

Roosevelt

Roosevelt Lake

Tonto
National
Monument

Red Rock

To Phoenix

88

San Carlos
Indian
Reservation

Apache
Junction

SUPERSTITION
MOUNTAINS

Claypool

Miami

Globe

A

Besh-Ba Gowah
Archeological Park

San
Carlos

M

60

60

Superior

C

PINAL MOUNTAINS

Icehouse
Canyon

I

70

H **G**
Peridot

L

77

3

San Carlos
Lake

McFarland
State Historic Park

79

177

Gila   River

Kearny

Casa Grande
Ruins
National
Monument

E

287

Florence

D

Coolidge

Dudleyville

287

87

Eloy

Picacho

To
Casa
Grande

J

K

77

Mammoth

Picacho Peak
State Park

10

B

Oracle

SANTA CATALINA MOUNTAINS

Catalina

To Tucson

N

0 SCALE   25
       KILOMETERS   25
                MILES   ——— ROAD   ══ HIGHWAY   ✕ POINT OF INTEREST

SIGHTSEEING HIGHLIGHTS

★★★★ **BOYCE THOMPSON ARBORETUM**
Highway 60, Superior; 520/689-2811
This 300-acre mosaic of gardens and natural areas was founded in
1924 by mining magnate William Boyce Thompson. It's both a
National Historic District and an Arizona State Park, as well as
Arizona's oldest botanical garden. You'll find miles of easy nature
trails, a hidden canyon, specialty herb gardens, a streamside forest,
picnic grounds, and many natural habitats. Pick up a guidebook, which
recommends self-guided tours, or purchase a plant at the greenhouse. While you're on the property, take a guided tour of Colonel
Thompson's 26-room castle, **Rose's Picketpost**, 520/689-2845,
overlooking the arboretum. It's filled with antiques and more than
300 porcelain dolls.
   *Details: Daily 8–5. $4 adults, $2 ages 5–12, under 5 free. Call
ahead to tour the castle, which is open Mon–Sat. $5 adults, $2.50 ages
5–12, under 5 free. (2–4 hours)*

★★★★ **CASA GRANDE RUINS NATIONAL MONUMENT**
1100 Ruins Drive, Coolidge; 520/723-3172
This 650-year-old Hohokam ruin, standing four stories high, is a
credit to the ingenuity of its creators. Four-foot-thick lower walls
support this 2,800-ton mass, and 600 wood beams were used in the

SIGHTS
Ⓐ Besh-Ba Gowah
Ⓑ Biosphere 2
Ⓒ Boyce Thompson Arboretum
Ⓓ Casa Grande Ruins National
   Monument
Ⓔ McFarland State Historic Park
Ⓕ Salt River Canyon
Ⓖ San Carlos Apache Cultural Center

FOOD
Ⓔ Murphy's Soup and Salad

LODGING
Ⓗ Best Western Apache Gold Casino
   Resort
Ⓘ Hideaway B&B

CAMPING
Ⓗ Apache Gold RV Resort
Ⓙ Picacho KOA
Ⓚ Picacho Peak State Park
Ⓛ Pinal Mountains Campground
Ⓜ San Carlos Apache Tribe

Note: Items with the same letter are located in the same place.

ceiling. Because trees were not native to the area, the logs may have been floated down the Gila River from the north. Miles of sophisticated irrigation ditches surround the community. Windows were sited to facilitate astronomical observations and ceremonies. Ask about ranger-guided tours and stop at the visitor center, which has numerous exhibits on the Hohokam, including large intact pots and irrigation techniques.

Details: Daily 8–5. $2 adults, children free. (1–2 hours)

★★★★ SALT RIVER CANYON
Highway 60 between Globe and Show Low

You can experience the red canyon walls and travertine waterfalls of the scenic Salt River Canyon in two different ways: by car or by raft. The breathtaking drive runs along the twisted, rugged ravine as the road plunges down into the canyon, then crosses the Salt River before winding its way back to the top. You'll find plenty of turnouts and picnic spots along the way, and a rest area at the bottom has interpretive displays. A walking bridge spans the Salt River, and paved paths lead to the river's edge.

Feeling more adventurous? Consider a raft trip. Blue Sky Whitewater, 800/425-5253 or www.blueskyww.com, offers options ranging from calm family-oriented float trips to Class III–IV whitewater rafting.

Details: Rafting season: daily Mar–June. $90–$255 per person for one- to two-day trips. Children must be over 6. (full day)

★★★ BESH-BA GOWAH ARCHEOLOGICAL PARK
1.25 miles on Jess Hayes Road off U.S. 60, Globe
800/804-5623

This 700-year-old pueblo ruin is unique in that visitors are encouraged to walk inside its rooms and even climb ladders to the upper stories. A nearby museum has the world's largest single-site display of Salado pottery as well as clothing, tools, and other artifacts. In this visitor-friendly place, you can watch a history video, walk the interpretive trails, and visit an ethnobotanical garden in which you can grind corn with prehistoric Indian tools.

Details: Daily 9–5. $3 adults, $2 seniors, under 13 free. (1–2 hours)

★★★ BIOSPHERE 2
Highway 77, Oracle; 800/828-2462

In 1991, eight volunteer scientists locked themselves in this airtight, three-acre greenhouse with animals and self-sustaining plants for two years to conduct experiments on how Earth supports life and to determine if life could be maintained within an artificial facility. Although no one currently lives in Biosphere 2, scientists still conduct many experiments. You can't go inside, but multimedia presentations and guided tours explain the project. Adults can visit the Ocean Viewing Gallery and Biome Ecology Laboratories, while children enjoy an interactive display area.

Details: Daily 8–5. $12.95 adults, $6 ages 6–17, under 6 free. (2–4 hours)

★★ COBRE VALLEY CENTER FOR THE ARTS
101 N. Broad Street, Globe; 520/425-0884

Local artists banded together several years ago to restore the 1907 Gila County Courthouse, thus providing an outlet for their handcrafted merchandise. In this National Register building you'll find stained glass, ceramics, paintings, sculpture, and jewelry. In the Hand Weaving Studio on the lower level, you can watch weavers working their looms. A community theater group occupies the top floor.

Details: Daily 10–4. Free. (1 hour)

★★ McFARLAND STATE HISTORIC PARK
Main and Ruggles, Florence; 520/868-5216

The original Pinal County Courthouse, sheriff's office, and jail was built in 1878. It was used as a county hospital at the turn of the century. Visitors can now see the old jury box, wooden pews, and judge's bench, as well as twentieth-century hospital exhibits. The building was named after Ernest W. McFarland, author of the G.I. Bill of Rights and chief justice of the Arizona Supreme Court.

Details: Thu–Mon 8–5. $2 adults, $1 ages 12–17, under 12 free. (1 hour)

★★ SAN CARLOS APACHE CULTURAL CENTER
Highway 70, Peridot; 520/475-2894

Here you'll discover the history of the San Carlos Apaches from exhibits about their spiritual beginnings, historical pictures, artifacts, and a life-size diorama of the Changing Woman ceremony (known today as the Sunrise ceremony). You'll also learn about the Mountain Spirit Dancers and the cultural legacy left by the people who lived on the land for thousands of years. The gift shop is a great place to purchase authentic Apache arts and crafts, including beadwork, wood carvings, and dolls.

Details: Tue–Sat 9–5. $3 adults, $1.50 seniors, $1 students, under 12 free. (1 hour)

★ HIGHWAY MINE TOUR
Highway 60, Globe-Miami

If you're interested in the mining industry, you'll enjoy this self-guided auto tour of six mines. One is the Old Dominion Mine, which began operating in the late 1800s. Others are still producing copper, while the Sleeping Beauty Mine produces turquoise. For a spectacular view into an open-pit operation, take Highway 177 out of Superior to the **Ray Mine Overlook**.

Details: Call the Globe-Miami Chamber of Commerce, 800/804-5623, for a free map and brochure. (2 hours)

★ WALKING TOUR OF HISTORIC DOWNTOWN GLOBE

Globe was established in 1876, when the lure of gold, silver, and copper attracted thousands of entrepreneurs and fortune-seekers to the area. This walking tour takes you past a host of turn-of-the-century buildings in styles ranging from Victorian to Neoclassical Revival. You'll see a rare steam locomotive and the old railroad depot. One unusual structure was designed in the shape of the state of Arizona; it's currently an antique quilt store.

Details: Call the Globe-Miami Chamber of Commerce, 800/804-5623, for a free map and brochure. (1–2 hours)

FITNESS AND RECREATION

During summer, you can spend a day lazily floating the **Gila River** on a guided raft trip. The gentle Gila is ideal for families, though children must be 5 or older. Call Blue Sky Whitewater, 800/425-5253.

The **San Carlos Apache Reservation** has several scenic lakes for waterskiing, sailing, swimming, and fishing. **San Carlos Lake**, almost 20,000 acres, has excellent bass, cat, and crappie fishing. Boat and Jet Ski rentals are available. The high country boasts several beautiful trout-filled mountain lakes and numerous hiking trails. Guided hunting trips are also popular. Contact the San Carlos Reservation Recreation and Wildlife Department, 520/475-2653, for information.

GLOBE AREA

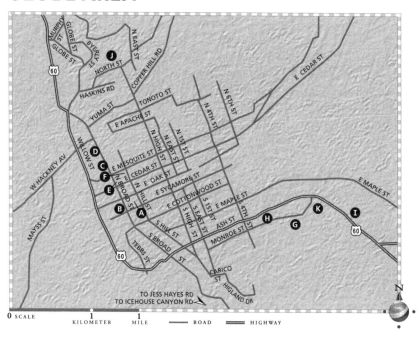

SIGHTS
A Cobre Valley Center for the Arts
A Walking Tour of Historic Downtown
Globe

FOOD
B Java Junction
C La Casita
D Mesquite Restaurant & Bar
E Peg's Kitchen

LODGING
F Cedar Hill B&B
G Comfort Inn
H El Rey Motel
I Holiday Inn Express
J Noftsger Hill Inn

CAMPING
K Gila County RV Park

Note: Items with the same letter are located in the same place.

The **Pinal Mountains**, towering 8,000 feet high, make for a cool summer getaway. The U.S. Forest Service, 520/425-7179, has maps and information on picnic areas and hiking trails, including the **Icehouse Canyon Trail**, which is dotted with remnants of ice ponds once used to haul ice to Globe and Miami. Further up the mountain, you'll find horse corrals.

You can take a car trip along the **Pinal Pioneer Parkway**, Highway 79, the old highway from Phoenix to Tucson. Along the way are interpretive signs identifying desert plants, plus picnic tables, scenic turnouts, and a memorial to cowboy film star Tom Mix, who died in a car crash here in October 1940.

On nearby I-10 at exit 219, you'll find **Picacho Peak State Park**, 520/466-3183. Picacho Peak rises 1,500 feet above the desert. Hiking trails ring the lower slopes, and there are trails to the summit if you're up for a hard climb. In spring, wildflowers can be seen for miles around. There's a $4 day-use fee.

FOOD

You won't find a lot of gourmet eateries in this part of the state, but plenty of small-town cafés serve home-cooked meals. Along historic Broad Street in Globe are several good restaurants. **Mesquite Restaurant & Bar**, 598 N. Broad, 520/425-6707, is one of the best restaurants in town. Once a Broad Street bordello, it is filled with historic photos of Globe.

La Casita, 470 N. Broad, 520/425-8462, is a great Mexican restaurant in a historic downtown building. **Peg's Kitchen**, 247 S. Broad, 520/425-8432, serves Mexican and American food, homemade pies, and pastries in a '50s-style diner that was used in the film *Midnight Run*.

For breakfast or lunch, try **Java Junction**, 130 N. Broad, 520/425-8925, a unique espresso bar also known for its Italian sodas. In Florence, **Murphy's Soup and Salad**, 310 N. Main, 520/868-0027, is open for lunch Monday through Friday 11 to 2. You might recognize it from the James Garner/Sally Field movie *Murphy's Romance*, which was filmed in Florence.

LODGING

Cedar Hill B&B, 175 E. Cedar, is a restored historic residence in downtown Globe, 520/425-7530. **Noftsger Hill Inn**, 425 North St., 520/425-2260, is a 1907 Globe schoolhouse converted into a lovely B&B. It's filled with antiques and still has the blackboards in each room. The **Hideaway B&B**, 9E Ice House Canyon, 520/402-0454, is in the scenic Icehouse Canyon.

El Rey Motel, 1201 Ash St., Globe, 520/425-7530, is a vintage Route 66 motor court offering a fun alternative to a standard motel room. Rates are under $45. You'll also find several chain motels in the Globe-Miami area, including **Comfort Inn**, 1515 South St. in Globe, 800/228-5150, with rates from $49 to $135; and **Holiday Inn Express**, Highway 60, 800/432-6655, with rates of $50 to $62. The **Best Western Apache Gold Casino Resort**, is conveniently located next to the Apache Casino, 520/425-7692.

CAMPING

The Pinal Mountains campgrounds offer stunning vistas at almost 8,000 feet. The narrow, winding road is not recommended for large RVs. Contact the Globe Ranger Station, 520/402-6200, for maps and details.

If you're looking for secluded campsites, check with the San Carlos Apache Tribe, 520/475-2343, about sites along the **Black and Salt Rivers**. The more popular Apache Reservation lakes also contain plenty of campsites.

RVers can stay at the **Apache Gold RV Resort**, Highway 70, 520/425-7692, and at the **Gila County RV Park**, 520/425-4653. The latter has full hookups and is next to a batting range near downtown Globe.

Picacho Peak State Park, 520/466-3183, has RV and tent sites with hookups for $10. Just north of the state park is **Picacho KOA**, 520/466-7401, where you'll find RV and tent sites from $16 to $23, along with a pool, rec room, groceries, and propane.

Old West Highway

The **Old West Highway** is a 203-mile stretch of road that encompasses the scenic and historic routes of Highways 60 and 70. It starts at Apache Junction, east of Phoenix, and winds its way southeast through the Superstition Mountains and past the San Carlos Apache Reservation to Lordsburg, New Mexico. In Globe, Highway 60 heads north into the Salt River Canyon, so pick up Highway 70 to continue on this historic trek. You'll drive through majestic canyons, past farm and ranch lands, ghost towns, Indian reservations, and ruins dating to A.D. 1100.

The Old West Highway's sites and stories were carved by the likes of the prehistoric Hohokam, Coronado, Geronimo, Billy the Kid, and Johnny Ringo. You'll see **Apache Leap**, named for the 75 warriors who leaped to their death to avoid surrendering to the cavalry in the 1800s. You can search for "Apache Tears," which are actually obsidian covered with perlite. Locals tell stories of lost gold mines in the Superstition Mountains, but **Mount Graham** is fabled to have even more hidden gold, buried by Mexican bandits.

Follow Highway 191 out of Safford to Mount Graham Drive, which takes you through five climate zones to 10,000 feet. Hiking, fishing, and camping information

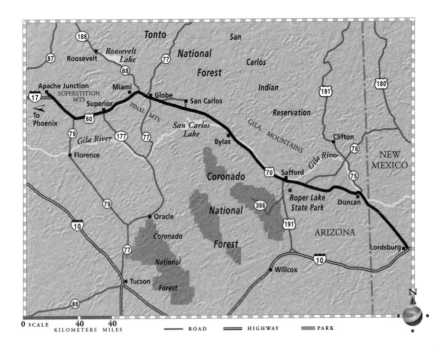

is available at the Safford Ranger District weekdays 8 to 5, 520/428-2522. Not far from Mt. Graham is **Roper Lake State Park**, 520/428-6760, a great birding and fishing spot that contains both a hot spring and a swimming beach on the lake. The park charges a $3 day-use fee and camping fees.

Safford's **Discovery Park**, 520/428-6260, includes an observatory open Wednesday through Monday from noon to 9. Both kids and adults enjoy this science-oriented park. Continue on Highway 70 to Lordsburg, New Mexico, where it ties into I-10, or take Highway 191 south to Cowboy Country and pick up I-10 just east of Willcox.

For an informative guide to the Old West Highway, call the **Globe Chamber of Commerce**, 800/804-5623, and ask for The History, Legends and Tales of the Old West Highway. This interesting book is free by mail or $2 at the Chamber offices, 1360 N. Broad.

9
COWBOY COUNTRY

In 1878, word of Ed Schieffelin's silver strike spread from wagon trains to mining camps, luring hardy prospectors and fortune seekers through dangerous Apache country to the new boomtown of Tombstone, Arizona. The camp grew from a few hundred citizens to more than 15,000 in less than 10 years, while more than $30 million in silver was excavated. This wild, reckless town held 110 saloons open 24 hours a day, many with professional gambling tables featuring the popular games of monte and faro. Prostitution syndicates from San Francisco and New York kept miners supplied with "ladies of the evening," and the Bird Cage Saloon became nationally renowned.

On the blustery afternoon of October 26, 1881, the infamous fight at the O.K. Corral was waged. The event probably would have been forgotten, except for an exaggerated biography of Wyatt Earp published decades later. Hollywood loved it, and before long Earp and the Gunfight at the O.K. Corral became famous. Tombstone dwindled to 150 people after the silver mines flooded and much of the equipment burned, but, in the last 50 years, books and movies have transformed the town into a tourist mecca.

A PERFECT DAY IN COWBOY COUNTRY

Start at Kartchner Caverns State Park for a tour of one of the only living caves left to be explored. Then make the short drive to Tombstone, stopping first at

TOMBSTONE

N
GLEESON RD
CAMINO SAN RAFAEL RD
NORTH DR
OLD BISBEE HWY
14TH ST
13TH ST
11TH ST
TOUGHNUT ST
9TH ST
BRUCE ST
NORTH ST
80
6TH ST
5TH ST
4TH ST
3RD ST
2ND ST
1ST ST
FITCH ST
FULTON ST
FREMONT ST
N SUMNER ST
HASKELL ST
GUN CLUB RD
Comstock Hill
W ALLEN ST
SCHIEFFELIN MONUMENT RD
CHARLESTON RD
A
B
C
D
E
F
G
H
I
J
K
L
M
N
0 SCALE
1 KILOMETER
1 MILE
ROAD
HIGHWAY

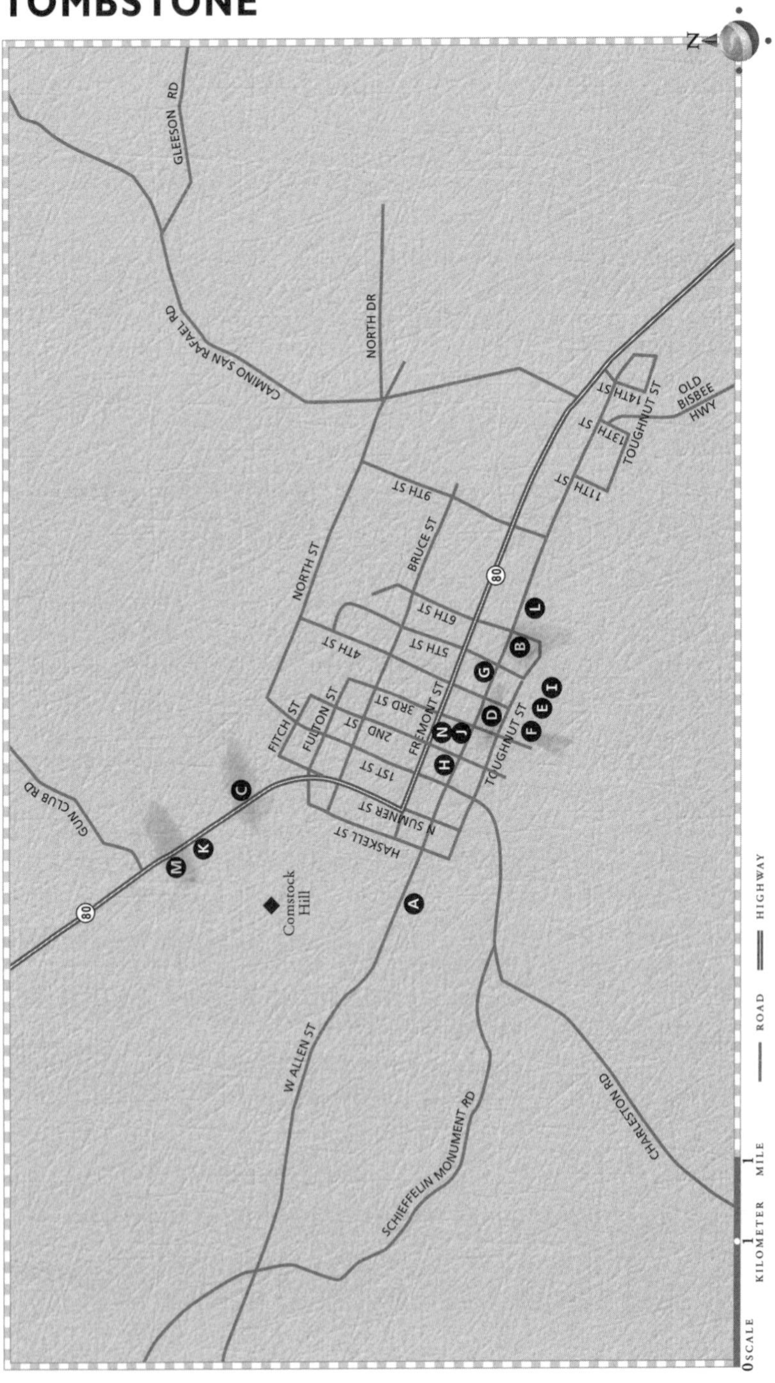

Boot Hill Graveyard for an overview of the colorful life of this wild town more than 100 years ago. Head to Allen Street and have a buffalo burger at the OK Cafe. Spend the afternoon meandering along the wooden sidewalks and catching the sites of old Tombstone. Take a stagecoach ride and be sure to witness a Wild West shootout. Have dinner at Nellie Cashman's or head to Benson's Skywatcher's Inn for a night of stargazing.

SIGHTSEEING HIGHLIGHTS

★★★★ ALLEN STREET
Tombstone

This is Tombstone's historic main street. You can just visualize Wyatt and Doc strolling along the dusty streets on their way to the O.K. Corral. Head first to Fourth and Allen to the **Tombstone Visitor's Center**, 520/457-9317, for walking-tour maps. Be sure and stop by the **Crystal Palace**, Fifth and Allen, 520/457-3611, built in 1879 and once Tombstone's most popular saloon. It's been completely restored and is still a saloon, though children are welcome. Back on Allen Street, you can catch the stagecoach for a fun tour around town, during which you'll likely see a gunfight or two.

Details: (2 hours to all day)

★★★★ BOOT HILL GRAVEYARD
Highway 80, Tombstone; 520/457-3348

The West's original Boot Hill sits on the outskirts as you enter Tombstone. Its 250 permanent residents, many dating from 1879, include those killed in the famous O.K. Corral gunfight. While some of

SIGHTS
- **A** Allen Street
- **B** Bird Cage Theater
- **C** Boot Hill Graveyard
- **D** OK Corral and Fly Photo Studio
- **E** Rose Tree Inn Museum
- **F** Tombstone Courthouse State Historic Park

FOOD
- **G** Longhorn Restaurant
- **H** Ms. Clanton Coffee and Natural Juice Company
- **I** Nellie Cashman's Restaurant
- **J** OK Cafe

LODGING
- **K** Best Western Lookout Lodge
- **L** Silver Nugget Bed & Breakfast

CAMPING
- **M** Tombstone Hills KOA
- **N** Wells Fargo RV Park

the epitaphs are quite humorous, they are still a reminder of the harsh, often short lives of these early pioneers.

Details: Enter through the Boot Hill Gift Shop. Open daily 7:30–6. No entrance fee, but donations are accepted. (1 hour)

★★★★ KARTCHNER CAVERNS STATE PARK
Highway 80, Benson; 520/586-7257
www.pr.state.az.us

This "living" cave was discovered more than 20 years ago but kept secret until responsible development was assured. It has been a lengthy, expensive undertaking for the Arizona Parks Department, but the end results are spectacular in what is now Arizona's largest state park, with plenty of hiking and picnicking areas. The caverns boast more than 2½ miles of underground passageways, with two main rooms exceeding 100 feet high. Before entering, you can learn about spelunking, visit the Cave-a-torium, and view fascinating exhibits in the visitor center.

Details: Daily 8–5. $10 per vehicle. Cave tours $12 adults, $4 ages 7–13. Tour reservations required: 602/542-4174. (2–4 hours)

★★★ AMERIND FOUNDATION MUSEUM
One mile from I-10 exit 318, Dragoon; 520/586-3666

This is probably one of the best archaeological museums in the country—a nice surprise given its unusual location. It houses thousands of Native American artifacts, many discovered in the vicinity. It also displays antique and contemporary Native American arts and crafts, including tribal pottery, Hopi kachinas, Pima willow baskets, Zuni fetishes, and Navajo weavings. Other exhibits explore the religious ceremonies and dances of the major Southwestern tribes. Be sure to visit the small but excellent museum store. The drive to Amerind takes you through Texas Canyon, an area of dramatic and colorful boulders where Cochise spent 11 years dodging the U.S. Army.

Details: Take I-10 between Benson and Willcox to exit 318 (Triangle T-Dragoon), then proceed one mile southeast. Sept–May daily 10–4; June–Aug Wed to Sun 10–4. Closed state holidays. $3 adults, $2 seniors and ages 12–18, under 12 free. (1–2 hours)

★★★ SAN PEDRO & SOUTHWESTERN RAILROAD
793 E. Country Club Drive, Benson; 800/269-6314

MOCK GUN BATTLE IN TOMBSTONE

Cochise County Tourism Council

Hop aboard the San Pedro for a relaxing rail excursion. You'll leave Benson and head into the San Pedro Riparian National Conservation Area. Birders, don't forget your binoculars. Guides will point out old miners' shacks, ghost towns, and Cochise's hideout, while they share stories of the Old West and nearby Tombstone. You can choose to ride in a historic parlor car, a covered open car, or the totally open caboose. Purchase refreshments at the on-board snack bar or bring your own food and drink. (No alcoholic beverages.) Themed excursions (mystery, jazz, etc.) run regularly. Call for schedules.

Details: *Sat 11 a.m. departure. Reservations recommended. $30.10 adults, $26.88 seniors, $24.43 students grades K–12. Optional barbecue lunch $9.50. (4 hours)*

★★ BIRD CAGE THEATER
Allen Street and Sixth, Tombstone; 520/457-3421

The Bird Cage attained national repute during Tombstone's 1880s heyday, spawning the refrain, "She's only a bird in a gilded cage." This hoppin' joint was open 24 hours a day, and in the small boxes, or "cages," that line the saloon's second floor, ladies of the evening were always available. When the town went bust, the Bird Cage was boarded up for decades, with everything left intact. The lobby now houses a variety of Western antiques and memorabilia, and the main saloon has been preserved in its original condition.

Details: *Daily 8–7, shorter hours in off season. $3.50 adults, $3 seniors, $1.75 children. (30 minutes–1 hour)*

★★ O.K. CORRAL AND FLY PHOTO STUDIO
Allen Street between Third and Fourth, Tombstone; 520/457-3456

Yep! This is it—the site of America's most famous gunfight. It lasted less than a minute but has created an entire industry of Earpmania, including movies, books, and a host of "experts" espousing their particular version of the gun battle. Inside the corral, you'll find life-size replicas of each man in the fight as well as the hearse that carried the unfortunate losers to Boot Hill. On the first and third Sundays of each month at 2 p.m., you can catch re-enactments of the actual fight. Also included is the studio of Camillus Fly, a photographer during Tombstone's boom period. He captured much of the town's history on film, and many of his photos are displayed.

Details: *Daily 8:30–5. Over age 6 $2.50. Next door is Tombstone's Historama, which runs hourly 9–4 and is an additional $2. (1 hour)*

★★ TOMBSTONE COURTHOUSE STATE HISTORIC PARK
Third and Toughnut, Tombstone; 520/457-3311

Tombstone was Cochise County's original county seat until 1931, when it was moved to nearby Bisbee. Tombstone's Courthouse, built in 1882, is today a historical museum containing the courtroom and sheriff's office, plus numerous exhibits on Wyatt Earp, Tombstone founder Ed Schieffelin, and other county history. You can even visit the reconstructed gallows, a frequent site of Old West hangings.

Details: *Daily 8–5. $2 adults, $1 children. (1 hour)*

★ ROSE TREE INN MUSEUM
Fourth and Toughnut, Tombstone; 520/457-3326

This is a fun little museum with period items from 1880s Tombstone, but the biggest attraction is the world's largest rosebush. The rose seedling was sent to a homesick bride from her native Scotland in 1885. Today it covers more than 8,000 square feet and is listed in the *Guinness Book of World Records*.

Details: *Open daily 9–5 except Christmas Day. $2.50 over age 13, under 14 free. (30 minutes)*

★ WILLCOX

This small town has a strong cowboy-and-Indian heritage. It was once home to the Chiricahua Apache tribe, then it became a railroad stop as the West developed. Singing cowboy Rex Allen hails from Willcox, and his Hollywood and western singing career is featured in the **Rex Allen Arizona Cowboy Museum**, 150 N. Railroad Ave., in historic downtown. One gallery features working cowboys and the ranching history of the area. Also downtown is the new **Chiricahua Regional Museum and Research Center,** where you can view minerals, old cavalry weapons, artifacts of the Chiricahua Apaches, and displays about Cochise and Geronimo. On Circle I Road is **Stout's Cider Mill**, 520/384-3696, where you'll find delicious concoctions of almost anything made with apples. From July to October, orchards and farms throughout the area feature "pick your own" markets, where you can head into the fields and pick apples, beans, and squash. Call the Willcox Chamber of Commerce, 520/384-2272, for times and prices. You can also visit the **Kokopelli Winery**, 520/384-3800, for wine tasting most weekends from noon to 5.

Details: *Willcox is located on I-10 35 miles east of Benson. AZ 186 heads southeast toward Fort Bowie and the Chiricahua National Monument. (half day)*

FITNESS AND RECREATION

If you're looking for some history and hiking, head to the **Fort Bowie Historical National Site**, 520/847-2500. Drive 25 miles south of Willcox on AZ 186, where you'll turn at the signs and continue another six miles on a dirt road. From there, it's a 1½-mile hike to the adobe remains of the fort, which was built in 1862, primarily to protect the stage from Apache attacks. A small visitor center is open from 8 to 5.

Back on AZ 186, head southeast about 10 miles to the spectacular yet relatively unknown **Chiricahua National Monument,** 520/824-3560. This was home to the Chiricahua Apache, who called it "the land of the standing-up rocks." More than 25 million years ago, volcanic eruptions created gravity-defying boulders and rock formations. You can camp, picnic, hike, bird-watch, or see the visitor center (daily 8 to 5). Stop by for information on ranger talks

COWBOY COUNTRY

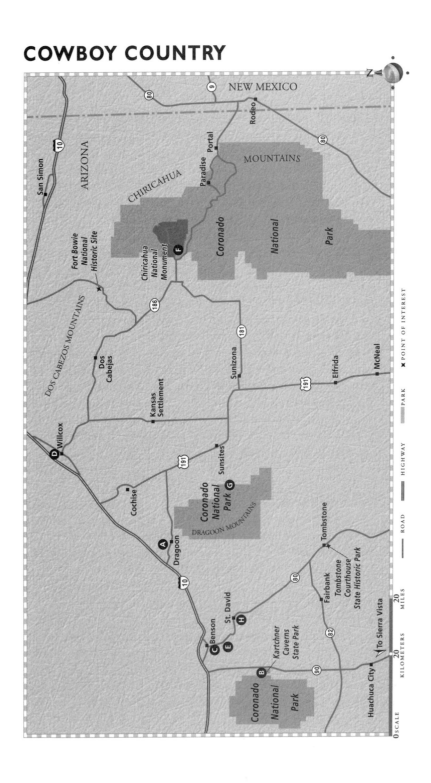

as well as maps on where to see some of the more unusual formations with equally unusual names: Sea Captain, China Boy, and Organ Pipe Rocks. Take an eight-mile scenic drive or hike into the more remote canyons (one-quarter-mile to over nine miles). Admission is $6 per vehicle.

Ask the rangers about the condition of the 15-mile gravel road to **Cave Creek Canyon**, one of the premier bird-watching sites in America. Many rare birds have been sighted here, and it is the northernmost habitat of the colorful elegant trogon. Birders will also find a wide variety of waterfowl around Willcox, particularly sandhill cranes. Between October and March, as many as 12,000 of these majestic birds gather in the area, and in January, there's an annual **Wings over Willcox** celebration.

If you'd like to explore other Apache homelands, head to the rock out-croppings of **Cochise Stronghold**, in the foothills of the Dragoon Mountains, 520/364-3468. From I-10, turn south onto U.S. 191 until you see the signs near Sunsites. Apache Chief Cochise battled and eluded the U.S. Army in this rocky fortress during the 1860s, and he's reportedly buried here. A few years later, another famous Apache, Geronimo, raided and hunted these same lands. Today the Stronghold is a recreation area within the Coronado National Forest. You'll find self-guided nature trails, historic walks, and nature trails leading into the Dragoons.

If you want a guided tour off the beaten path, contact High Desert Adventures Classic Jeep Tours, 520/586-9309. For a Hollywood trip through the Old West, call Gammons Gulch Movie Set, 520/212-2831. And book lovers will want to make the effort to find the Singing Wind Bookshop, outside Benson on Winifred Bundy's working cattle ranch, 520/586-2425. Although the hundreds of titles focus mainly on the Southwest, you'll find great children's

---

SIGHTS

Ⓐ Amerind Foundation Museum
Ⓑ Kartchner Caverns State Park
Ⓒ San Pedro & Southwestern Railroad
Ⓓ Willcox

FOOD

Ⓒ Chute-out Steakhouse
Ⓓ The Dining Car
Ⓒ Horseshoe Cafe
Ⓓ Saxon House

LODGING

Ⓓ Best Western Plaza Inn
Ⓒ Best Western Quail Hollow Inn
Ⓔ Skywatcher's Inn

CAMPING

Ⓒ Butterfield RV Resort
Ⓕ Chiricahua National Monument Campground
Ⓖ Cochise Stonghold
Ⓗ Holy Trinity Monastery RV Park

Note: Items with the same letter are located in the same place.

books as well. Take I-10 exit 304 in Benson, drive north 2.25 miles, then turn right. You can't miss the mailbox full of buckshot holes. And don't forget to shut the gate.

FOOD

You won't find much gourmet cuisine in Cowboy Country, even though in the 1880s many Tombstone restaurants rivaled San Francisco with their fancy fare. Most restaurants here today serve cowboy or Western food, and Tombstone has the best selection. A couple of choices in historic settings include **Nellie Cashman's Restaurant**, Fifth and Toughnut, 520/457-3950. The current restaurant, housed in Nellie's popular boardinghouse of the 1880s, serves moderately priced fare ranging from Mexican to burgers. It offers the best chicken, shrimp, and steak entrees in town.

At Allen and Fifth you'll find the **Longhorn Restaurant**, 520/457-3969, serving all three meals in a historic building drenched in cowboy ambiance. At the **OK Cafe**, Third and Allen, 520/457-3980, you have a choice of buffalo, beef, veggie, and even ostrich burgers. For breakfast or a light soup-and-sandwich lunch, try **Ms. Clanton Coffee and Natural Juice Company**, at Second and Allen. Just 20 miles from Tombstone, in Benson, you'll find several fast-food restaurants. For a great steak, try the **Chute-Out Steakhouse and Saloon**, 161 S. Huachua Blvd., 520/586-3481. **Horseshoe Cafe**, 154 E. Fourth St., 520/586-3303, has the best homestyle cooking for miles.

In Willcox, enjoy dinner at the historic **Saxon House**, 308 S. Haskell Ave., 520/384-4478. This renovated "city house" of area rancher Henry Saxon was built in 1916. The restaurant now features American and continental cuisine. Check out the prime rib and chef's special. Another fun choice is the **Dining Car**, 130 E. Maley, 520/384-0515, where lunch and dinner are served in a vintage railroad car; specialties are gourmet burgers and other American entrées.

LODGING

Lodging choices are somewhat limited around Tombstone, but some motor inns rent rooms for less than $80 per night. The best motel choice is the **Best Western Lookout Lodge**, one mile northeast of Tombstone on Highway 80, 520/457-2223. Benson also has the **Best Western Quail Hollow Inn**, 699 N. Ocotillo St., 520/586-3646. For rates of under $60 you'll find a heated pool but no restaurant. In Willcox, the **Best Western Plaza Inn**, 1100 W. Rex Allen Dr., also has a pool, plus a Jacuzzi in some rooms and an excellent restaurant, The Solarium. You can reserve a room at any of the above Best Westerns by calling 800/528-1234.

For a more intimate setting, try the **Silver Nugget Bed & Breakfast**, 520 E. Allen St., Tombstone, 520/457-3844. This is small and fairly plain, but the second-floor verandah overlooking Allen Street can't be beat. Stargazers should check out the **Skywatcher's Inn**, 520/586-0600, a small bed-and-breakfast four miles from Benson. It sits on the grounds of the **Vega-Bray Observatory**, which has six telescopes, a planetarium, and night-sky programs for $70 to $150 per group.

CAMPING

Tombstone Hills KOA, two miles northwest of Tombstone, 520/457-3829, has RV and tent sites, plus "Kamping Kabins." Other amenities include a playground, pool, groceries, and a free shuttle into town. **Wells Fargo RV Park**, Fremont and Third, 520/457-3966, also has some tent sites within walking distance of downtown. For a serene spot, try the **Holy Trinity Monastery RV Park**, near the artesian wells in St. David. Benson's **Butterfield RV Resort**, 520/586-4400, is a large new park with a pool, library, and even a computer room.

RV and campsites are available at **Cochise Stronghold**. Contact the Douglas Ranger District, Box 228-R, Douglas, AZ 85607; 520/364-3468. Or check out sites in the **Chiricahua National Monument Campground**, 520/824-3560.

NIGHTLIFE AND SPECIAL EVENTS

If you're looking to get out in the evening, try some of the local restaurant clubs and saloons. Tombstone has several annual events that pack the town. Reserve in advance and plan on some longer waiting times at local restaurants. The most popular events are **Territorial Days**, the first weekend in March; **Wyatt Earp Days**, Memorial Day weekend; **Vigilante Days**, the third weekend of August; **Rendezvous of Gunfighters**, Labor Day weekend; and **Helldorado Days**, the third weekend of October. For more information, call the Tombstone Visitor Center, 520/457-3929, or the Tombstone Office of Tourism, 800/457-3423, or visit the Web site www.cityoftombstone.com.

10
SOUTHEASTERN
ARIZONA

Centuries before Europeans arrived, Native Americans inhabited the hillsides and valleys of southeastern Arizona. Then, in 1540, Coronado marched through the region on his search for the Seven Cities of Gold. By the mid-1800s Americans were streaming into the area, lured by stories of silver and gold strikes. Clashes with the Apache brought the U.S. Army, and it wasn't until Geronimo surrendered in 1886 that the area was settled.

If you envision Arizona as a flat, hot desert, this corner of the state will surprise you. Here, rolling grasslands and valleys are flanked by dramatic mountain ranges. You'll enjoy a mild summer climate with warm, sunny days and nighttime temperatures that sometimes drop 40 degrees—perfect for snuggling by a fire. Avid birders come from all over the world to the region's preserves and wildlife areas. The mile-high city of Bisbee has a genteel charm developed nearly 100 years ago, when copper-mining barons poured their newfound fortunes into stately mansions and grand buildings. This is a great place to shop for art, taste some local wines, and enjoy nature.

A PERFECT DAY IN THE SOUTHEAST

Begin your day at the Fort Huachuca Museum, learning what the Old West was like more than a century ago. Then make the short drive to Bisbee, where you'll want to tour the Copper Queen Mine. Have lunch at the historic

BISBEE

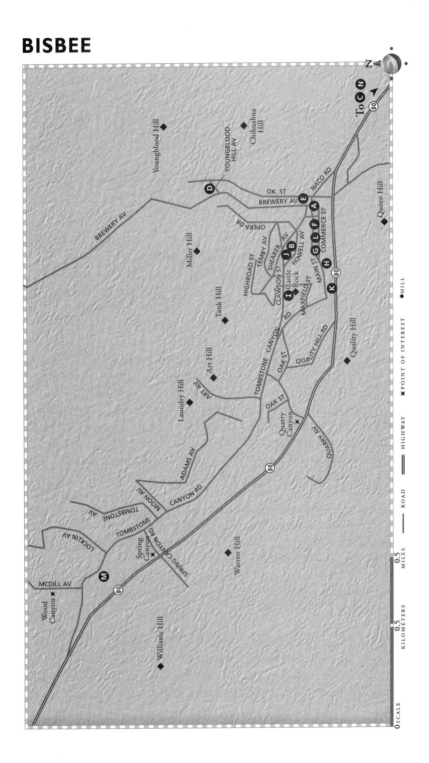

Copper Queen Restaurant and spend the afternoon exploring the shops of Brewery Gulch and the historic district. Pick one of Bisbee's great restaurants for dinner, then spend the night at a charming bed-and-breakfast.

SIGHTSEEING HIGHLIGHTS

★★★★ **COPPER QUEEN MINE TOUR**
118 Arizona Street, Bisbee; 520/432-2071
You'll be outfitted with a hard hat, bright yellow slicker, and miner's lamp before hopping on a mining train and riding 1,000 feet into this damp, dark, subterranean world. Most tour guides are former miners, so you'll learn firsthand about Bisbee's copper-mining era. The old mines remain a constant 47 degrees, so bring a sweater or jacket.
    Details: *Open daily. Tours at 9, 10:30, 12, 2, and 3:30. $10.75 adults and children over 11, $3.76 children 7–11, $2.15 children 3–6, under 3 free. (1¹/₂ hours)*

★★★★ **FORT HUACHUCA MUSEUM**
Fry Boulevard, Fort Huachuca; 520/533-5736
This is the oldest active cavalry post in the nation, today serving as the U.S. Army Intelligence Center. The 1892 museum building originally housed the post chapel and then the officers' club. You'll see exhibits on Apache uprisings, skirmishes with Pancho Villa, the famous Buffalo Soldiers, and displays of period uniforms. Nearby, the museum annex tracks the history of the fort, from an 1870s campsite to the installation

SIGHTS
Ⓐ Bisbee Mining and Historical Museum
Ⓑ Brewery Gulch Walking Tour
Ⓒ Copper Queen Mine Tour
Ⓒ Copper Queen Surface Tours
Ⓓ Muheim Heritage House Museum

FOOD
Ⓔ Brewery Restaurant
Ⓕ Cafe Cornucopia
Ⓖ Cafe Roka
Ⓔ Stock Exchange Bar

LODGING
Ⓗ Bisbee Grand Hotel
Ⓘ Clawson House atop Castle Rock
Ⓙ Copper Queen Hotel
Ⓚ Inn at Castle Rock
Ⓛ Main Street Inn
Ⓜ School House Inn B&B

CAMPING
Ⓝ Queen Mine RV Park

Note: Items with the same letter are located in the same place.

it is today. In 1995, the Military Intelligence Corps Museum opened to focus on the newer aspects of the fort's military operations.

Details: 2 miles west of Sierra Vista. Mon–Fri 9–4, Sat–Sun 1–4. Free. Fort Huachuca has controlled access; visitors might have to check in at the main gate and get a pass. Bring your driver's license, car registration, and proof of insurance. (2–4 hours)

★★★ BISBEE MINING AND HISTORICAL MUSEUM
5 Copper Queen Plaza, Bisbee; 520/432-7071

This 1897 building was originally the opulent headquarters of the Copper Queen Consolidated Mining Company and later home to the town's main employer, copper-mining giant Phelps Dodge. You'll find historic photos and antique mining equipment, along with fascinating details of Bisbee's history.

Details: Open daily 10–4. $3 adults, $2.50 seniors, children under 17 free. (1 hour)

★★★ BREWERY GULCH WALKING TOUR
Downtown off Howell Avenue, Bisbee

Explore the twisted streets and endless stairways of one of the most famous streets in America. As the town boomed in the 1880s, the canyon was lined with saloons and brothels. Today you can browse for antiques or contemporary art in the historic area, which has been reborn as an artists community.

Details: (1–3 hours)

★★★ COPPER QUEEN SURFACE TOURS
118 Arizona Street, Bisbee; 520/432-2071

Climb aboard for a van tour to glimpse the vastness of Bisbee's mining operations. You'll be escorted onto private Phelps Dodge Mining Company property to see the giant **Lavender Pit**, which is more than a mile long and 950 feet deep. Forty-one million tons of rich copper ore was excavated here before the mine was closed more than 20 years ago. The tour lets you view mining equipment and the Mule Mountains' terrace mining areas.

Details: Open daily. Tours at 10:30, 12, 2, and 3:30. $7.53 adults and children over 3, children under 3 free. (1 1/2 hours)

★★ CORONADO NATIONAL MEMORIAL
4101 E. Montezuma Canyon Road, Hereford; 520/366-5515

The memorial was created to honor the 1540 expedition of Francisco Vasquez de Coronado, although his actual trail is several miles away. A small visitor center features details of Coronado's journey through the Southwest, along with Spanish armor and weapons. The 5,000-acre memorial preserves a wide array of flora and fauna, including such high-desert plants as yucca, bear grass, and desert spoon. Deer, coyote, and javelina live here, and you might even spot the elusive bobcat, black bear, or mountain lion. Along its numerous hiking trails and scenic vistas, more than 140 bird species have been sighted.

Details: 25 miles west of Bisbee on AZ 92. Visitor center open daily 8–5. Free. (1–3 hours)

★ **MUHEIM HERITAGE HOUSE MUSEUM**
207 Youngblood Hill, Bisbee; 520/432-7698
This Victorian-era home is listed on the National Register of Historic Places. It's been restored with period furnishings, and tour guides share lots of local history and stories. Perched on a hill overlooking Old Bisbee, the Muheim House offers a panoramic view of the surrounding mountains and homes on Brewery Gulch.

Details: Open winter Fri–Mon 10–4, summer Thu–Mon 10–5, or by appointment. $2 donation suggested. (1 hour)

★ **SLAUGHTER RANCH STATE PARK**
Douglas; 520/558-2474
John Slaughter, a former Texas Ranger and Cochise County sheriff, bought this 140-acre valley near the Mexican border in 1884. Thanks to recent preservation efforts, the Slaughter Ranch has been returned to its turn-of-the-century grandeur and is now a National Historic Landmark.

Details: Go east 16 miles out of Douglas on 15th Street, which turns into unpaved Geronimo Trail. Wed–Sun 10–3. $3 adults, children under 12 free. (1 hour)

WINERY TOURS OF SONOITA AND ELGIN

Surprisingly, Arizona has 13 bonded wineries, and several vineyards are clustered in the rolling hills and high-elevation valleys near Sonoita and Elgin. If you enjoy quality wines, this is a treat. Sonoita's **Callaghan Vineyards**, 520/455-5322, offers wine tasting by appointment. Ken Callaghan's wines were described as "one of America's best-kept wine secrets" by Robert M.

Parker Jr. of the *Wine Advocate*. The wines of **Sonoita Vineyards Ltd.**, 520/455-5893, were selected for President George Bush's 1989 inaugural food and wine gala. It's open daily except on holidays. Call for directions. All the wines from the **Village of Elgin Winery**, 520/455-9309, are hand-crafted by owners Gary and Kathy Reeves. Check their Web site at www.concentric.net/~elgnwine. They're open from 10 to 5 daily. **Santa Cruz Winery**, Patagonia, 520/394-2888, is the only kosher winery between New York and California. Kosher wines are bottled under the Naveh Vineyards label. The winery's elegant tasting room is open every day (except Tuesday) from 11 to 5.

BIRD-WATCHING

Southeastern Arizona is a hot spot for bird-watching. The most notable place is the Nature Conservancy's **Ramsey Canyon Preserve**, 520/378-2785, where you can see 14 hummingbird species as well as sulfur-bellied flycatchers, warblers, elegant trogons, golden eagles, and dozens of butterfly species. Parking is limited to 13 vehicles, so reservations are a must even to visit this secluded canyon, open 8 to 5 daily. Ramsey Canyon is five miles south of Sierra Vista on AZ 92, then three miles west on Ramsey Canyon Road.

Just seven miles east of Sierra Vista on Highway 90 is the visitor center for the **San Pedro Riparian Nature Conservation Area**, 520/459-2555, open daily from 9:30 to 4:30. Two-thirds of North America's inland bird species have been spotted along the San Pedro River, including the gray hawk, vermilion flycatcher, green kingfisher, and crissal thrasher.

South of Sierra Vista, in the Coronado National Forest, is **Carr Canyon**, the most reliable spot for viewing buff-breasted flycatchers and other high-altitude species. And **Garden Canyon**, located on Fort Huachuca, is famous for its Mexican spotted owls and Montezuma quail. It is considered the most picturesque canyon in the Huachuca Mountains, and encompasses eight miles of hiking trails. It's open Wednesday through Friday 11 to 7, weekends 10 to 6, unless military maneuvers are occurring. For pass information, call the Fort Huachuca Wildlife Office, 520/533-7083.

At the Nature Conservancy's **Patagonia-Sonoita Creek Preserve**, 520/394-2400, 100-year-old cottonwoods tower over a permanently flowing creek. The area supports more than 260 bird species and several rare and endangered native fish and plants. The preserve, located just outside Patagonia, is open Wednesday to Sunday 7:30 to 3:30. A $3 donation is suggested.

And finally, six miles north of Sonoita on Highway 83, you'll find the **Empire-Cienega Resource Conservation Area**, managed by the BLM.

This grass-and-woodland area is home to the rare gray hawk. Call 520/722-4289 for access information.

Each summer in mid-August, Sierra Vista hosts a four-day **Southwest Wings Birding Festival**, featuring programs, activities, field trips, and exhibits about the area's diverse habitats and wildlife. For information, call the Sierra Vista Chamber of Commerce, 800/288-3861.

FITNESS AND RECREATION

Even if you're not an avid birder, all of the areas listed above are great places to explore, hike, and picnic. The **Coronado National Forest** also has numerous hiking trails. The region contains two great fishing and boating lakes. **Patagonia State Lake Park** is seven miles south of Patagonia on Highway 82, 520/287-6965. Day use per vehicle is $5. This is a great family swimming spot. **Parker Canyon Lake** is 30 miles south of Sonoita on Highway 83, 520/455-5847. Fifteen of these miles are unpaved. For guided horseback day trips, call Arizona Trail Tours at 520/394-2701. Golfers can head to **Pueblo del Sol Golf Club**, Sierra Vista, 520/378-6444; **Kino Springs**, 15 miles south of Patagonia, 520/287-8800; or the18-hole **Turquoise Valley Golf Course,** near Bisbee, 520/432-3091.

FOOD

Karen Callaghan, whose family owns the Callaghan Winery, has the most upscale restaurant in the area. **Karen's Wine Country Café**, on Highway 82 in Sonoita, 520/455-5282, features Southwestern cuisine supplemented by a great wine list and a fabulous view. Join her for lunch or dinner Thursday through Sunday; reservations are advised. Sierra Vista has the greatest variety of restaurants. A favorite Mexican place is **La Casita**, 465 E. Fry Blvd., 520/458-2376. **The Beef Baron**, at the corner of Fry and Fab, 520/459-2719, boasts great steaks and a big salad bar. For an unusual selection, **The Peacock Restaurant**, 80 S. Carmichael Ave., 520/459-0095, features gourmet Vietnamese entrées.

A more casual lunch or dinner choice is the **Ovens of Patagonia**, 292 Naugle St., Patagonia, 520/394-2483, an interesting spot with Cuban-influenced dishes and a bakery that draws people from miles around.

After walking through Bisbee, take a break at **Cafe Cornucopia**, 14 Main St., 520/432-3364, for a yummy fruit smoothie or sandwich. Or, for heartier appetites, order mesquite-grilled steaks and ribs at the **Brewery Restaurant**, 15 Brewery Ave., 520/432-9924, open daily. After dinner, drop by the adjoining **Stock Exchange Bar**, which has live entertainment on weekends.

SOUTHEASTERN ARIZONA

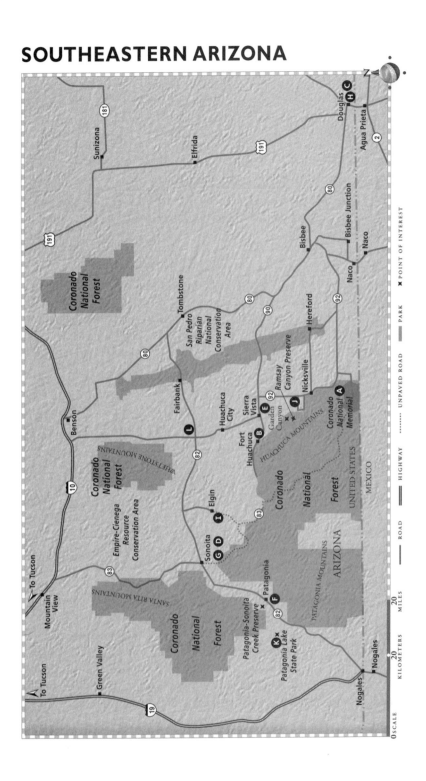

N

✕ POINT OF INTEREST

▬ PARK

········ UNPAVED ROAD

▬ HIGHWAY

▬ ROAD

SCALE

0   20
KILOMETERS

0   20
MILES

To Tucson

Green Valley

Nogales

Nogales

19

Mountain View

To Tucson

83

Coronado National Forest

SANTA RITA MOUNTAINS

Patagonia-Sonoita Creek Preserve ✕

Patagonia Lake State Park

K ✕

82

F

Patagonia

PATAGONIA MOUNTAINS

Empire-Cienega Resource Conservation Area

10

Coronado National Forest

WHETSTONE MOUNTAINS

Benson

82

Elgin

I

Sonoita

G D

83

ARIZONA

Coronado National Forest

UNITED STATES

MEXICO

181

Sunizona

191

Elfrida

191

Coronado National Forest

80

Tombstone

Fairbank

San Pedro Riparian National Conservation Area

80

L

Huachuca City

Sierra Vista

Fort Huachuca

B

80

90

Garden Canyon ★ ★

E

Ramsay Canyon Preserve

92

J

Nicksville

HUACHUCA MOUNTAINS

Coronado National Memorial

A

191

Bisbee

80

Hereford

92

Bisbee Junction

Naco

Naco

Douglas

H

C

Agua Prieta

2

If you're looking for a sophisticated dinner, try the contemporary Italian cuisine of **Cafe Roka**, 35 Main St., Bisbee, 520/432-5153. Reservations are suggested at this local favorite.

LODGING

If you like bed-and-breakfasts, this part of the state has some great choices. The historic **Crown C Ranch,** three miles west of Sonoita, 520/455-5739, www.flash.net/~crownc., is a renovated 60-year-old adobe ranch house with spacious rooms and a pool. Guests have full use of the kitchen. The **Vineyard B&B**, P.O. Box 1227, Sonoita, AZ 85637, 520/455-4749, sits on a hilltop surrounded by rolling grasslands and stunning mountain vistas. It was built in 1916 as the Hacienda Los Encinos. Also on the property is a nicely decorated casita, which costs a little more.

In nearby Elgin, the heart of wine country, are two additional inns. The **Rain Valley B&B**, HC2 Box 672, Elgin, AZ 85611, 520/456-2911, offers a two-room suite with a wet bar. The **Yee Haa Guest Ranch**, P.O. Box 888, Sonoita, AZ 85637, 520/455-9285, has three Western-themed rooms, each with a private entry and sitting area. The **Dusquesne House B&B**, 357 Duquesne Ave., 520/394-2732, was originally a miner's boardinghouse at the turn of the century.

Birders should check out the charming **Ramsey Canyon Inn B&B**, 31

SIGHTS

- **A** Coronado National Memorial
- **B** Fort Huachuca Museum
- **C** Slaughter Ranch State Park
- **D** Winery Tours of Sonoita and Elgin

FOOD

- **E** The Beef Baron
- **F** Karen's Wine Country Cafe
- **E** La Casita
- **G** Ovens of Patagonia
- **H** Peacock Restaurant

LODGING

- **E** Best Western Mission Inn
- **F** Crown C Ranch
- **G** Dusquesne House B&B

LODGING (continued)

- **H** Gadsden Hotel
- **E** Gateway Studio Suites
- **I** Rain Valley B&B
- **J** Ramsey Canyon Inn B&B
- **E** Super 8 Motel
- **F** Vineyard B&B
- **E** Windmere Hotel
- **F** Yee Haa Guest Ranch

CAMPING

- **A** Coronado National Forest
- **H** Douglas Golf and Social Club
- **K** Patagonia Lake State Park
- **G** Patagonia RV Park
- **J** Ramsey Canyon Campground
- **L** San Pedro Riparian Conservation

Note: Items with the same letter are located in the same place.

Ramsey Canyon Rd., Hereford, AZ 85615, 520/378-3010. It's located just outside the Preserve's gates, along the creek. Two cottages with kitchens and six inn rooms are available for around $100 per night. Contact **Ramsey Canyon Preserve**, 27 Ramsey Canyon Rd., Hereford, AZ 85613, 520/378-2785. Reserve well in advance for spring and summer.

Bisbee has several historic B&Bs. If you're looking for something artsy and somewhat funky, check out the **Inn at Castle Rock**, 112 Tombstone Canyon Rd., 800/566-4449, an 1890 miners' boardinghouse. The **School House Inn B&B**, 818 Tombstone Canyon Rd., 800/537-4333, was built as a schoolhouse in 1918. The 1888 **Main Street Inn** sits at the center of the historic district, while the **Clawson House atop Castle Rock** was built in 1895 as an executive home for the Copper Queen Mine manager. Both B&Bs can be reached at 800/467-5237.

For an authentic turn-of-the-century experience, try the **Bisbee Grand Hotel**, 61 Main St., Bisbee, 800/421-1909, situated in the heart of the historic district. The **Copper Queen Hotel**, 11 Howell Ave., 800/247-5829, was Bisbee's grand hotel for decades, entertaining the likes of Teddy Roosevelt during the town's boom period. Another grand hotel is the 1907 **Gadsden Hotel** in Douglas, which is listed on the National Register of Historic Places. The lobby has massive columns and a 42-foot stained-glass skylight. Among the celebrities who have stayed here are Amelia Earhart, Eleanor Roosevelt, and Paul Newman.

In Sierra Vista, the **Windemere Hotel and Conference Center**, 2047 S. Highway 92, 800/825-4656, offers guests a free breakfast buffet, health-club passes, and complimentary cocktails. At the entrance to Fort Huachuca, the new **Gateway Studio Suites**, 203 S. Garden Ave., 877/443-6200, has rates from $50 to $60.

CAMPING

At the **Patagonia Lake State Park**, 520/287-6965, campsites are near the lake, and amenities include flush toilets. Full hookups are $15; no hookups, $10. You can reserve ahead at the **Patagonia RV Park**, 520/394-2491, where full hookups are $15. The **San Pedro Riparian Conservation Area** contains low-fee primitive RV and campsites. They're managed by the Bureau of Land Management, Huachuca City, 520/457-2265.

Coronado National Forest has some camping. RVers can reserve wooded sites in the small **Ramsey Canyon Campground**, 520/378-0549, or stay at the **Queen Mine RV Park**, 1 Dart Avenue, Bisbee, 520/432-5006. The **Douglas Golf and Social Club,** P.O. Box 1220, Douglas, 520/364-3722, is a combined RV park and 18-hole golf course.

11
SOUTHERN LANDS

In 1539, only 47 years after Columbus landed at Santo Domingo, a Franciscan monk entered the region now considered Arizona's southern lands. By 1687, Padre Eusebio Kino, a Jesuit missionary, began establishing a string of 21 missions in northern Sonora, Mexico, and southern Arizona to convert Native Americans to Christianity. He built one at Guevavi, north of Nogales; then at Tumacacori, further north; and San Xavier del Bac, southwest of Tucson, which is often described as "the White Dove of the Desert."

A presidio, or fort, was founded at Tubac in 1752, to guard the area's rich mineral resources and combat rebellions from local Indians. By 1822, Mexico had gained its independence from Spain, and the territory was under Mexican control. Finally, the area from the Gila River to the Mexican border was purchased from Mexico in 1853, and the U.S. flag finally flew over the land. This region, established before the settlements at Jamestown and Plymouth, richly blends Mexican, Native American, and Anglo culture and history.

Today the old fort at Tubac is one of the country's top arts communities. Just a few miles away are the shopping bargains of Nogales, Sonora, Mexico. Two world-renowned observatories sit perched atop two different mountain peaks, where you'll also find hiking, birding, and a wildlife refuge. Championship golf courses and warm, sunny winter days make this a popular vacation spot.

SOUTHERN LANDS

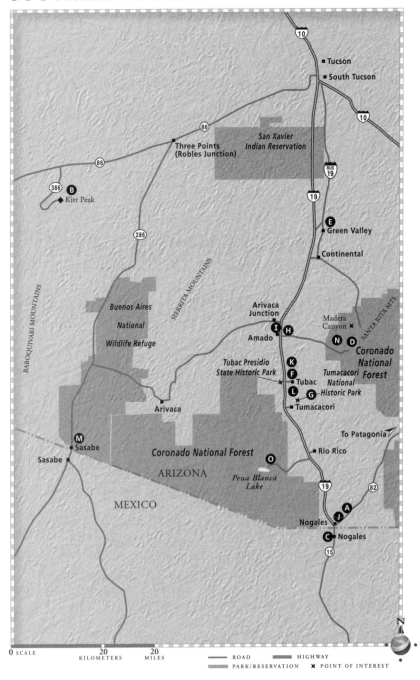

Tucson
South Tucson

10

10

86
Three Points
(Robles Junction)
San Xavier
Indian Reservation

BUS
19

386 **B**
◆ Kitt Peak

E
Green Valley

286
Continental

19

SIERRITA MOUNTAINS

Buenos Aires
National
Wildlife Refuge

Arivaca
Junction
Madera
Canyon ✕
SANTA RITA MTS.

I **H**
Amado
N **D**
Coronado
National
Forest

BABOQUIVARI MOUNTAINS

Tubac Presidio
State Historic Park
K
F ■ Tubac
L ✕
G ■
Tumacacori
National
Historic Park
Tumacacori

Arivaca

To Patagonia

M
■ Sasabe
Sasabe ■

Coronado National Forest

O
■ Rio Rico

ARIZONA
Pena Blanca
Lake

19
82

MEXICO
J **A**
Nogales
C Nogales

15

N

0 SCALE   20   20
        KILOMETERS   MILES

━━━ ROAD   ▦▦ HIGHWAY
▬▬ PARK/RESERVATION   ✕ POINT OF INTEREST

A PERFECT DAY IN THE SOUTHERN LANDS

Catch the 9 a.m. tour of the Titan Missile Museum in Green Valley, then drive to Tubac and check out the Tubac Presidio State Historic Park. After having lunch on the patio at Tosh's Hacienda, spend the afternoon wandering through Tubac's fascinating shops. In the evening, dine at the Stables Restaurant at the Tubac Golf Resort.

SIGHTSEEING HIGHLIGHTS

★★★★ TUBAC

In this town "Where Art and History Meet," you'll find a great collection of art galleries and interesting boutiques along ancient, dusty streets. This artists' community features hand-blown glassware, fiber and leather arts, sculpture, paintings, and Native American crafts. **Hal Empie**, a territorial-born native artist, has a gallery on Tubac Road, and internationally known artist **Hugh Cabot** has his studio/ gallery in Old Town. You'll also want to check out the **Lee Blackwell Studios**, Plaza Road, for the intriguing selection of copper fountains and sculptures. The **Tubac Center for the Arts**, also on Plaza Road, 520/398-2371, features local, regional, and national exhibits, as well as a great selection of collectible crafts. The center is

---

SIGHTS

- Ⓐ Arizona Vineyards
- Ⓑ Kitt Peak National Observatory
- Ⓒ Nogales, Sonora, Mexico
- Ⓓ Smithsonian's Whipple Observatory
- Ⓔ Titan Missile Museum
- Ⓕ Tubac
- Ⓖ Tubac Presidio State Historic Park
- Ⓖ Tumacacori National Historical Park

FOOD

- Ⓗ Amado Cafe
- Ⓕ Cafe Fiesta
- Ⓘ Cow Palace
- Ⓒ El Cid
- Ⓖ La Roca
- Ⓙ Mr. C's Supper Club
- Ⓚ Stables Restaurant
- Ⓕ Tosh's Hacienda Restaurant
- Ⓛ Wisdom Cafe

LODGING

- Ⓔ Best Western Green Valley
- Ⓘ Best Western Time Motel

LODGING (continued)

- Ⓙ Motel 6
- Ⓜ Rancho de la Osa
- Ⓖ Rancho Santa Cruz
- Ⓡ Rex Ranch
- Ⓝ Santa Rita Lodge
- Ⓙ Super 8 Motel
- Ⓕ Tubac Golf Resort

CAMPING

- Ⓝ Bog Springs Campgrounds
- Ⓔ Green Valley RV Resort
- Ⓞ White Rock Campground

Note: Items with the same letter are located in the same place.

open daily from mid-November to mid-April, with limited hours during the summer.

Shop for southwestern Christmas ornaments at the **Crowe's Nest** or browse through the cookbooks and spices at the **Chile Pepper**. Be sure to stop in at **Tortuga Books**, an independently owned bookstore that specializes in Southwest subjects, architecture and the arts, and beautifully illustrated children's books. It also has a great selection of unusual stationery products. During the **Tubac Arts Festival,** held the first full week of February, scores of artists set up booths along the streets and in the surrounding fields.

Details: South on I-19, take exit 40 (Chavez Siding Road/Tubac), cross under the highway, and continue south on the Frontage Road about two miles. Most stores are open daily in winter but have shorter summer hours. (half to full day)

★★★★ **TUBAC PRESIDIO STATE HISTORIC PARK**
Tubac; 520/398-2252
In 1974 archaeologists excavated portions of this circa-1752 presidio, which are part of an interesting underground exhibit. The park also includes the old Tubac schoolhouse (built in 1885), a visitor center, and a museum with artifacts from Tubac's unique history. The state's first newspaper, the *Weekly Arizonian,* in 1859 was cranked off an old flatbed printing press, which is also on display. For fascinating reading, pick up a copy of the newspaper and scan its classifieds ads, including such items as a vegetable painkiller, native wines, Colt's Revolving Guns & Pistols, and the $150 fares for a stagecoach ride from San Antonio to Tucson. Sunday afternoons from October to March, Spanish soldiers and settlers give living-history presentations.

Details: Open daily 8–5. $2 adults, $1 children 7–14, under 7 free. (1 hour)

★★★ **KITT PEAK NATIONAL OBSERVATORY**
Highway 86, 520/318-8726
If you're interested in astronomy, don't miss this observatory, perched on a 7,000-foot-high site. Here you can enjoy panoramic daytime views of the surrounding desert and stunning nighttime glimpses into the heavens. Visitors can tour five giant telescopes, including McMath, the world's largest solar telescope, and the 158-inch Mayall, which has a 30,000-pound quartz mirror and can view distant regions of the universe. To learn more about the starry heavens, check out the visitor

center, gift shop, and museum, which also features exhibits on a variety of telescopes. Be sure to pack a picnic—there are no food vendors—and toss in a jacket to be comfortable on this chilly mountaintop.

Details: Take I-19 south of Tucson to AZ 86 and drive about 40 miles. Daily 9–4. Guided tours at 10, 11:30, 1, and 2:30. Free admission, but $2 donation suggested. Evening stargazing by reservation: $35 adults; $25 seniors, students, and children under 18. Price includes box dinner. (half to full day)

★★★ TUMACACORI NATIONAL HISTORICAL PARK
Tumacacori; 520/398-2341

Father Kino established the Mission San Jose de Tumacacori in 1691, and much of the old adobe structure is still intact. Walk through the mission, then visit the small interpretive center nearby. The center displays several relics from the old church, interpretive exhibits about mission life, and a video on the missionaries' work with Native Americans.

Details: Open daily 8–5. $2 adults, children under 17 free. (1 hour)

★★★ SMITHSONIAN INSTITUTION'S FRED L. WHIPPLE OBSERVATORY
I-19, exit 56, Amado, 520/670-5707

Dark skies and a dry climate have made this the site for good "optical seeing" since October 1968. The observatory has six different telescopes. Its Multiple Mirror Telescope is the largest in the world.

Details: Visitor Center open weekdays 8:30–4. Free. Observatory tours by reservation Mar–Nov Mon, Wed, Fri. $7 adults, $2.50 children 6–12. (6 hours)

★★ TITAN MISSILE MUSEUM
Duval Mine Road, Green Valley; 520/625-7736

Eighteen Titan missile silos circled Tucson before the SALT Treaty called for their deactivation. One of the missiles in its underground silo and the surrounding command center are open to the public. This is a fascinating view of America's nuclear-warhead capabilities. On your guided tour, you'll pass through 6,000-pound doors and walk through a space-age corridor for a simulated countdown and launch. You can view the silo from above and check out the empty nuclear warhead nearby.

Details: Daily Nov–Apr, May–Oct Wed–Sun 9–5. Tours are given on the hour; the last one is at 4. Reservations suggested. $6 adults, $5 seniors and active military, $4 children 10–17. (1 hour)

★ ARIZONA VINEYARDS
1830 Patagonia Road, Nogales; 520/287-7972

This almost 20-year-old rustic winery features some eclectic proprietary blends like Apache Red, Tino Tinto, and Rattlesnake Red. You can sample the vineyard's offerings in a nineteenth-century-style tasting room.

Details: Look for the signs two miles east of Nogales on Highway 82. Daily tours and tastings 10–5. (1 hour)

★ SHOPPING IN NOGALES
Sonora, Mexico

This is the best and biggest of Arizona border towns. Shopping in Mexico is fun and easy if you follow a few simple rules. Park on the American side and walk through customs, where you simply need to declare your American citizenship for stays of less than 72 hours. Most everyone speaks English, and American cash is accepted. Take lots of $1 bills. Plan on some fun bargaining and don't feel awkward about offering at least half the posted price as a starting point. Many Arizonans cross the border regularly for prescription drugs and pharmaceuticals. Liquor (especially Mexican tequila), name-brand perfumes, leather items, glassware, and curios are just a few of Mexico's shopping bargains. Each person can bring back up to $400 in duty-free merchandise and one quart of liquor. Since this is a border town, many restaurants cater to tourists, but if you're uncomfortable "drinking the water," carry some bottled drinks and packaged snacks.

For longer stays, you'll need a Mexican Tourist Card and an automobile permit. Check with the Mexican Consulate, 553 S. Stone Avenue, Tucson, 520/882-5595, for details. Never drive into Mexico without Mexican auto insurance, which is available along the border.

Details: Take I-19 south to exit 8, which becomes Grand Avenue. This will take you to downtown Nogales, Arizona. At the border, you'll find several parking lots charging around $5 per day. You may encounter a line to cross back into the United States, especially on weekends.

FITNESS AND RECREATION

Drive to the **Madera Canyon National Forest Recreation Area** for some spectacular bird-watching and hiking. Parking is limited, so pack a picnic and head out early. In Green Valley, take I-19 to exit 63 east. Go about 12 miles and follow the signs. The canyon is open dawn to dusk. Suggested donation is $2; camping is available for $5.

The **Buenos Aires National Wildlife Refuge**, 520/823-4251, is also a great spot for bird-watchers. Turn west off I-19 at Arivaca Junction and look for the signs just outside Arivaca. Ten miles west of I-19 (exit 12, Ruby Road) is scenic **Pena Blanca Lake**, just the place for some quiet fishing. The lake is stocked with trout in winter. No motors or swimming is allowed.

For a historic hike, start at the **Anza Trailhead** at the Tubac Presidio State Historic Park and follow the trail 4 1/2 miles along the Santa Cruz River to Tumacacori. Take binoculars—the bird watching is great. This is part of the Juan Bautista de Anza National Historic Trail, which runs from Nogales to San Francisco.

Golfers can try the 18-hole course at the **Tubac Golf Resort**, 800/848-7893, where Kevin Costner filmed *Tin Cup*, or the **Rio Rico Resort & Country Club**, 800/288-4746, a few miles north of Nogales. Book tee times at least one week in advance.

FOOD

Driving south on I-19 past Green Valley, you can't miss the **Cow Palace**, 520/398-2201. Take exit 48 in the small town of Amado to the long, red, saloon-style building. Another small building with huge cowhorns sits in front of the restaurant. The inside is equally "cowboy," with wagon-wheel lights and lots of mounted horns, and the hearty menu ranges from huevos rancheros for breakfast to burgers and steaks for dinner. Across the highway is the **Amado Cafe**, 520/398-9211, a newer restaurant offering lighter Mediterranean and Southwestern cuisine for lunch and dinner.

Just north of Tubac is the **Stables Restaurant**, at the Tubac Golf Resort, which offers American entrees with a Southwestern flair. It's fun to look at the displayed vintage photos of celebrities and politicians, who have flocked here since the '30s.

If you're exploring Tubac, walk across the footbridge off Tubac Road to **Cafe Fiesta**, 520/398-2332, for a light lunch of soup, salad, or a sandwich. Open daily 11 to 3. Another Tubac lunch or dinner option is **Tosh's Hacienda Restaurant**, 520/398-3008, a great Mexican food spot featuring an outdoor patio with mountain views. Open 11 to 8 daily, with shorter summer hours.

Locals head to the **Wisdom Cafe**, 520/398-2397, a small family-owned Mexican restaurant in Carmen, north of Tumacacori, for lunch and dinner. The Wisdom family has operated a restaurant from this historic landmark for years.

For more authentic Mexican food, continue south of the border to Nogales, Sonora, Mexico. **El Cid**, 124 Obregon Ave. (within walking distance of the border), 011-52-631-21944, has been popular with Americans for Mexico City–style lunch and dinner since its opening in 1927. Ask to be seated near the second-floor balcony overlooking the bustling street. **La Roca**, 91 Calle Elias, 011-52-631-20545, is the fanciest place in Nogales, with formal waiters and candlelit tables. You find sizzling shrimp and great margaritas. This popular bar and restaurant, only two blocks from the border, is open daily from 11 a.m. to midnight. Both of these restaurants advertise American water and ice, and both take major credit cards.

Back in the States, you'll find plenty of fast-food restaurants in Nogales, Arizona. If you'd like a nicer lunch or dinner, try **Mr. C's Supper Club**, 282 W. View Point Dr., Nogales, 520/281-1852, perched on top of a hill overlooking town. This rather expensive restaurant features fresh fish with daily specials. Green Valley, 40 miles north of Nogales, has a variety of chain and fast-food restaurants along I-19.

LODGING

This part of the state has some great historical lodges. The **Tubac Golf Resort**, P.O. Box 1297, Tubac, 85646, 800/848-7893, is part of an old Spanish land-grant ranch. The charming casitas have fireplaces and patios, and the resort has a pool, pro shop, 18-hole golf course and great dining facilities. Rates range from $75 to $125, with steep discounts during summer. The nearby **Rex Ranch**, P.O. Box 636, Amado, AZ 85645, 800/547-2696, is the place to go for some real pampering. Rates are $125 to $225 per night, and you can enjoy a masseuse, several therapy packages, and healthful European cuisine. The **Santa Rita Lodge**, 520/625-8746, has been a birders' paradise for over 50 years. It offers rustic accommodations nestled near a meandering creek in Madera Canyon and extensive natural history programs on birding and other aspects of life in the canyon. During the busy winter season, there is a two-day minimum stay at $70 to $80 per night. **Rancho Santa Cruz**, P.O. Box 8, Tumacacori, AZ 85640, 800/221-5592, is a small historic guest resort. You'll find walking trails, horseback riding, a restaurant, and a swimming pool. Rates range from $60 to $80. **Rancho de la Osa**, P.O. Box 1, Sasabe, AZ 85633, 800/872-6240, became a guest ranch in the 1920s. It sits across from the Buenos Aires Wildlife Refuge. The rooms are beautifully renovated with sitting areas and fireplaces, but no TVs or phones—so prepare to relax. A three- or four-night stay runs $250 a night. Both Green Valley and Nogales offer several chain motels, including the **Best Western Green Valley**, 111 S. La Canada, 520/625-2250. Rates range from $75 to more than $100. Nogales also has a **Motel 6**, 141 W. Mariposa Rd., 520/281-2951, **Super 8 Motel**, 547 W. Mariposa Rd., 520/281/2242, and **Best Western Time Motel**, 921 N. Grand Ave., 520/287-4627 at less than $75 per night.

CAMPING

Bog Springs Campground in Madera Canyon has RV and tent sites for $7 per night. There are no hookups but you'll find toilets, water, and picnic tables. The **Green Valley RV Resort**, off I-19 on exit 69, Duval Mine Rd., 800/222-2969, has full hookups for under $30. It also has a pool, showers, laundry facilities, and a fantastic view of the Santa Rita Mountains. **White Rock Campground**, off I-19 at exit 12, is near Pena Blanca Lake. It's a scenic area with picnic tables and barbecues but no hookups.

12
TUCSON

The ancient Hohokam Indians farmed here in the first century, but by the time the Spanish explored the area, the Pima and Tohono O'odham tribes were established. The city of Tucson was founded as a military post in 1775 and was controlled by Spain until 1821, when Mexico gained its independence. The old fort was retained by Mexico until 1853, when the United States acquired it as part of the Gadsden Purchase. Tucson continues to blend Native American, Hispanic, and Anglo cultures. Once a rowdy frontier town, it still retains hints of its Old West beginnings.

This is a casual town with an outdoors orientation, a community proud of its cowboy poets and Western writers. However, it's also a sophisticated city with a major university, symphony, theater company, ballet, and opera. Tucson's warm, sunny winters draw visitors from around the world to golf or horseback ride. So whether you're looking to lounge by the pool or to explore the Sonoran Desert, Tucson will lure you back time and again.

A PERFECT DAY IN TUCSON

Start early and spend several hours enjoying the fabulous exhibits at the Arizona-Sonoran Desert Museum. After lunch, explore the nature trails and waterfalls of Sabino Canyon. Enjoy some of the city's most spectacular views over dinner at a restaurant in the foothills.

TUCSON

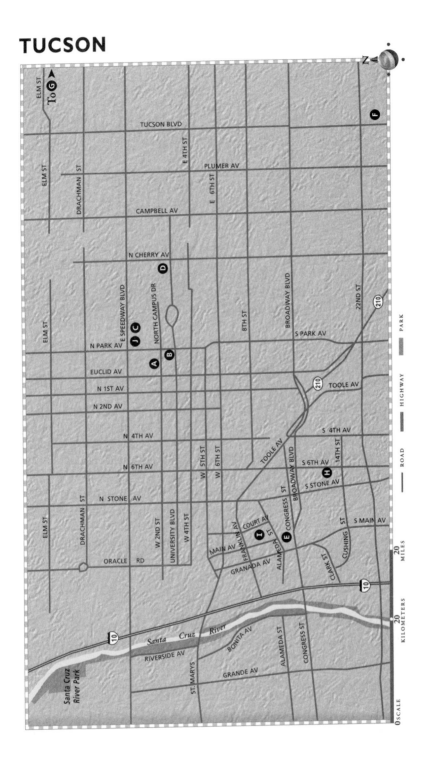

ORIENTATION

You'll probably enter Tucson on I-10, which runs east to northwest, toward Phoenix. I-10 intersects I-19, which heads south to Nogales. From I-10, take the Congress exit to downtown or the Ina Road exit for the Catalina foothills.

SIGHTSEEING HIGHLIGHTS

★★★★ ARIZONA-SONORAN DESERT MUSEUM
2021 N. Kinney Road; 520/883-2702

At this living museum, you'll find an amazing variety of natural landscape displays complete with plants and animals. The Life Underground exhibit features nocturnal desert dwellers, from tarantulas to kit foxes. You'll see beaver, river otter, and desert fishes in the Underwater Exhibit, while the Desert Grassland area provides an up-close view of black-tailed prairie dogs. Visitors can walk through a Hummingbird Aviary and a cave leading to a fine collection of rare and beautiful regional gems and minerals. Enjoy the area's best display of cacti and succulents, plus colorful Arizona wildflower and pollinator gardens.

Details: Open daily Oct–Feb 8:30–5, Mar–Sept 7:30–6. $8.95 adults, $1.75 ages 6–12, under 6 free. (half-day)

★★★★ FLANDRAU SCIENCE CENTER AND PLANETARIUM
Cherry Avenue and University Boulevard; 520/621-4515
www.seds.org/ flandrau/

This planetarium and science museum offers programs on stars,

SIGHTS

- **A** Arizona Historical Society Museum
- **B** Arizona State Museum
- **C** Center for Creative Photography
- **D** Flandrau Science Center & Planetarium
- **E** Historic Walking Tours
- **F** Reid Park Zoo
- **G** Tucson Botanical Gardens
- **H** Tucson Children's Museum
- **I** Tucson Museum of Art
- **J** University of Arizona Museum of Art

dazzling laser light shows set to music, and an excellent mineral specimen displays. Visitors can participate in hands-on exhibits about holography and radio waves and gaze through the center's 16-inch telescope.

Details: Open daily Mon–Fri 9–5, Sat–Sun 1–5, and evenings Wed–Thu 7–9, Fri–Sat 7–midnight. Telescope viewing Wed–Sat evening 7–10. Exhibit admission $3 adults, $2 children. Planetarium $5 adults, $4.50 seniors and students, $4 ages 3–12. Telescope viewing free. (2–3 hours)

★★★★ **MISSION SAN XAVIER DEL BAC,**
Nine miles south of I-19; 520/294-2624

The "White Dove of the Desert" was built in the late 1700s by Spanish Franciscans. Located on the San Xavier reservation, it still serves Native Americans. The Mission San Xavier del Bac incorporates Moorish, Byzantine, and Mexican Renaissance architectural styles and is considered the finest example of mission architecture in the United States. It has recently undergone a renovation, and the once-faded colors are restored to their original vibrancy.

Details: Church, museum, and gift shop open daily 9–5. Free. Donations accepted. Mass Tue–Fri 8:30 a.m., Sat 5:30 p.m., Sun 8, 9:30, 11, and noon. (1–2 hours)

★★★★ **OLD TUCSON STUDIOS**
201 S. Kinney Road; 520/883-6437

Originally built for the 1939 movie *Arizona*, this studio was later used for the filming of John Wayne favorites *McClintock* and *Rio Lobo*, and TV series *Little House on the Prairie* and *The High Chaparral*. In addition to seeing movie backdrops, you'll enjoy this Old West theme park's live entertainment and train and stagecoach rides. The studios have been rebuilt after a devastating 1995 fire and now include good historical educational shows as well as video presentations of local Native American and Anglo history.

Details: Open daily summer 10–6, winter 9–7. $14.95 adults, $9.45 ages 4–11. (2–4 hours)

★★★★ **PIMA AIR & SPACE MUSEUM**
6000 E. Valencia Road; 520/574-9658

This museum traces the evolution of American aviation with more than 200 aircraft, including replicas of the 1903 Wright brothers'

Wright Flyer and the X-15, the world's fastest aircraft. You can also tour the president's quarter and Secret Service compartments of the DC-6 that served as Air Force One for Presidents Kennedy and Johnson. Space artifacts and exhibits include X-15 and Mercury space capsule mockups.

Details: *Open daily 9–5. $6 adults, $5 seniors and military, $3 ages 10–17, under 10 free. (1–2 hours)*

★★★★ SABINO CANYON
Sabino Canyon Road; 520/749-2327

This is one of Tucson's favorite coolin'-off spots. Sabino Creek runs through a rugged canyon and forms waterfalls and pools. Several popular hiking trails include the Telephone Line Trail. A 45-minute (round-trip) tram stops at picnic areas and trailheads. Stop #6 is your best bet for bird-watching. Shuttles from the tram station also stop at the less crowded **Bear Canyon**. A **Coronado National Forest Visitor Center** near the tram station features several interpretive exhibits and information on the different trails.

Details: *Visitor center open daily 8–4:30. Tram runs Dec–May every half-hour 9–4:30. $5 adults, $2 ages 3–12. Bear Canyon tram runs less often. $3 adults, $1.25 ages 3–12. For a moonlight tram ride, call 520/749-2327. (half-day)*

★★★ CENTER FOR CREATIVE PHOTOGRAPHY
Speedway and Olive; 520/621-7968

The center houses more than 500,000 negatives, 200,000 study prints, and 60,000 master prints, including the world's largest collection of works by Ansel Adams and Alfred Stieglitz. Year-round photography exhibits are just part of this research facility dedicated to preserving photographers' complete archives. If you'd like to study the works of a particular photographer, call ahead for an appointment.

Details: *Mon–Fri 11–5. Free. (1 hour)*

★★★ COLOSSAL CAVE
I-10 exit 279 (Vail); 520/647-7275, www.colossalcave.com

Due to a lack of water, formations no longer grow in this "dry" cave. But thanks to the hard work of the Civilian Conservation Corps, who constructed the buildings and walkways during the mid-1930s, you can tour a half-mile of the cave. A favorite hideout for turn-of-the-century bandits, the cave displays cowboy items that have been found inside.

GREATER TUCSON

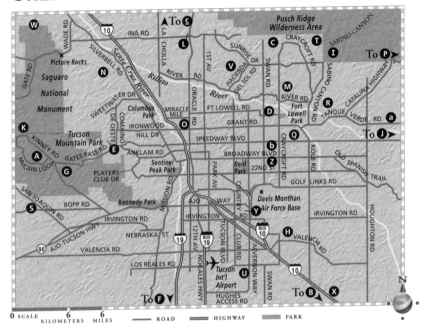

SIGHTS

- **A** Arizona-Sonoran Desert Museum
- **B** Colossal Cave
- **C** De Grazia Gallery
- **D** Fort Lowell Museum
- **E** International Wildlife Museum
- **F** Mission San Xavier del Bac
- **G** Old Tucson Studios
- **H** Pima Air & Space Museum
- **I** R. W. Webb Winery
- **J** Sabino Canyon
- **J** Saguaro National Park East
- **K** Saguaro National Park West
- **L** Tohono Chul Park

FOOD

- **M** Boccata
- **I** Hidden Valley Inn
- **N** L'il Abner's Steakhouse
- **O** La Fuente
- **P** Mt. Lemmon Cafe
- **D** Penelope's
- **Q** Rancher's Club
- **J** Saguaro Corners
- **R** Tack Room
- **L** Tohono Chul Tea Room
- **S** Triple C Chuckwagon Suppers
- **T** Ventana Room

LODGING

- **K** Casa Tierra
- **Q** DoubleTree
- **U** Embassy Suites
- **V** Hacienda del Sol

LODGING (continued)

- **W** Lazy K Bar Ranch
- **T** Loews Ventana Canyon Resort
- **X** Motel 6
- **Y** Red Roof Inn
- **Z** Super 8–Tucson East
- **a** Tanque Verde Ranch
- **b** Viscount Suite Hotel
- **L** Westward Look

CAMPING

- **B** Cactus Country RV Resort
- **C** Catalina State Park
- **X** Crazy Horse RV Park
- **G** Gilbert Ray Campground
- **P** Mount Lemmon Recreation Area

Note: Items with the same letter are located in the same place.

Details: Open daily mid-Mar to mid-Sept 8–6. Mid-Sept to mid-Mar 9–5. Extended hours on Sun. $6.50 adults, $5 ages 11–16, $3.50 ages 6–10, under 6 free. (1½ hours)

★★★★ **HISTORIC WALKING TOURS**
800/638-8350, www.arizonaguide.com/visittucson

Downtown Tucson contains two good walking tours. The **El Presidio Historic District** is named for the Spanish military garrison that once stood on this site. This was the city's most affluent neighborhood in the 1880s. Many of the homes have been restored and now contain restaurants and art galleries. The **Barrio Historico District** is another nineteenth-century neighborhood characterized by Sonoran-style adobe houses. You'll fine some art galleries and a few restaurants, but most of the buildings serve as offices. It overlaps the Downtown Arts District, home to galleries, boutiques, and nightclubs.

Details: Contact the Metropolitan Tucson Convention and Visitors Bureau, 800/638-8350, for a historic district map and free visitor guide or the Tucson Museum of Art, 520/624-2333, for docent-led tours. (3–4 hours per district)

★★★ **SAGUARO NATIONAL PARK**
East Visitor Center, 3693 S. Old Spanish Trail
520/733-5100. West Visitor Center, 2700 N. Kinney Road
520/733-5158.

The Sonoran Desert of Arizona and Mexico is the only place in the world that the stately saguaro cactus grows. Thick concentrations of them, many more than 200 years old, cluster in the park's west section. The east side is larger, at more than 60,000 acres, and is set in the Rincon Mountains. The park climbs through five climate zones. Both visitor centers offer trails information, saguaro displays, and a driving guide that leads you through eight-mile Cactus Forest Drive in the Rincon foothills.

Details: West side open 24 hours daily. Free. East side park open daily 7–sunset. $4 per car; $1 per biker or hiker. Both visitor centers open daily 8:30–5. (2–4 hours)

★★★ **TUCSON BOTANICAL GARDENS**
2150 N. Alvernon Way; 520/326-9686

This is a collection of gardens set on 5½ acres. Cactus and wildflower gardens accompany a garden with crops typical of early Native Americans. The Xeriscape Demonstration Garden exhibits water conservation methods essential to a desert environment. The gift shop sells many nice gardening and gift items.

Details: *Open daily 8:30–4:30. $4 adults, $3 seniors, under 12 free. (1 hour)*

★★★ UNIVERSITY OF ARIZONA MUSEUM OF ART
Park Avenue and Speedway Boulevard; 520/621-7567

Rated one of the finest university museums in the West, this art collection consists of more than 4,000 pieces. Holdings encompass fifteenth-century Spanish paintings, as well as European and American works from the Renaissance to the twentieth century, including Rembrandt, Picasso, O'Keeffe, and Warhol.

Details: *Labor Day to mid-May 9–5, Sun noon–4; shorter summer hours. Free. (2 hours)*

★★ ARIZONA HISTORICAL SOCIETY MUSEUM
949 E. Second Street; 520/628-5774

Arizona's oldest historical museum is both a fabulous research facility and the sponsor of many informative exhibits. Highlights include a full-scale reproduction of an underground mine tunnel, plus displays about Arizona's mining history and cattle business. One hands-on exhibit features the daily lives of three children from different ethnic backgrounds—Mexican, Anglo, and Native American—in the 1870s.

Details: *Mon–Sat 10–4, Sun noon–4. Free. (1–2 hours)*

★★ ARIZONA STATE MUSEUM
University Boulevard and Park Avenue; 520/621-6302

This museum collects wide-ranging artifacts from prehistoric to modern Native American cultures. One exhibit features the extinct Hohokam and their ancient desert-farming culture, while another presents an excellent overview of the Apache lifestyle. There's everything from cave archeology info to an Arizona animals exhibit.

Details: *Mon–Sat 10–4, Sun noon–5. Free. (1–2 hours)*

★★ INTERNATIONAL WILDLIFE MUSEUM
4800 W. Gates Pass Road; 520/617-1439

You can't miss this building, a combination castle/fort that contains

SABINO CANYON TRAM RIDE

© Thomas Wiewandt/Metropolitan Tucson CVB

more than 300 stuffed animal varieties from all over the world. The museum shows videos on wildlife conservation and threats to the rain forest. Kids will love its dramatic dioramas and interactive computers.

Details: Open daily 9–5. $5 adults, $3.75 seniors and students, $1.50 ages 6–12, under 6 free. (1 1/2 hours)

★★ TOHONO CHUL PARK
7366 N. Paseo del Norte; 520/575-8468

In the middle of Tucson is this fine desert preserve, hosting nature trails, a tearoom, greenhouse, many gardens, and a variety of plants, birds, and wildlife. A 1937 restored adobe building furnishes a number of changing exhibits. Pick up a self-guiding tour booklet to help identify the trail's flora and fauna, or take one of several guided tours.

Details: Grounds open daily 7–sunset. Exhibit House Mon–Sat 9:30–5, Sun 11–5. Free admission, but $2 donation appreciated. (1–2 hours)

★★ TUCSON CHILDREN'S MUSEUM
200 S. Sixth Avenue; 520/792-9985

Your kids won't want to miss this interesting museum, filled with hands-on activities that are both fun and educational. They can experiment with magnets, make giant bubbles, and join special weekend programs.

Details: Wed–Fri 9–5, Sat 10–5, Sun noon–5. $5 adults, $4 seniors, $3 ages 3–16, under 3 free. Third Sun of each month, free to all. (1–2 hours)

★★ TUCSON MUSEUM OF ART
140 N. Main Avenue; 520/624-2333

The recently renovated and expanded museum houses more than 4,000 works of art, including a sizable group of pre-Columbian artifacts and large collections of Western art. The museum presents 15 to 20 changing exhibitions each year.

Details: Mon–Sat 10–4, Sun noon–4. Closed Mon June–Aug. $2 adults, $1 students and seniors, under 13 free. Free to all on Tue. (2 hours)

★ DE GRAZIA GALLERY
6300 N. Swan Road; 520/299-9191

Ted De Grazia is probably the most reproduced artist in the world. His brightly colored Southwestern subjects are found on everything from notecards to refrigerator magnets. This small museum preserves De Grazia's rustic gallery and displays a selection of his originals. Visit the gift shop.

Details: Open daily 10–4. Free. (1 hour)

★ FORT LOWELL MUSEUM
2900 N. Craycroft Road; 520/855-3832

This part of Fort Lowell Park is a reconstruction of the military camp established in 1873 to protect American citizens from Apaches. Its commanding officer's quarters contain period furnishings and historical displays. This was originally the site of a Hohokam village, and artifacts unearthed during archaeological digs are also displayed.

Details: Wed–Sat 10–4. Free. (1 hour)

★ REID PARK ZOO
1100 S. Randolph Way; 520/791-4022

Although the zoo is small, this is an important breeding center for several endangered species, such as giant anteaters, white rhinoceroses, and zebras. You'll see a well-rounded collection of animals, from hippos to primates to several species of bird. Reid Park, next door, has a great kids' playground.

Details: *Open daily 9:30–5. $3.50 adults, $2.50 seniors, 75 cents ages 5–14. (2 hours)*

★ **R. W. WEBB WINERY**
I-10 exit 279 (Vail); 520/762-5777
Arizona's first winery opened after Prohibition uses only Arizona grapes for its entire line of 13 wines. You can tour and taste. Its sister microbrewery, Dark Mountain, produces Prickly Pear beer, a brew with a Sonoran flair.

Details: *Mon–Sat 10–5, Sun noon–5. $1 admission applied to purchase. (1 hour)*

FITNESS AND RECREATION

Mount Lemmon Recreation Area sits at the end of Catalina Highway, which spirals along the foothills of the Catalina Mountains to the piney forest of Mount Lemmon. Several lookouts provide impressive views across the Tucson Basin below. This part of the Coronado National offers plenty of hiking trails. Information is available at the Santa Catalina Ranger District, 5700 N. Sabino Canyon Rd., 520/749-8700.

This is also the site of the nation's southernmost ski area. **Mount Lemmon Ski Valley**, 520/576-1321, is 35 miles northeast of Tucson and encompasses 15 slopes for beginning to experienced skiers. During its December to April ski season, lift tickets are $27 adults, $12 children. Be sure to check snow conditions before going. In summer, ride the lifts for a fabulous view.

Tucson Mountain Park, west of Tucson at the end of Tucson Boulevard, 520/883-4200, offers desert wilderness for picnics, hiking, and biking. This scenic area in the Tucson Mountain foothills allows day use from 7 a.m. to 10 p.m. A viewpoint at the top of **Gates Pass** is a great place to watch the sunset.

From **Catalina State Park**, 11570 N. Oracle Rd., 520/628-5768, located on the northwest face of the Santa Catalina Mountains, hiking trails lead into the **Pusch Ridge Wilderness. Romero Pools** are a refreshing day-hike destination. Park admission is $4. Mountain bikers can purchase a mountain-biking map for $12 from Arizona Offroad Adventures, 800/689-BIKE, who offers half- and full-day trips in the Tucson area. Tucson Bicycles, 4743 E. Sunrise Dr., 520/577-7374, also has guided mountain bike rides. Full Cycle,

3232 E. Speedway, 520/327-3232, and Bargain Basement Ride, 428 N. Fremont Ave., 520/628-1015, rent bikes for $18 to $33 per day.

To follow the old National Mail stagecoach route through the Sonoran Desert on horseback, check with Colossal Cave Mountain Park Stables, 520/647-3450. Desert-High Country Stables, 6501 W. Ina Rd., 520/744-3789, offers a variety of rides in the Tucson Mountains and Saguaro National Park West for $15 per hour to $60 for a full day. El Conquistador Stables, 520/742-4200, and Walking Wind Stables, 10811 N. Oracle Rd., 520/742-4422, both at the entrance to Catalina State Park, offer hourly rates plus a 1 1/2-hour sunset ride for $23. Reservations required.

Golf is a favorite Tucson pastime, and the area holds more than 20 courses. You'll find them detailed in the *Tucson & Southern Arizona Golf Guide*, 520/322-0895. **Raven Golf Club at Sabino Springs**, 9777 E. Sabino Springs, 520/749-3636, has won several awards, including *Golf Digest's* "Top Ten Best New Courses." Jack Nicklaus and Tom Fazio captured the essence of desert golf with their designs at the **Westin La Paloma Resort & Country Club**, 3660 E. Sunrise Dr., 520/299-1500, and the **Lodge at Ventana Canyon**, 7000 N. Resort Dr., 520/577-4015. You'll also find five municipal golf courses around Tucson. Call 520/791-4873 for information. Tucson also caters to tennis players, with more than 220 public tennis courts. **Randolph Tennis Center**, 50 S. Alvernon Way, 520/791-4896, has 25 lighted courts.

Looking for some outdoor action? You might enjoy a cattle drive with Cocoraque Ranch Cattle Drives, 520/682-8594, who operate from an 1890s cattle ranch. Old Pueblo Archaeology Center, 520/798-0577, offers tours of ancient Indian ruins and hands-on opportunities to learn about Arizona's extinct cultures.

Award-winning photographer Dave Banks will take you on a behind-the-scenes workshop where you'll get to photograph rodeos, Native American ceremonies, and working ranches. Call Photographic Journeys, 888/355-8400. Tours of Tucson, 3325 N. Christmas, 520/325-2450, gives a full two-hour city tour from the perspective of an 1870s saloonkeeper for $25 per person. Lost Corner Tours, 520/884-7880, will take you off the beaten path, while the guides at Trail Dust Jeep Tours, 1665 S. Craycroft Rd., 520/747-0323, share the ecology and archaeology of the Sonoran Desert.

During baseball's spring training you can watch the **Arizona Diamondbacks** and the **Chicago White Sox**, 520/319-9501. For ticket info, call 888/683-3900. Tucson also hosts the **Colorado Rockies** Baseball Club, 520/327-9467. To order tickets, call 800/388-ROCK. Stock-car races are held March through October on Saturday night at **Tucson Raceway Park**, 12500 S.

Houghton Rd., 520/762-9200. For ice hockey fans, the **Tucson Gila Monsters**, 520/903-9000, battle WCHL teams from October through March.

FOOD

As a resort town, there's no shortage of quality dining in Tucson. Probably the most spectacular setting is the **Ventana Room** at the Loews Ventana Canyon Resort, 7000 N. Resort Dr., 520/299-2020. Diners enjoy views of the canyon waterfall and the twinkling lights of Tucson in the valley below. The Ventana's new American cuisine is accompanied by the sounds of a harpist. The chef's five-course tasting menu is $75, $55 without wine. Otherwise, entrees range from $18 to $36.

Also nestled in the Catalina foothills is the **Tack Room**, 7300 E. Victor Ranch Trail, 520/722-2800, a legendary Five Diamond restaurant. You'll be treated to impeccable service in an atmosphere of casual elegance. It's one of the most expensive places in town, with entrees on its Southwestern/American menu ranging from $25 to $35.

Built in 1930, the **Arizona Inn**, 2200 E. Elm St., 800/933-1093, has all the charm and ambiance of an Old West resort. It serves predominantly Southwestern fare, with entrees around $20. Patio dining overlooks manicured gardens, while a patio bar offers more casual service. Lunch entrees range from $5 to $11. Sunday brunch is a favorite.

The **Ranchers Club,** 5151 E. Grant Rd., 520/321-7621, is the best, and most expensive, place to get a steak. Its classic Old West decor incorporates animal trophies, old saddles, and steer horns. Chefs grill the prime beef and fresh seafood over a combination of mesquite, hickory, and sassafras woods. Main courses for lunch and dinner vary widely, from $17 to $64.

Looking for a cowboy experience? Mosey on over to **L'il Abner's Steakhouse**, 8500 N. Silverbell, 520/744-2800, formerly a stagecoach stop. Sit down at a picnic table to enjoy mesquite-grilled steaks served with beans and all the fixin's, and two-step to a live country band weekend nights.

Hidden Valley Inn, 4825 N. Sabino Canyon, 520/299-4941, is a popular family steak house tucked into an Old West town facade. Specialties include mesquite-broiled steaks, prime rib, and even seafood. Lunch and dinner entrees start at $8.95. Another favorite family destination is the **Triple C Chuckwagon Suppers**, 8900 W. Bopp Rd., 800/446-1798, located on an old cattle ranch. Your choice of barbecue beef or chicken is dished up from an old chuck wagon. The complete meal, for $14 adults and $7 children, includes a Western dinner show.

Tucson offers many authentic Mexican food choices. **La Fuente**, 1749 N.

TUCSON

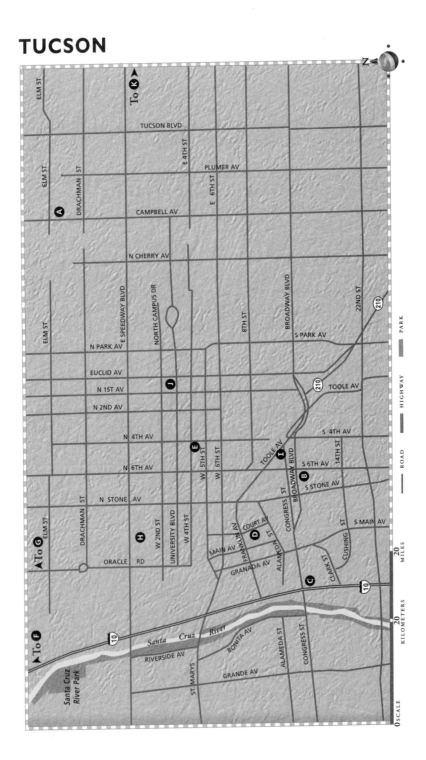

Oracle Rd., 520/623-8659, features mariachis nightly and a great champagne Mexican Sunday brunch. **El Charro Mexican Cafe**, 311 N. Court Ave., 520/622-1922, is the oldest family-operated Mexican restaurant in the country. They use sun-dried beef in their famous *carne seca*, and the taste is unique. **Carlos Murphy's**, 419 W. Congress St., 520/628-1958, serves Mexican food in a historic old train depot. Kids love the place. **Cafe Poca Cosa**, 88 E. Broadway Blvd., 520/622-6400, offers some unique versions of Mexican and Southwestern food. The menu changes daily but often includes tequila marinades and unique mole sauces. They're open for lunch and dinner; evening entrees range from $11 to $15.

For classical French cuisine, try **Penelope's**, 3071 N. Swan Rd., 520/325-5080, set in a charming adobe ranch house with fireplaces and stained glass. Specialties include escargot and quail. Open for lunch and dinner; entrees from $13 to $22. The fixed-price six-course meal is $29.50, $42.50 with wine. Another dining experience with a fabulous foothills view is the upscale **Boccata**, 5605 E. River Rd., 520/577-9309. Its Italian/American menu offers entrees with unusual glazes, and the desserts are heavenly. Dinner only; entrees range from $12 to $23.

If you're looking for unique casual dining, consider lunch or dinner at **Saguaro Corners**, near the entrance of Saguaro National Park entrance, 520/886-5424. This rustic restaurant offers Southwestern fare with wonderful views of the desert landscape. Located in a Territorial-style building at Tohono Chul Park, the **Tohono Chul Tea Room**, 7366 N. Paseo del Norte, 520/797-1222, serves breakfast, lunch, and afternoon tea amid fountains on the courtyard and garden patios.

For something healthy, the **Sundance Cafe & Juice Bar**, 621 N. Fourth St., 520/620-1699, is the best vegetarian restaurant in town for lunch and dinner. And if you're headed up to Mount Lemmon, stop by the **Mount**

FOOD

- Ⓐ Arizona Inn
- Ⓑ Cafe Poca Cosa
- Ⓒ Carlos Murphy's
- Ⓓ El Charro Mexican Cafe
- Ⓔ Sundance Cafe & Juice Bar
- Ⓕ Tohono Chul Tea Room

LODGING

- Ⓐ Arizona Inn
- Ⓖ Best Western Ghost Ranch Lodge
- Ⓗ Clarion Santa Rita Hotel & Suites
- Ⓓ El Presidio Inn
- Ⓘ Hotel Congress
- Ⓙ Peppertrees B&B Inn
- Ⓚ Smuggler's Inn Campground

Note: Items with the same letter are located in the same place.

Lemmon Cafe on Catalina Highway in Summerhaven, 520/576-1234. The café features Pennsylvania Dutch cooking and has its own smokehouse.

LODGING

Those visiting Tucson to play golf or lounge at a resort will find plenty of fabulous choices. The **Loews Ventana Canyon Resort**, 7000 N. Resort Drive, 800/234-5177, is nestled in the Santa Catalina foothills. Amenities include two golf courses, full-service spas, and four restaurants. A short nature trail leads to the waterfall visible from the resort. But this pampering doesn't come cheap. During peak winter months, doubles range from $235 to $400, with suites commanding up to $2,400. However, summer rates are often half.

The **Westin La Paloma**, 3800 E. Sunrise Drive, 800/937-8461, is also in the foothills and offers sweeping panoramic views, 12 tennis courts, a 27-hole golf course, and spa services. This kid-friendly resort also furnishes a children's lounge, game room, and new 170-foot waterslide. Peak rates begin at $325 to $495 for a suite, while summer rates plunge to $110.

One of Tucson's most reasonably priced resorts is the **Westward Look Resort**, 245 E. Ina Road, 800/722-2500, which opened in 1929 as a dude ranch. It has Old World charm with such modern amenities as three pools and spas, eight tennis courts, a fitness center, and horseback riding. Summer rates start at $69, with peak season from $159 to $339. Another favorite historic lodge is the **Arizona Inn**, 2200 E. Elm Street, 800/933-1093, which opened in 1930. This classic adobe structure provides a peaceful oasis amid manicured gardens and courtyards—even a croquet court. Peak rates range from $165 to $215.

If you want history without the resort setting, stay downtown at the **Hotel Congress**, 311 E. Congress, 800/722-8848, built in 1919. Its simple rooms retain much of the original furniture. Public Enemy #1, John Dillinger, stayed here in the 1930s. This budget hotel attracts many young people for its youth-hostel dormitory rooms. Its Club Congress is a popular nightclub, and Cybar has ten computers, Internet access, and lots of games. Rates range from $31 to $45.

If you want to stay near the arts and historic district, the **Clarion Santa Rita Hotel & Suites**, 88 E. Broadway Blvd., 800/488-8276, features newly renovated guest rooms, saunas, and pool. Rates run from $69 to $225. The hotel's Cafe Poca Cosa serves some of the best Mexican food in town.

If you're looking for a suite motel, another good choice is **DoubleTree**

Guest Suites, 6555 E. Speedway Blvd., 800/222-TREE. Decorated in Southwestern style, the motel offers a small pool and exercise room. Peak rates range from $133 to $147 and start at $74 during summer. The **Tucson Viscount Suite Hotel**, 4855 E. Broadway, 800/527-9666, features upscale rooms with a contemporary feel for $99 to $145 per night. A complementary breakfast and afternoon cocktails are served in a four-story garden atrium. Another option is **Smuggler's Inn**, 6350 E. Speedway Blvd., 800/525-8852, which offers spacious rooms and suites overlooking lush interior gardens from private patios. Kids enjoy the lagoon, filled with wild ducks and giant goldfish. Peak rates run from $99 to $119. At the **Embassy Suites-Tucson International Airport**, 7051 S. Tucson Blvd., 800/262-8866, all suites have a kitchenette, two phones, and two TVs. Rates start at $89 in summer and at $134 during winter.

The **Lodge on the Desert**, 306 N. Alvernon Way, 800/456-5634, has the charm and ambiance of the Arizona Inn, without the expense. It's owned by the same family who started it in 1936, and many guests return year after year. The pool has a view of the Santa Catalina Mountains; other niceties include a shuffleboard court, croquet court, and library. Peak rates, including continental breakfast, are $92 to $118.

The **Best Western Ghost Ranch Lodge**, 801 W. Miracle Mile, 800/456-7565, was a desert resort opened in 1941. It's situated on eight acres amid cactus gardens and an orange grove. The rooms have been refurbished with Western flair, and there's a small pool and game room. Rates in peak season range from $52 to $110.

Tucson has several bed-and-breakfasts set in historic homes. The **Peppertrees B&B Inn**, 724 E. University Blvd., 800/348-5763, is a 1905 Victorian-style home furnished with family antiques. It's conveniently located just two blocks from the University of Arizona. Rates run from $98 per double to $165 per suite. **El Presidio Inn**, 297 N. Main, 800/349-6151, is set in an 1880 historic adobe mansion within walking distance of restaurants, museums, and the downtown arts district. Antique-adorned rooms decorated accompany romantic lush garden courtyards. In addition to a hearty breakfast, the inn provides complementary drinks, fruit, and treats in the afternoon and evening. Located in the Sonoran Desert west of Tucson, **Casa Tierra**, 11155 W. Calle Pima, 520/578-3058, is a rustic adobe home with all the charm of an Old Mexico hacienda. While enjoying spectacular mountain views and brilliant sunsets, you'll be treated to full vegetarian breakfast, a hot tub, and some great birding and hiking.

If you want to play cowboy, stay at **Tanque Verde Ranch**, 14301 E. Speedway Blvd., 800/234-DUDE, which was founded in the 1880s. Set near the Saguaro National Park and the Coronado National Forest, it offers scenic nature trails for hiking, horseback riding, and bird-watching. Its nature center has live snakes and other desert life. Rates range from $250 to $365. **Lazy K Bar Ranch**, 8401 N. Scenic Dr., 800/321-7018, was homesteaded in 1933 and converted to a dude ranch in 1936. Ranch activities include riding and hiking, plus hayrides, cookouts, and square dances. Rates range from $185 to $275, with a three-night minimum. The casual **Hacienda Del Sol**, 5601 N. Hacienda del Sol Rd., 800/728-6514, was once a girls' prep school that now features cowboy barbecues, ecological nature tours, and horseback riding. Room, suites, and casitas are available from $120 to $285.

If you're looking for basic accommodations, Tucson's numerous chain motels include the **Red Roof Inn**, 3700 Irvington Rd., 520/571-1400, **Motel 6**, 1031 E. Benson Hwy., 520/628-1264, and **Super 8-Tucson East**, 1990 S. Craycroft Rd., 520/790-6021.

CAMPING

Catalina State Park, 520/628-5798, furnishes tent and RV sites for $8 per night, with hiking and nature trails into Coronado National Forest. **Mount Lemmon Recreation Area** 520/670-4552, maintains several campgrounds off the highway in Coronado National Forest, 520/749-8700. The **Gilbert Ray Campground**, in Tucson Mountain Park, 8451 W. McCain Rd., 520/883-4200, has RV sites and tent camping close to Old Tucson and Saguaro National Park. **Crazy Horse RV Park Campground**, 6600 S. Craycroft Rd., 800/279-6279, has full hookups and a pool. **Cactus Country RV Resort**, 10195 S. Houghton Rd., 800/777-8799, has RV and tent sites with pool, laundry, and a spa.

NIGHTLIFE AND SPECIAL EVENTS

You'll find plenty of options for evening activities in the Tucson area. Most of the other foothills resorts also have lounges open to nonguests that often feature excellent entertainment and unequaled panoramic vistas.

To purchase tickets for the performing arts, including Tucson's symphony, opera, and ballet companies, call Dillard's, 800/638-4253, or TicketMaster, 520/321-1000. The **Tucson Jazz Society**, 520/743-3399, sponsors several concerts each year. Or, if you're looking for country, **New West**, 4385 W. Ina Rd., 520/744-7744, is the biggest and best dance floor in Tucson. You can even get dance lessons.

The most popular annual event, drawing thousands to town, is the February **Tucson Gem & Mineral Show**. For weeks before and after the official show, all over town you'll see booths and tents with gemstones, petrified rock, and fossils for sale. This is a great time to visit, but be sure to book your room early. Also in February is the **Tucson Rodeo and Parade**, 520/741-2233. Preseason major-league baseball begins in March.

Other Tucson events include numerous golf tournaments and tennis classics, as well as music festivals and Indian powwows. Check with the Visitors Bureau, 800/638-8350, www.arizonaguide.com/visittucson, for current events.

Tucson to Yuma

If you're heading west to Yuma, consider traveling on State Highway 86. You'll pass the exit to Kitt Peak National Observatory (see Chapter 11), sitting nearly 7,000 feet high atop the Quinlan Mountains, then enter the Tohono O'odham Nation Indian Reservation. **Sells** *and* **Quijotoa** *are popular stops for bargains on goods handmade by tribal artisans.*

Arizona's largest, most remote national monument is your next stop. **Organ Pipe Cactus National Monument,** *520/387-6849, is open 24 hours; its visitor center is open from 8 to 5. The rare organ-pipe cactus resembles the saguaro, but instead of forming a single main trunk it forms many trunks, some 20 feet tall, resembling organ-pipes. Two loop drives run through the park: the 53-mile* **Puerto Blanco Drive,** *on which you'll pass* **Quitobaquito Spring,** *and the 21-mile* **Ajo Mountain Drive.** *Park admission is $4 per car; camping fees are $8 per night.*

Back on Highway 85, you'll pass through **Ajo,** *which offers a lookout access and the mining exhibits of the* **New Cornelia Mine,** *open Tuesday through Saturday 10 to 4 (closed in summer). Admission is $1. Highway 85 then takes you to I-8 and* **Gila Bend,** *where you'll proceed west to Yuma.*

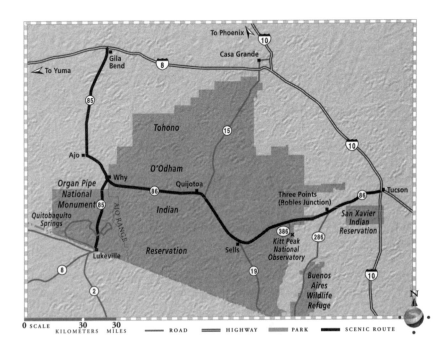

13
THE SOUTHWEST CORNER: YUMA AND BEYOND

Yuma sits at the confluence of the Gila and Colorado Rivers. Although the raging waters have been tamed through a series of dams, the Spanish explorers who first ventured into the area in 1540 saw bubbling, turbulent rivers. Eight different Native American tribes farmed along the banks of the rivers and alternated between friendship and war with the intruding Europeans.

When American troops were assigned to Arizona Territory in the mid-1800s, they traveled across the established northern routes to San Francisco. After transferring to steamer ships, they sailed along the California coast past Mexico, and then up the inland waterways to Yuma. Up and down the Colorado River chugged huge barges and stern-wheelers transporting soldiers and supplies to various ports upstream. Horses, mules, and wagons then carried the troops to the remote outposts of the Arizona Territory.

By the turn of the century, railroads had reduced the need for water routes, and Yuma's population began to decline. Eventually, the dams turned the raging river into a mild stream, creating a variety of scenic lakes and waterways and transforming the old port into a popular retirement destination.

The U.S. Weather Service claims Yuma is the sunniest spot in the country, making it a magnet for winter visitors. The summer months are hot, and you'll want to stick to early morning activities. This low-key, casual town offers lots of golf, tennis, birding, hiking, fishing, and rockhounding.

YUMA

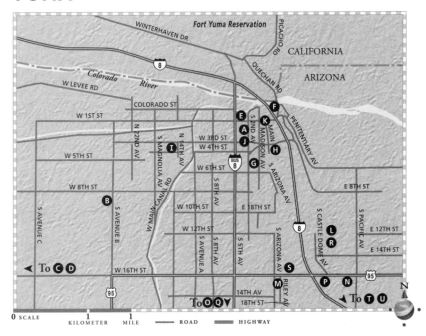

SIGHTS

A Century House Museum
B Ehrlich's Date Garden
C Peanut Patch
D Saihati Camel Farm
E Yuma Crossing State Historic Park
F Yuma Territorial Prison State Park
G Yuma Valley RR

FOOD

H California Bakery
I Chretin's Mexican Foods
J The Garden Cafe and Rio Colorado Coffee Co.
K Lutes Casino

LODGING

L Best Western Inn Suites Yuma
M Comfort Inn
N Days Inn
O Holiday Inn Express
P La Fuente Inn & Suites
Q Radisson Suites Inn Yuma
R Shilo Inn Hotel
S Super 8 Motel
T Westwind Golf & RV Resort
U Winterhaven RV Park

A PERFECT DAY IN THE SOUTHWEST CORNER

Start out at the Yuma Territorial Prison State Park to learn about life in this notorious penitentiary. Then head back into the sunshine for a short hike to the Yuma Crossing State Historic Park. Have a relaxing lunch among the cool gardens and aviaries at the Garden Cafe, then tour the Century House Museum. Fill in the afternoon by checking out the Peanut Patch or the Date Gardens. To top off the day, schedule a sunset dinner cruise along the Colorado River.

SIGHTSEEING HIGHLIGHTS

★★★★ **YUMA CROSSING STATE HISTORIC PARK**
201 N. Fourth Avenue, Yuma; 520/329-0471
Stroll among the buildings from the original Quartermaster Depot, which was authorized by Congress in 1865. For the next 20 years, this was the distribution point for troops, supplies, and several hundred head of mules bound for the remote outposts of Arizona Territory. The park's other attractions include an early adobe house, stagecoaches, mule wagons, a steam train, a historic adobe corral, and an interesting visitor center.
   Details: Open daily 10–5. Adults $3, seniors $2.50, children 7–13 $2, under 7 free. (1–2 hours)

★★★★ **YUMA TERRITORIAL PRISON STATE PARK**
Giss Parkway and Prison Hill Road, Yuma; 520/783-4771
The subject of numerous Hollywood movies and television shows, this penitentiary happens to be Arizona's most visited state historic park. Between 1876 and 1909, its thick adobe walls and steel bars confined some of Arizona's most notorious criminals—plus several adulterers and polygamists. The scorching desert sun often sent the temperature soaring inside the prison cells, and the dungeon was known as the "snake pit." After a new facility was built, the building served as the town high school from 1910 to 1914 and as a homeless shelter during the Depression. A total of 3,049 men and 29 women were incarcerated at the Yuma prison. You can check out their mugs at the museum, which chronicles the history of this famous prison.
   Details: Open daily 8–5. Closed Christmas. Interpretive programs at 11, 2, and 3:30. Adults $3, children 7–13 $2, under 7 free. (1–2 hours)

★★★ CENTURY HOUSE MUSEUM
240 S. Madison Avenue, Yuma; 520/782-1841

You'll step back in time as you enter the lavish 1870s adobe home of pioneer merchant E. F. Sanguinette and gaze at his family's period clothing, photos, and furnishings, including an elaborate Victorian pump organ. The extensive gardens and aviaries filled with colorful cockatoos, peacocks, parrots, and mynah birds are maintained as they were more than a century ago. Don't be surprised if a few of the birds strike up a conversation! You can also browse through the historical library and gift shop next door, and have breakfast or lunch at the adjoining **Garden Cafe**.

Details: Tue–Sat 10–4. Free, but donation suggested. Call for special tours, films, and lectures. (1–2 hours)

★★ COLORADO RIVER TOURS

The importance of the Colorado River in the development of the Southwest is often overlooked because the river has been dammed. In the river's heyday, the turbulent water was jammed with riverboats and barges as it moved settlers, soldiers, and supplies up and down the coast. For one of the most interesting tours in Yuma, take a cruise on an authentic double-decker stern-wheeler. Listen to historic yarns from Captain Ron and his crew while aboard the **Colorado King I**, 520/782-2412. In addition, Yuma River Tours, 520/783-4400, offers a variety of jet-boat tours past Indian petroglyphs, mining camps, and old ranch sites, and through bird-watching areas at the Imperial Wildlife Refuge. The company also offers custom three-hour lunch tours and sunset dinner cruises.

Details: Both companies launch from Fisher's Landing, about 30 miles north of Yuma. Tours run $25–$75 each, $15 and up for children. Call for specific times, cost, and directions. (half- to full day)

★★ YUMA VALLEY RAILWAY
Fifth Street and Second Avenue, Yuma, 520/783-3456

Hop aboard and travel along the winding banks of the Colorado River within sight of Mexico. As you pass rolling farmlands, a local historian will share some of the region's history and folklore. Passengers ride in a comfortable 1922 Pullman coach pulled by a 1941 diesel locomotive or a 1952 Davenport Bessler. This is a delightful 22-mile excursion.

Details: Oct–May only. Call Yuma County Live Steamers for schedule. Adults $10, seniors $9, children 5–16 $5. Picnic tables. (2 hours)

★ EHRLICH'S DATE GARDEN
868 Avenue B, Yuma; 520/783-4778

The date is one of the oldest cultivated tree crops on Earth, having been around for more than 5,000 years. At this garden, one of the leading Medjool date producers, the fruit is harvested from September to November, but you'll find fresh dates, produce, nuts, and candies year-round.

Details: Open daily 9–5. (1 hour)

★ PEANUT PATCH
4322 E. County 13th Street, Yuma; 800/USA-PNUT

You can watch the peanut harvest in nearby fields from October to December. Tour the processing facility from October to spring and watch them make peanut brittle, fudge, and other goodies (free samples!). Head to the gift shop for fresh peanuts, peanut brittle, peanut fudge, and lots of other peanutty foods.

Details: Gift shop open Mon–Sat 9–6. Closed in summer. Free tours Tue and Fri at 10. (1 hour)

★ SAIHATI CAMEL FARM
5672 S. Avenue 1E, Yuma; 520/627-2553

You'll get a close-up look at some of the Arabian Desert's rare and endangered animals, including Arabian camels and oryx, African pygmy goats, Asian water buffalo, Watusi cattle, and some of the largest camel herds in North America.

Details: Tours are given Mon–Sat at 10 and 2, Sun at 1. Closed June 1–Sept 30. Admission $3. Call for reservations. (1–2 hours)

FITNESS AND RECREATION

Since the sun shines 93 percent of the time in Yuma, outdoor activities are featured. *Golf Digest* rated Yuma's 11 challenging public golf courses the seventh best in the United States. **Desert Hills Municipal Golf Course**, 520/344-GOLF, was rated Arizona's top municipal course.

Hikers enjoy the **Riverside Path** and **Levee Trail,** less than a mile walk that leads from the prison to Yuma Crossing and on to the Quartermaster Depot. For longer hikes and birding, drive to the **Imperial National Wildlife Refuge**, located about 40 miles northeast of Yuma, 520/783-3371. It protects two unique environments: the desert and the Colorado River ecosystem. A little further north is the **Cibola National Wildlife Refuge,**

QUARTZSITE

Head north on Highway 95 to the crossroads of I-10, and you'll find the unusual community of Quartzsite. During summer it just looks like a few old buildings and a population of under 1,000. But venture there during the warm winter months, and you'll be amazed at the sea of RVs, pickup campers, tents, etc., as the crowds mushroom to more than 20,000. This is not an improved RV or campsite area, but simply an open-ended patch of desert where snowbirds (Arizonans' affectionate term for retired wintertime visitors) park, roll out some Astroturf, and plunk down the lawn chairs. They provide their own water and electricity, but the rates are cheap. Call the Yuma BLM Office for info on short- and long-term RV parking.

This area is a rockhound's paradise between January and February. Each year, 11 local gem and mineral shows attract more than a million visitors. It's like a giant flea market, with opportunities to buy huge chunks of petrified wood, fossilized dinosaur poop, and all kinds of rocks and minerals from 6,000-plus vendors. You'll also find antiques and collectibles, a huge variety of food booths, and lots of homemade crafts. The **Quartzsite Gemboree** is a combination of three shows: the **Main Event, Quartzsite PowWow** (the largest gem and mineral show in the world), and **Tyson Wells Sell-A-Rama**. For details, contact the Quartzsite Chamber of Commerce, P.O. Box 85, Quartzsite, AZ 85346, 520/927-5600.

While in town, check out the small **Quartzsite Museum**, which is the old Tyson Wells stage stop on the Main Street drag. This free museum is open Wednesday through Saturday from 10 to 3 during winter. In the cemetery at the west end of town, you'll find the **Hi Jolly grave site**. Hadji Ali ("Hi Jolly") was a Syrian camel herder who stayed in the area after the failed U.S. Army Camel Corps disbanded in the 1860s.

520/857-3253, a four-mile drive offering close views of wintering waterfowl, especially Canada geese and sandhill cranes. Near Mittry Lake is **Betty's Kitchen**, a 10-acre wildlife interpretive area with a half-mile self-guided tour, easy walking, bird-watching, and fishing. For guided tours, call 520/627-2773. A few miles to the east is the **Kofa National Wildlife Refuge**, 520/783-

7861, which protects 665,400 acres of mountainous Sonoran Desert habitat and encompasses the Kofa and Castle Dome Mountain Ranges. Although they are not especially high, the Castle Dome Mountains are extremely rugged and rise sharply from the surrounding desert plains, providing ideal bighorn sheep habitat. Take your binoculars.

Of the only three places in the United States where palm trees grow naturally, one is in a remote area of the Kofa Refuge. The entrance to **Palm Canyon** is a 10-mile curvy dirt road off Highway 95. Park in the lot at the end of the road. It's a tough one-mile hike. Besides the few dozen palms, you'll see a variety of birds. including red-tailed hawks and an occasional golden eagle.

Numerous lakes and scenic waterways exist along the Colorado River for boating and fishing. The cool waters are home to bass, catfish, and bluegill. Contact the BLM, 520/317-3200, or Arizona Game and Fish, 520/342-0091, for specific information including licensing. From November to March, the Colorado River near the Mexican border near Algodones is stocked with trout. For information on permits and licenses, contact the **Quechan Indian Tribal Fish and Game**, 760/572-0544. You'll find boat rentals at **Hidden Shores** and **Martinez Lake**.

If you're interested in rockhounding, the numerous gem fields within 80 miles of Yuma are happy hunting grounds for kaynite, garnet, tourmaline, talc, pyrite, agate, jasper, chalcedony roses, cat's-eye quartz, petrified wood, etc. Check with some of the local rock shops or the Yuma Convention and Visitors Bureau, 520/783-0071, for maps and information.

Twenty miles west of Yuma, pure white sand dunes surround both sides of I-8. It is illegal to go into the dunes from the rest stop on the highway, so head west on I-8 to the Gray's Well exit, then to the Frontage Road leading to the dunes.

Yuma's **Marine Corps Air Station** welcomes civilians to visit their premier aviation training base. For information on winter tours and air show schedules, call 520/341-2275. And at the **Yuma Speedway**, 520/726-9483, five miles south of town, the Napa Auto Parts Desert Racing Series features weekly racing events from February to June and September to December, plus a Fourth of July celebration. Prices vary for special events.

FOOD

If you're looking for a relaxed atmosphere, you'll find plenty of choices in Yuma. In fact, no restaurant requires a coat and tie, and dress is fairly casual everywhere in town. The **Garden Cafe and Rio Colorado Coffee Co.**, 250 S. Madison Ave., 520/783-1491, sits in back of the Century House Museum, amid

SOUTHWEST CORNER

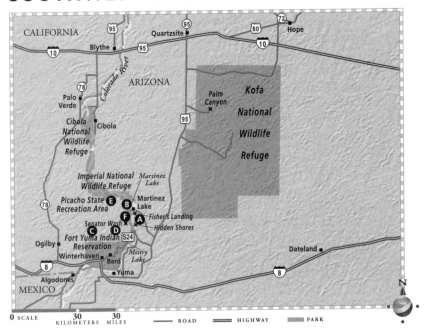

SIGHTS
A Colorado River Tours

FOOD
B Martinez Lake Restaurant and Cantina

LODGING
B Martinez Lake Resort

CAMPING
C Gold Rock Ranch
D Imperial Dam Recreation Area
E Picacho State Recreation Area
F Senator Wash and Squaw Lake Campground

aviaries and colorful gardens. It's a favorite for breakfast and Sunday brunch, with rich coffees and sumptuous pancakes. Tempting lunches include gourmet sandwiches, quiche, salads, and decadent desserts. Misters cool the outside patio, and inside dining is also available. Another excellent spot for lunch or dinner is the **California Bakery**, 284 S. Main St., 520/782-7335. Housed in a historic building, this charming restaurant features a yummy tortilla soup and pasta that is handmade daily.

For a taste of local life, head to **Lutes Casino**, 221 Main St., 520/782-2192, a Yuma tradition since the 1920s. It's the oldest continuing pool hall and domino parlor in the state. Any of the burgers are great, but Lutes is best known for the "especial," a cheeseburger/hot dog combination.

For authentic Mexican food, try **Chretin's Mexican Foods**, 485 S. 15th Ave., 520/782-1291. a family restaurant started in 1946 that still feels like an old border-town café. Sample their great margaritas. For lunch or dinner with a view, head north of town to the **Martinez Lake Restaurant and Cantina**, at the west end of Martinez Lake Rd., 520/783-0253, overlooking the lake. Its full menu offers burgers, steaks, fish, and daily specials. Live music keeps the place hopping on weekends.

LODGING

Yuma is filled with quality chain motels, most providing a pool, complimentary breakfast, and airport shuttle. Many also have restaurants. Also in town are several suite hotels, some with kitchenettes. Probably the most luxurious is the **Shilo Inn Hotel,** 1550 S. Castle Dome Rd., 800/222-2244, which furnishes kitchenettes within its bright, comfortable guest rooms, some with desert views. Amenities include a refrigerator, microwave, and VCR, for rates of $125 to $250 per night.

The **Radisson Suites Inn Yuma**, 2600 S. Fourth Ave., 520/726-4830, has 164 two-room suites. Extras include a heated pool/spa, guest laundry, use of a local fitness center, and complimentary cocktails from 5 to 7. Other options include **Best Western Inn Suites Yuma**, 1450 Castle Dome Ave., 520/783-8341, which has tennis courts and a nearby golf course for $90 to $160; and the Southwestern-style **La Fuente Inn & Suites**, 1513 E. 16th St., 520/329-1814, whose many amenities include guest barbecue grills by the pool, at $60 to $85.

You'll also find a good choice of newer budget motels, including **Holiday Inn Express**, 3181 S. Fourth Ave., 520/344-1420; **Days Inn**, 1671 E. 16th St., 520/329-7790; **Super 8 Motel**, 1688 S. Riley Ave., 520/782-2000; and **Comfort Inn**, 1691 S. Riley Ave., 520/782-1200. The Comfort Inn has a heated pool and spa, and its room service is provided by Shoney's.

For something more unusual, try **Martinez Lake Resort**, at the west end of Martinez Lake Rd., 520/783-9589. It rents 30 standard motel units, plus rustic waterfront houses that sleep 4 to 12 (houses come with their own docks). Rates range from $35 to $200 per night.

All prices listed above are for peak winter months. During the blazing summer, rates can plunge by more than one-third.

CAMPING

If you're looking for adventure, go to **Gold Rock Ranch**, P.O. Box 728, Winterhaven, CA 92283, 22 miles northwest of Yuma. The Walker family allows camping and prospecting and runs a rock and antique shop. Since they don't have a phone, you'll need to write for more specific info on dates and rates.

At **Picacho State Recreation Area**, 23 miles north of Yuma, you'll find improved campsites with solar showers, toilets, hiking trails, and fishing. From October to May, weekend campfire programs and guided nature walks take place. In addition, plenty of campsites exist in the wildlife refuge areas and near the lakeshores surrounding Yuma. Call the Bureau of Land Management for fee and regulation info about the **Imperial Dam Recreation Area**, **Senator Wash**, and **Squaw Lake Campground**.

Yuma has no shortage of RV parks, all with varying amenities. **Westwind RV Resort, Golf & Country Club**, 9797 E. Highway 80, 520/342-2992, is a large full-service RV resort with pool, spa, golf course, driving range, activity center, and planned functions. Roger's also offers TV and phone hookups. The **Winterhaven RV Park**, 6580 E. Highway 80, 520/726-0284, has a homey atmosphere with a pool, cable TV, Bingo, and potluck dinners. Check with the visitors bureau for a complete list of RV parks.

14
ARIZONA'S
WEST COAST

The story of Arizona's "west coast" is closely tied to the water of the Rio Colorado. This wild and raging river took millions of years to cut the Grand Canyon. For several millennia Native Americans farmed along the fertile banks of this bubbling red torrent. When the West was being settled, American troops and pioneers were shuttled up and down the river by paddlewheel steamboats. Yet in the last century, this country has diverted, dammed, and altered the Colorado River. To deal with the river's unpredictable nature, a series of seven dams has been constructed, creating thousands of miles of shoreline and several recreational lakes that have turned the western edge of Arizona into an aquatic playground amid an arid desert landscape. It's become a Fort Lauderdale–type getaway for the college crowd, while families rent paddleboats and relax on the sandy beaches, and the retired flock to Laughlin to gamble. No matter what your age, Arizona's west coast has plenty to offer.

A PERFECT DAY ON ARIZONA'S WEST COAST

Drive across the Hoover Dam and take a Behind-the-Scenes tour. Explore the coastline along the Colorado until you reach Lake Havasu City. Play around the beaches, shop the English Village, and check out the London Bridge. Book a sunset dinner cruise or head back to Laughlin for a little nighttime gambling or a show.

WEST COAST REGION

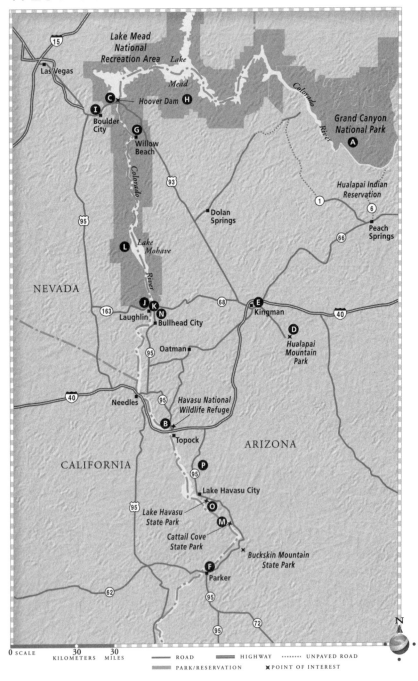

Lake Mead National Recreation Area

Lake Mead

15 Las Vegas

C ✗ Hoover Dam   H

I Boulder City

G Willow Beach

Colorado

93

Dolan Springs

Colorado River

Grand Canyon National Park

A ✗

Hualapai Indian Reservation

1

6

66

Peach Springs

Lake Mohave

River

95

L

NEVADA

163   J K N

Laughlin   Bullhead City

68

E Kingman   40

D ✗ Hualapai Mountain Park

95   Oatman

40   Needles

95   Havasu National Wildlife Refuge

B

Topock   ARIZONA

CALIFORNIA

P 95

Lake Havasu City

95   Lake Havasu State Park   O

M

Cattail Cove State Park   ✗ Buckskin Mountain State Park

F Parker

62   95

95   72

N

0 SCALE
KILOMETERS   30   30   MILES

——— ROAD   ═══ HIGHWAY   ········ UNPAVED ROAD
PARK/RESERVATION   ✗ POINT OF INTEREST

SIGHTSEEING HIGHLIGHTS

★★★★ HOOVER DAM

Highway 93, eight miles east of Boulder City in Black Canyon; 702/293-8321

Highway 93 takes you across the top of Hoover Dam, where you can stop at a new multimillion-dollar visitor center. There you'll learn about the dam's construction—an incredible engineering feat. At 726 feet high, it's the tallest concrete dam in the Western Hemisphere. It's 1,244 feet wide at the crest, 660 feet thick at the base, and required almost 4 million cubic yards of concrete to build. Five thousand men worked 'round the clock to complete the dam in 1935.

Diverting the flow of the Colorado River formed **Lake Mead**, at 110 miles long the largest artificial lake in the United States. **Lake Mohave**, to the south, is 67 miles long and ends at **Davis Dam**. You can take a free, self-guided dam tour from 7:30 to 3:30 daily.

Details: Visitor center open daily 8:30–6:30, Pacific time. Basic tour lasts 35 minutes and plunges you 500 feet into the dam. $6 adults, $5 seniors, and $2 ages 6–16. Tours leave every 10 minutes. One-hour Behind-the-Scenes Tours leave every 30 minutes and cost $25. You get to keep the hard hat. (1–2 hours)

SIGHTS

- **A** Grand Canyon West
- **B** Havasu National Wildlife Refuge
- **C** Hoover Dam
- **D** Hualapai Mountain Park
- **E** Mohave Museum of History and Arts
- **F** Parker
- **G** Willow Beach National Fish Hatchery

FOOD

- **H** Captain's Table
- **I** Happy Days Diner

FOOD (continued)

- **J** Mr. D'z
- **J** Rick's Restaurant
- **J** Tiffany's
- **G** Willow Beach Resort Restaurant

LODGING

- **F** Best Western Kings Inn
- **K** Edgewater Hotel & Casino
- **K** Harrah's Laughlin
- **L** Lake Mohave Resort
- **F** Quality Inn
- **K** Riverside Resort Hotel & Casino

LODGING (continued)

- **H** Temple Bar Resort
- **G** Willow Beach Resort

CAMPING

- **M** Cattail Cove State Park
- **N** Davis Camp County Park
- **L** Katherine Landing
- **O** Lake Havasu State Park
- **K** Riverside RV Park
- **H** Temple Bar
- **P** Windsor Beach State Park

Note: Items with the same letter are located in the same place.

★★★★ LONDON BRIDGE
Highway 95, Lake Havasu City

Yes! This is the famous London Bridge, which spanned the Thames River from 1824 until 1968, when it was purchased for almost $2.5 million by entrepreneur Robert McCulloch. Its new owner had it dismantled and shipped to the Arizona desert. The 900-foot bridge now connects Lake Havasu shoreline to a small island with an authentic English village beneath the bridge. Tourist shops and restaurants surround the bridge, and you can book a lake cruise.

Details: (1–2 hours)

★★★ GRAND CANYON WEST
Hualapai Reservation; 888/255-9550

This is the *other* South Rim of the Grand Canyon but without the crowds and noise. It was opened in 1988 and, as a part of the Hualapai Indian Nation, is still a pristine wilderness area. A four-mile guided bus tour provides insight into the culture and lifestyle of the Hualapai. Hualapai River Runners offers one- and two-day family-oriented rafting trips from $245 to $365. A million acres of the **Wildlife Conservation Area** is home to herds of elk, bighorn sheep, and mountain lion; and offers hiking trails, camping facilities ($7), and fishing ($8). You can also fly into the Grand Canyon via helicopter for $30 to $70.

Details: About 1 1/2 hours from Kingman. $7 entry fee. Check road conditions after rain. (full day)

★★★ WILLOW BEACH NATIONAL FISH HATCHERY
Lake Mohave; 520/767-3456

More than a million trout are released into Lake Mohave and Lake Mead from the hatchery each year. You'll observe the hatching room and trout at all stages of growth, plus exhibits on Colorado River history.

Details: 15 miles south of Hoover Dam on Highway 93, then 4 miles west to Willow Beach. Daily 7 a.m. to sunset. Free. (1–2 hours)

★★ HAVASU NATIONAL WILDLIFE REFUGE
I-40 and the Colorado River, 760/326-3853

The Refuge is a favorite wintering area for waterfowl, so it's a great bird-watching spot. You may even see wild burros and desert bighorn sheep. The **Topock Gorge**, bordered by the Wildlife

LONDON BRIDGE

Refuge, is one of the last stretches of the Lower Colorado River still virtually unchanged by humanity. The gorge is accessible only by boat or on foot. Both the London Bridge Watercraft Tours, 800/732-3665, and Western Arizona Canoe and Kayak Outfitters (WACKO), 520/453-6212, offer guided excursions to Topock Gorge.

> *Details: 19 miles north of Havasu City. (1 hour)*

★★ MOHAVE MUSEUM OF HISTORY AND ARTS
400 W. Beale Street, Kingman; 520/753-3195

This is a terrific place to learn about the history of northwestern Arizona. A re-created Mohave village accompanies dioramas depicting the area's settlement and an exhibit on actor Andy Devine, who grew up in Kingman. An outdoor display features mining equipment and a nineteenth-century wooden Santa Fe caboose. To learn about life in the early 1900s, tour the **Bonelli House**, 430 E. Spring St., which was built in 1915 and has retained much of its original furnishings. It's open Thursday through Monday 1 to 5. Admission is free, but they'd appreciate a donation.

> *Details: Mon–Fri 9–5, Sat–Sun 1–5. $2 adults, children free. (1 hour)*

★★ **PARKER**
Highway 95
If you head down the coast to the Parker area, you'll come to **Parker Dam**. Self-guided tours are available Monday through Friday 8 to 5. The cottonwood and willow forest of the **Bill Williams River National Wildlife Refuge** is home to many rare and endangered species of bird, reptile, mammal, and fish. Vehicle access is via a dirt road just south of Bill Williams Bridge off Highway 95. Guided tours are available through Outback Off-Road Adventures, 520/680-6151. Some of the most scenic areas of the Colorado are preserved as part of the **Buckskin Mountain State Park**, 520/667-3231, which incorporates river beaches and hiking trails into the Buckskin Mountains. Parker's **Colorado River Indian Tribes Museum**, 520/669-9211, ext. 335, allows you to learn about several Colorado River tribes' history. It's open Monday through Friday from 8 to 5 (closed for lunch). Admission is free. You can rent canoes and explore remote sections of the Colorado at the **Ahakhav Tribal Preserve**, 520/669-8831.
Details: (half day)

★ **HUALAPAI MOUNTAIN PARK**
Hualapai Mountain Road, 877/757-0915
In the midst of semiarid to desert countryside, the Hualapai Mountains climb to 8,500 feet. This pine-forested park is accented by granite rock formations and clear mountain streams. You'll find majestic views and more than 16 miles of hiking trails. In the higher forests you may see mule deer, elk, mountain lion, fox, and a variety of birds. Overnight possibilities include campsites, an RV park, and several rustic cabins.
Details: Advance cabin reservations required May–Sept. Trail system maps available at the Park Office at the park's entrance. (2–4 hours)

FITNESS AND RECREATION
Lake Mead Recreation Area, 702/293-8906, encompasses the land along the shores of **Lake Mead** and **Lake Mohave**. Between the two reservoirs are hundreds of miles of shoreline that annually attract more than 8 million visitors to fish, boat, swim, and ski. Several marinas offer resorts, restaurants, general stores, campgrounds, and bait shops. At Temple Bar, 520/767-3211, and Lake Mohave Resort, 520/754-3245, you'll find all kinds of boats and

HAVASU CANYON

Six miles east of Peach Springs on Route 66 is Indian Route 18, which carries you to Hualapai Hilltop, eight miles from the Supai village on the Havasupai Reservation. This is the trailhead into one of the most beautiful and remote corners of the Grand Canyon.

You'll have an easy eight-mile hike into the village, where you'll continue by foot another two miles down to the waterfalls and blue-green pools of Havasu Canyon. If you're not up for a 10-mile hike, you can travel by horseback for $110 round trip. You can also book rides one way (hike in and ride out).

The entry fee at the canyon is $15 from April to October and $12 from November to March. There are 340 campsites at $10, and they fill quickly in peak season. There's a lodge, café, and small museum in Supai. For more information call the Havasupai Tourist Enterprise office at 520/448-2141, the campground at 520/448-2121, or the lodge at 520/448-2111.

equipment for rent from $60 to $225 per day. Personal watercraft are available from $50 an hour to $250 per day.

Swimming beaches and picnic areas line the shore of **Katherine Landing** on Lake Mohave near Bullhead City, and **Temple Bar**, 26 miles from mile marker 19 on U.S. 93, on Lake Mead. **Willow Beach**, on the north end of Lake Mohave, hosts a marina, ranger station, boat rentals, and the nearby fish hatchery.

Lake Mead Cruises, 702/293-6180, offers paddle-wheeler cruises around the lake on the *Desert Princess*. Choose from a basic two-hour cruise to a breakfast, dinner, and even a dinner-dancing cruise. Rates range from $17 to $43. Back Bay Canoes & Kayaks, 1450 Newberry Dr., Bullhead City, 520/758-6242, has half-day trips through Black Canyon, just below Hoover Dam to Willow Beach, for $50 per person. For a fun, family-oriented float trip down the Colorado, contact Black Canyon Raft Tours, 1297 Nevada Hwy., Boulder City, 800/696-RAFT.

Fishing for bass and trout is popular on both lakes, which are stocked during winter and spring. Whichever bank you fish from, you'll need a license from that state. Fishing on water requires a license from one state and a special-use stamp from the other. Check at bait shops or ranger stations for details.

Miles of hiking trails run throughout the recreation area. Check with the ranger stations at Katherine Landing, Cottonwood Cove, Temple Bar, Las Vegas Bay, Callville Bay, Echo Bay, or Overton Beach for maps and information. Houseboat rentals are available from Seven Crown Resorts, 800/752-9669, at $1,000 to $2,500 per week.

Bullhead City is the gateway to the mini–Las Vegas gambling destination of Laughlin, Nevada. Most folks are lured here by its dozen major gambling casinos, which supply incredibly cheap food and lodging in exchange for gambling dollars.

But plenty of outdoor activities exist as well. Paddle-wheelers *Little Belle* and *Fiesta Queen*, 800/228-9825, offer daily cruises along the Colorado. They leave from the Edgewater and Gold River Hotel docks; costs are $10 adults and $6 children. Harrah's, 2900 S. Casino Dr., Laughlin, Nevada, 800/74-BEACH, runs a boat trip at $12.95; and the Riverside Resort and Casino, 1650 S. Casino Dr., Laughlin, Nevada, 800/277-3849, sponsors five daily cruises.

Golf is a popular pastime, and both sides of the river contain golf courses. **Desert Lakes Golf Course**, four miles south of Bullhead City, 520/768-1000, has 18 holes with a driving range, pro shop, and lessons. The 18-hole **Emerald River Golf Course**, 1155 S. Casino Dr., 702/298-0061, is on the Laughlin side. In addition, several nine-hole courses can be found near Bullhead City.

Chet's Fishing Guide Service, 520/754-7111, offers guided fishing tours, as does Desert Recreation, 702/298-6828, which operates out of Harrah's. A variety of water-sports rental operations line the waterfront near Laughlin's casinos.

The 45-mile-long **Lake Havasu** includes several beaches: **Windsor Beach State Park**, two miles north of London Bridge, **Lake Havasu State Park**, south of town, and **Cattail Cove State Park,** 15 miles south of Lake Havasu City. The **London Bridge Beach**, near Island Inn Resort, is a sandy beach beneath plenty of palm trees.

Many companies offer boat tours on Lake Havasu, including Blue Water Charters, 520/855-7171, and World Jet Boat Tours, 888/505-3545, who have trips south to Topock Gorge or north to Laughlin. *Miss Havasupai* at Island Fashion Mall, Lake Havasu, 520/855-7979, offers pontoon-boat tours, while the *Dixie Belle* at English Village in Lake Havasu, 520/855-0888, gives a paddle-wheel riverboat trip. The pontoon *Kon Tiki*, also at English Village, will take you to scenic Copper Canyon, nine miles from Lake Havasu City, for $10.

If you want to learn to water-ski, contact Havasu Adventures Water Ski

LAKE HAVASU CITY

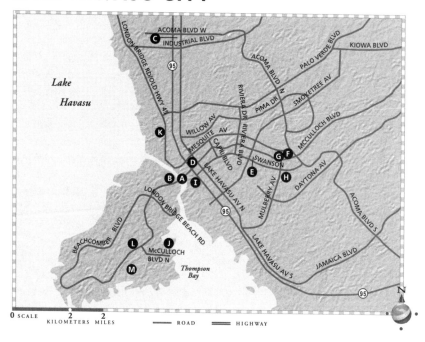

SIGHTS
Ⓐ London Bridge

FOOD
Ⓑ Barley Brothers Brewery and Grill
Ⓒ Big John's Steak 'n Pub
Ⓓ London Arms Pub & Brewery
Ⓔ Nicolino's Italian Restaurant
Ⓑ Shugrue's
Ⓕ Taco Hacienda

LODGING
Ⓖ Days Inn
Ⓗ Hidden Palms
Ⓘ London Bridge Resort
Ⓙ Nautical Inn Resort
Ⓚ Super 8

CAMPING
Ⓛ Crazy Horse Campground
Ⓜ Islander RV Resort

Note: Items with the same letter are located in the same place.

School, 1425 McCulloch, Lake Havsu City, 520/855-6274. At the Fun Center at English Village, 520/453-4386, you can rent pedalboats and aqua cycles or try your hand at parasailing. Havasu Springs Resort in Parker, 520/667-3361, rents four different houseboat sizes, for $1,200 to $1,700 per week.

Golfers will enjoy the **Havasu Island Golf Club,** 1040 McCulloch Blvd., 520/855-5585, Lake Havasu City, or Parker's **Emerald Canyon Golf Course**, 72 Emerald Canyon Dr., 520/776-3366, which plays through a rugged canyon and past red-rock cliffs. American Golf, 800/GO-TRY-18, can book tee times at London Bridge Golf Club's two championship courses.

Outback Off-Road Adventures, 520/680-6151, has guided jeep tours to 26,000-acre **Crossman Peak Natural Scenic Area**, where the Mohave and Sonoran deserts converge to create a natural area of amazing plant and animal diversity. The Lords and Ladies Club, 520/855-3341, leads free desert walks around Lake Havasu the second Saturday of each month.

FOOD

At the Temple Bar Resort on Lake Mead, the **Captain's Table**, 520/767-3211, has a great lake view and a seafood menu. **Willow Beach Resort Restaurant**, 520/767-3311, also has a lake view.

Over the Hoover Dam to Boulder City, **Happy Days Diner**, 512 Nevada Hwy. (Ave. B), 702/294-4637, is a '50s-style casual diner. **Tiffany's**, in the historic Boulder Dam Hotel, 1305 Arizona St., 702/294-1666, serves Italian and American fare nightly from 4 to 11.

In Kingman, **Mr. D'z**, 106 Andy Devine Ave., 520/718-0066, is another fun '50s diner open for lunch and dinner. **Rick's Restaurant**, south of Davis Dam bridge, 520/754-2201, has a riverfront view and serves basic American fare from 6 a.m. to 11 p.m.

Lake Havasu City's varied choices range from old English pubs to cozy Italian bistros. **London Bridge Brewery**, 422 English Village, 520/855-8782, offers great views of the bridge from the patio. The brewery serves traditional English and American fare but is best known for its selection of handcrafted beers and ales. For authentic Mexican cuisine, check out **Taco Hacienda**, 200 Mesquite Ave., 520/855-8932, which also features patio dining.

Big John's Steak 'n Pub, 717 N. Lake Havasu Ave., 520/453-5858, is a popular steak joint with a sports pub next door. **Nicolino's Italian Restaurant**, 86 S. Smoketree Ave., 520/855-3484, is a family-run restaurant with pasta dinners, seafood, and a good wine selection. It's open for lunch and dinner. Other popular restaurants include **Shugrue's**, 520/453-1400, and

Barley Brothers Brewery and Grill, 520/505-7837, both located in the Island Fashion Mall at 1425 McCulloch Boulevard.

LODGING

At Lake Mohave, three nice lakeside resorts with marina facilities rent rooms for $50 to $75 per night: the **Temple Bar Resort**, Lake Mead, 800/752-9669, **Willow Beach Resort**, Lake Mohave, 520/767-3311, and **Lake Mohave Resort**, 520/754-3245.

Laughlin boasts several huge hotel/casino complexes and lots of restaurants with good, inexpensive meals. Some of the largest are **Harrah's Laughlin**, 2900 S. Casino Dr., 800/447-8700, **Riverside Resort Hotel & Casino**, 1650 S. Casino Dr., 800/227-3849, and the **Edgewater Hotel & Casino**, 2020 S. Casino Dr., 800/677-4837.

Lake Havasu City has several good facilities: the waterfront **London Bridge Resort**, 1477 Queens Bays, 800/624-7939, and the **Nautical Inn Resort**, 1000 McCulloch Blvd., 800/892-2141, with beachfront and lake views from every room. Both rent rooms for $50 to $250 per night. **Hidden Palms**, 2100 Swanson Ave., 800/254-5611, is an all-suite inn at $49 to $79 per night. In addition, local chain motels include the **Days Inn**, 2190 Birch Square, 800/982-3622; and Lake Havasu's **Super 8**, 305 London Bridge Rd., 800/800-8000. In Kingman try **Quality Inn**, 1400 E. Andy Devine Rd., 800/228-5151, and **Best Western Kings Inn**, 2930 E. Andy Devine Rd., 800/528-1234. Houseboat rentals include **Sand Point Marina**, 15 miles south on Lake Havasu, 520/855-0549, and **H2O Houseboats** on Lake Havasu, 800/242-2628.

CAMPING

Camping and RV sites are plentiful throughout the west coast area. At Lake Mohave's **Katherine Landing** and Lake Mead's **Temple Bar**, 520/767-3211, you can camp close to the water. North of Bullhead City, **Davis Camp County Park**, 520/754-4606, rents sites for $8 to $15. In Laughlin, try the **Riverside RV Park**, 1650 S. Casino Dr., 800/227-3849.

Lakefront campgrounds in Lake Havasu City include **Crazy Horse Campground**, 1534 Beachcomber Blvd., 520/855-4033, and **Islander RV Resort**, 751 Beachcomber Blvd., 520/680-2000. For $10 to $15, you can camp at **Windsor Beach State Park**, 520/855-2764, **Lake Havasu State Park**, 520/855-7851, and **Cattail Cove State Park**, 520/855-1223. Lake Havasu and Cattail Cove have almost 200 boat-in campsites.

Old Route 66

If you want to experience some of the historic old towns and eateries along America's favorite highway, then pick up Route 66 in **Oatman**, where the old road runs through Main Street past shops and saloons. Wild burros, let loose by miners years ago, wander the streets, and you're likely to see an Old West gunfight. Be sure and go in the old **Oatman Hotel**.

Next you'll reach Kingman, where you can stay at the Quality Inn on Andy Devine Avenue, which is actually Route 66. The lobby is filled with fun memorabilia. **Mr. D'z Route 66 Diner** is housed in an old gas station/café and serves blue-plate specials and malts. The Historic Route 66 Association of Arizona, 520/753-5001, is based in Kingman, and each April the Route 66 Fun Run Weekend occurs here.

Follow the signs along the winding road through Valentine and Peach Springs, which will take you into a bygone era. **Grand Canyon Caverns**, 520/422-3223, is still a favorite stop along the Mother Road. You'll plunge 21 stories into the earth and tour these magnificent caverns on lighted and paved pathways. Admission is $8.50 for adults and $5.75 for children. In Seligman, have lunch at the Snow Cap Drive-In or stop in Pope's General Store. You can pick up I-40 again in the Ash Fork area.

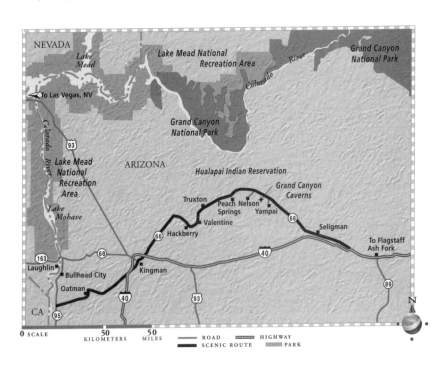

15
CENTRAL ARIZONA

Central Arizona encompasses the edge of the Sonoran Desert near Wickenburg to the pine-forested Prescott region. The Apache had lived here for decades when, in 1863, mountain men and pioneers discovered gold in Prescott and Wickenburg. With this discovery came streams of Americans and the U.S. Army. In 1864, Prescott was designated capital of the Arizona Territory, mainly because the only other contender, Tucson, had supported the Confederacy just a few years before.

Prescott is unmistakably eastern. Wickenburg, on the other hand, is definitely western, looking much the same as it did decades ago, when it lured folks from back east to its neighboring dude ranches. Jerome was built up a 30-degree slope, and the streets switchback from one level of houses to the next. Jerome has known several incarnations: first a gold town, then a copper town, and most recently a popular artists' community.

A PERFECT DAY IN CENTRAL ARIZONA

Plan to stay at least one day in Wickenburg and another in the Prescott/Jerome area, if possible. Schedule a jeep tour or horseback ride in Wickenburg and make sure it includes some old mining sites. Shop the antique stores downtown as you take the self-guided historic walking tour. For a real taste of Old West hospitality, stay at a guest ranch.

WICKENBURG

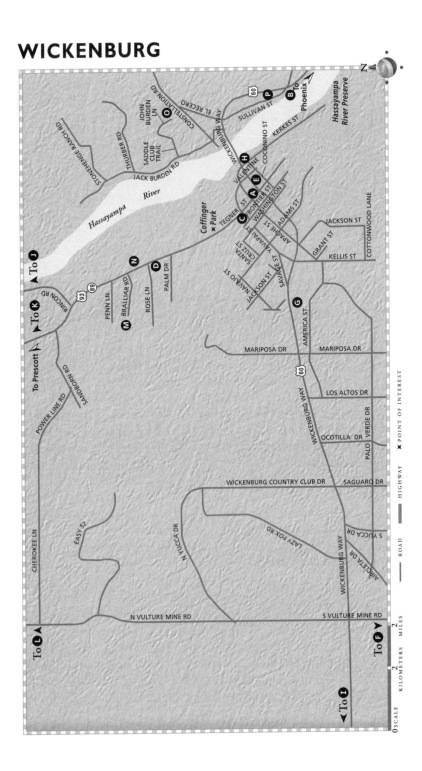

STONEHENGE RANCH RD

THURBER RD

JOHN BURDEN LN
SADDLE CLUB TRAIL

CONSTELLATION RD

EL RECREO

WICKENBURG WAY

JACK BURDEN RD

Hassayampa River

Coffinger Park

TEGNER ST

FRONTIER ST
WASHINGTON ST

SANTA CRUZ ST
YAVAPAI ST
APACHE ST
ADAMS ST

SULLIVAN ST

60 ○P
○B To Phoenix

COCONINO ST
KERKES ST

Hassayampa River Preserve

N

○O

○H

VALENTINE
○A ○E
○C

JACKSON ST
GRANT ST
KELLIS ST

COTTONWOOD LANE

JACKSON ST

SAVAGE ST

NAVAJO ST

○G
AMERICA ST

60

MARIPOSA DR

MARIPOSA DR

LOS ALTOS DR

WICKENBURG WAY

OCOTILLA DR

PALO VERDE DR

WICKENBURG COUNTRY CLUB DR

SAGUARO DR

○K ▲To K
▲To J

○N
○D
PALM DR
ROSE LN

93 89

PENN LN

BRALLIAR RD

○M

RINCON RD

To Prescott

POWER LINE RD

SANDBORN RD

CHEROKEE LN

EASY ST

N YUCCA DR

LAZY FOX RD

S YUCCA DR

AIRCHETA DR

WICKENBURG WAY

To L ▲

N VULTURE MINE RD

S VULTURE MINE RD

To F ▼

◀ To I

2 KILOMETERS
0 SCALE
2 MILES

ROAD ══ HIGHWAY ✖ POINT OF INTEREST

In Prescott, stroll around Courthouse Square, visit the Governor's Mansion, and drive past the many charming Victorian homes. Take a walk down historic Whiskey Row, then visit the ghost-town-turned-artist-community of Jerome. You can choose to explore anything from Western art museums to Indian ruins to the great outdoors.

SIGHTSEEING HIGHLIGHTS

★★★★ DESERT CABALLEROS WESTERN MUSEUM
21 N. Frontier Street, Wickenburg; 520/684-2272

This collection includes Remington, Russell, Moran, Bierstadt, and Cowboy Artists of America members. The popular Street Scene and Period Rooms contain more than 2,500 artifacts from the turn of the century. Other favorites include a Native American Gallery, and a Mineral and Gem Gallery with more than 200 specimens. Don't miss the black-lit mineral exhibit. The museum store features southwestern books, children's toys, and art. Also visit the museum park, at the corner of Tegner and Wickenburg Way.

Details: Mon–Sat 10–5, Sun noon–4. $5 adults, $4 seniors, $1 ages 6–16, under 6 free. (1–2 hours)

★★★★ PHIPPEN MUSEUM OF WESTERN ART
4701 Highway 89 N., Prescott; 520/778-1385

SIGHTS
- **A** Desert Caballeros Western Museum
- **B** Hassayampa River Preserve
- **C** Historical Walking Tour of Wickenburg

FOOD
- **D** Cowboy Cafe
- **E** House of Berlin
- **F** Rancho de los Caballeros
- **G** Santa Fe Grill & Cantina

LODGING
- **H** Best Western Rancho Grande
- **I** Flying E Ranch

LODGING
- **J** Kay El Bar Guest Ranch
- **K** Merv Griffin's Wickenburg Inn & Dude Ranch
- **F** Rancho de los Caballeros
- **L** Rancho Casitas Guest Ranch
- **I** Rincon Guest Ranch
- **M** Sombrero Ranch B&B
- **N** Super 8 Motel

CAMPING
- **O** Desert Cypress RV Park
- **P** Horspitality RV Park

Note: Items with the same letter are located in the same place.

After a six-mile drive through the scenic Granite Dells, you'll arrive at this excellent museum. It was named after local painter George Phippen, a cofounder of the Cowboy Artists of America. The museum displays paintings, prints, and sculpture from America's best Western artists. Special exhibits feature holdings from other museums and private collectors. Browse the museum store for an excellent choice of original artwork.

Details: *Mon, Wed–Sat 10–4. Sun 1–4. Closed Tue. $3 adults, $2 seniors, $1 students. (1–2 hours)*

★★★★ **SHARLOT HALL MUSEUM**
415 W. Gurley Street, Prescott; 520/445-3122
Several historic buildings are clustered on this three-acre site, including the **Governor's Mansion**, built for the territorial governor in 1864. Sharlot Hall came to Arizona Territory in 1882, when she was only 12. Fascinated with frontier life, she began collecting artifacts and writing about pioneering. In 1928, she opened the Governor's Mansion museum. Also on the grounds are the 1875 **John C. Fremont House**, built for the fifth territorial governor, and the 1877 Victorian **William Bashford House**. The **Sharlot Hall Building** houses Native American artifacts and Prescott historical exhibits. In addition, you can tour a schoolhouse, a blacksmith's shop, and a rose garden honoring famous Arizonan women.

Details: *Mon–Sat 10–5, Sun 1–5. Closes at 4 in winter. Suggested donation: $4 adults, $3 seniors, $5 family. (1–3 hours)*

★★★ **HASSAYAMPA RIVER PRESERVE**
Highway 60, three miles southeast of Wickenburg; 520/684-2772
This Nature Conservancy preserve consists of rare forest areas that support the endangered Southwest willow flycatcher and Arizona's rarest raptors, such as zone-tailed, Harris, and black hawks. Nature trails along the river lead to springfed Palm Lake, home to five rare native desert fish species. More than 230 bird species have also been spotted here, and the preserve offers free guided walks. Call for the current walk schedule and to make reservations. The Hassayampa Bookstore is a delight for nature lovers.

Details: *Open Wed–Sun 8–5 in winter, 6 a.m.–noon in summer. $5 suggested donation. (2–3 hours)*

★★★ **JEROME STATE HISTORIC PARK**
Highway 89A, Jerome; 520/634-5381
In 1916, copper baron James S. "Rawhide Jimmy" Douglas built this mansion overlooking his Little Daisy Mine and the Verde Valley. It had a wine cellar, billiard room, steam heat, and central vacuum system. Today the home incorporates history, mining, and geology exhibits, plus colorful ore samples and mining equipment.
    Details: Open daily 8–5. $2.50 adults, $1 ages 7–13, under 7 free. (1 hour)

★★★ **TUZIGOOT NATIONAL MONUMENT**
Off U.S. 89A, Clarkdale; 520/634-5564
This Sinagua ruin was occupied between 1125 and 1400. It's estimated that about 250 people at a time lived in the dwelling. It originally had 86 ground-floor rooms, some with second stories, that were entered using ladders through roof openings. Archaeologists who excavated the ruin in the 1930s found 450 burial sites.
    Details: Daily 8–5, with extended summer hours. $2 adults, under 17 free. (1 hour)

★★ **COURTHOUSE PLAZA AND WHISKEY ROW WALKING TOUR**
Gurley and Montezuma Streets, Prescott
When Prescott was established as the capital of Arizona Territory, many offices were filled by politically appointed Easterners. The Courthouse Square resembles that of a small town back east, and the nearby Victorian houses and historic buildings are unusual for Arizona. The square contains a gazebo and interesting sculptures.
    But don't forget that this was also a rowdy mining-town camp, and off the square is the famous Whiskey Row, a street lined with saloons and houses of prostitution. Although the bawdy women are gone, you can catch a glimpse of the Old West by visiting one of the saloons. Prescott Historical Tours, 520/445-4567, leads informative trips through this and other parts of the city for $7 per person.
    Details: Prescott Chamber of Commerce, 117 W. Goodwin, 520/445-2200. (2–4 hours)

★★ **HISTORICAL WALKING TOUR OF WICKENBURG**
Wickenburg Chamber of Commerce; 520/684-5479; www.wickenburgchamber. com

PRESCOTT

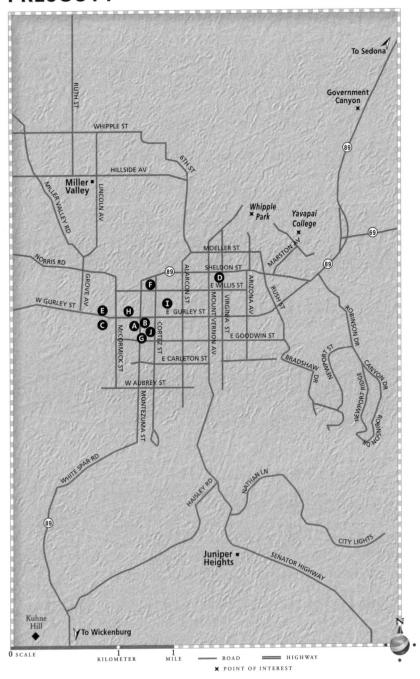

To Sedona

Government
Canyon ×

RUTH ST

WHIPPLE ST

6TH ST

HILLSIDE AV

MILLER VALLEY RD

Miller
Valley ■

LINCOLN AV

Whipple
Park ×

Yavapai
College ×

89

69

NORRIS RD

MOELLER ST

MARSTON AV

89

GROVE AV

89

SHELDON ST

F

ALARCON ST

E WILLIS ST

D

W GURLEY ST

E

H

I

E GURLEY ST

MOUNT VERNON AV

VIRGINIA ST

ARIZONA AV

RUSH ST

C

A B

J

CORTEZ ST

G

McCORMICK ST

E GOODWIN ST

E CARLETON ST

BRADSHAW DR

ROBINSON DR

NEWPORT ST

NEWPORT RIDGE

CANYON DR

ROBINSON DR

W AUBREY ST

MONTEZUMA ST

WHITE SPAR RD

HAISLEY RD

NATHAN LN

CITY LIGHTS

89

Juniper
Heights ■

SENATOR HIGHWAY

Kuhne
Hill
◆

To Wickenburg

N

0 SCALE   1   1
        KILOMETER   MILE   ——— ROAD   ═══ HIGHWAY
                                  × POINT OF INTEREST

The chamber offers a free brochure for a self-guided walking tour past 19 historic buildings, including the 1864 general store, an 1890 adobe brick home, and the 1895 Santa Fe Depot, now the chamber offices. The brochure includes a map and historic information about each place.

Details: Wickenburg Chamber of Commerce, 216 N. Frontier St., 520/684-5479. (2 hours)

★★ **ROBSON'S ARIZONA MINING WORLD**
Highway 71, 26 miles west of Wickenburg; 520/685-2609
Step back in time to the original site of the Nella-Meda gold mining camp in the Harcuvar Mountains. Twenty-six buildings in the ghost town are filled with antique mining equipment and artifacts. Visitors can eat at the Gold Leaf Saloon and spend the night in a boardinghouse. You can also tour the buildings, pan for gold, hike through a saguaro forest, and view prehistoric pictographs.

Details: Open Oct–May Mon–Fri 10–4, Sat–Sun 8–dark. $5 adults, 50 cents seniors, under 11 free. Gold panning $8 per person, including instructions. (2–4 hours)

★ **THE BEAD MUSEUM**
140 S. Montezuma, Prescott; 520/445-2431
This unique museum houses a collection of ancient Indian tribal beads, trade beads, and elaborately detailed beadwork from all over the world. Exhibits explain how natural and artificial beads have been used for centuries as trade, currency, religious symbolism, amulets, and social identification. The museum also has a large selection of beads for sale, along with art books and giftware.

Details: Open Mon–Sat 9:30–4:30. Free. (1 hour)

★ **SMOKI MUSEUM**
147 N. Arizona Street, Prescott; 502/445-1230

SIGHTS
Ⓐ The Bead Museum
Ⓑ Courthouse Plaza and Whiskey Row Walking Tour
Ⓒ Sharlot Hall Museum
Ⓓ Smoki Museum

FOOD
Ⓔ Gurley St. Grill
Ⓕ Murphy's
Ⓖ The Palace
Ⓗ Prescott Brewing Company

LODGING
Ⓘ Hassayampa Inn
Ⓙ Hotel Vendome

Although there is no real Smoki Tribe, this building incorporates elements of several Native American styles. You'll find Southwestern basketry, Hopi kachinas, stone artifacts, and textiles. In addition, the museum features a colorful collection of warbonnets, costumes, and beadwork from the Plains tribes.

Details: May–Sept Mon, Tue, Thu–Sat 10–4, Sun 1–4. Closed Wed. Open Fri–Sun in Oct. Closed Nov–Apr. Admission $2. (1 hour)

FITNESS AND RECREATION

The Wickenburg Chamber of Commerce has a free hiking guide outlining four different local trips. If you climb to the top of **Vulture Peak**, the chamber will even give you a certificate. Hike around the historic **Vulture Gold Mine**, 520/859-2743, where you can look at the remaining buildings and mine site and pan for gold.

You can see Wickenburg and nearby ghost towns on a jeep tour with Wickenburg Desert Tours, 295 E. Wickenburg Way, 800/596-JEEP. No Fences, 18970 W. Moonlight Mesa Rd., 520/684-3308, offers custom horseback rides. Sixteen miles north of town on U.S. 93 is the **Joshua Forest Parkway**, one of the largest remaining Joshua tree stands left. These strange plants are not really trees but members of the lily family that grow up to 30 feet.

Prescott sits on the edge of the **Prescott National Forest**, 520/771-4700, which boasts 450 miles of hiking trails and 104,000-plus acres of wilderness. Nearby is the town's most prominent landmark, **Thumb Butte**, a basaltic monolith. It's a popular rock-climbing spot, and while the trail is steep, it's paved much of the way.

The **Granite Dells** is a scenic area of huge granite boulders tumbled around the hillside a few miles north of Prescott on AZ 89. **Watson Lake Park** is an artificial lake set in the middle of these boulders, with plenty of trails and picnic areas around it. Granite Mountain Stables, 520/771-9551, can take you on trail rides or a sunset dinner rides. Trail Horse Adventures, 800/SAD-DLE-UP, www.trailhorseadventures.com, offers overnight rides and half-day rides to **Granite Mountain Lake**. Kids must be at least six years old.

Off Highway 69 and Forest Road 197 is **Lynx Lake**, famous for its gold-bearing creeks. Pan for gold if you visit, but you're more likely to land one of the lake's stocked trout than a gold nugget.

Near Jerome, the **Mingus Mountain Recreation Area**, 520/567-4121, has camping, hiking trails, and spectacular views of the Verde Valley, San Francisco Peaks, and the edge of the Colorado Plateau. It's a favorite jumping-off point for local hang gliders. If you're ready for your own free-floating adventure, call Arizona Hang Gliding Center, 150 S. AZ 69, Dewey, 800/757-2442.

Golf Digest ranked Wickenburg's **Los Caballeros Golf Club**, 1551 S. Vulture Mine Rd., 520/684-2704, one of the top five courses in the state. Greens fees range from $40 in summer to $105 in peak season. If you're in Prescott, schedule a round at the **Hassayampa Golf Club**, 240 Hassayampa Village Lane, 800/834-4966, www.hassayampagolf.com.

FOOD

Wickenburg has several good cafés for all three meals, including **Custer's Cowboy Cafe**, 686 N. Tegner St., 520/684-2807. The **Santa Fe Grill & Cantina**, 683 W. Wickenburg Way, 520/684-3113, is a local favorite for steaks and prime rib. Be sure to try one of their specialty desserts. Town founder Henry Wickenburg was a German immigrant, and **House of Berlin**, 169 E. Wickenburg Way, 520/684-5044, serves German specials and European cuisine. The most elegant (and pricey) place for lunch or dinner is at Wickenburg's most exclusive guest ranch, **Rancho de los Caballeros**, 1551 S. Vulture Mine Rd., 520/684-5484. The restaurant requires jackets for men and appropriate dress for women. Reservations necessary. Closed summers.

Several historic buildings in Prescott now house popular restaurants. **Murphy's**, 201 N. Cortez, 520/445-4044, sits in an 1890 mercantile building that displays many antiques and original fixtures. At this favorite for steaks and seafood, main courses range from $12 to $18. **The Palace**, 120 S. Montezuma St., 520/541-1996, is a renovated turn-of-the-century frontier bar that also serves Southwestern cuisine and steaks. **Gurley St. Grill**, 230 W. Gurley St., 520/445-4488, and **Prescott Brewing Company**, 130 W. Gurley St., 520/771-2795, are both in old brick buildings near Courthouse Square. They're lively pasta, pizza, and burger joints with several beers and ales on tap.

The **English Kitchen**, 119 Jerome Ave., Jerome, 520/634-3123, in business since 1899, is one of Arizona's oldest restaurants. It's open daily for hefty breakfasts and casual lunches. The **House of Joy** on Hull Avenue, 520/634-5339, was once a bordello. This restaurant has just seven tables and is open only Saturday 3 to 9 and Sunday 3 to 8. Reservations are a must.

LODGING

For years, Wickenburg was known as the "Dude Ranch Capital of the World." **Rincon Guest Ranch**, three miles west of town, 520/684-2328, is a charming bed-and-breakfast. They specialize in horseback adventures, operated by the

CENTRAL ARIZONA

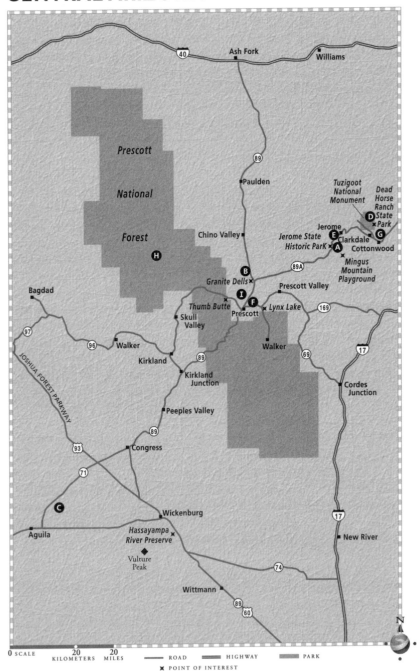

Ash Fork
Williams
40

Prescott

89
Paulden

National

Chino Valley

Tuzigoot
National
Monument
Dead
Horse
Ranch
State
Park
D
G

Jerome
E
Jerome State
Historic ParK
Clarkdale
A
Cottonwood

Forest
H

89A
Mingus
Mountain
Playground

Granite Dells
B

Prescott Valley
I
F

Thumb Butte
Lynx Lake
169

Bagdad
Prescott

Skull
Valley

97

Walker
96

Walker

Kirkland
69

17

89

Cordes
Junction

Kirkland
Junction

Peeples Valley

93

89

71

Congress

C
17

Wickenburg

Aguila
Hassayampa
River Preserve
New River

Vulture
Peak

74

Wittmann

89
60

N

0 SCALE   20   20
KILOMETERS MILES
ROAD   HIGHWAY   PARK
× POINT OF INTEREST

famous Mule Shoe Outfitters of Glacier National Park. The **Flying E Ranch**, 2801 E. Wickenburg Way, 520/684-2690, is a working cattle/guest ranch on a 2,400-foot mesa near Vulture Peak. Offerings include breakfast and lunch horseback rides (for an extra fee), chuck-wagon cookouts, and a pool and spa. Rates range from $185 to $250 per couple.

The adobe lodge and cottages of **Kay El Bar Guest Ranch**, Rincon Rd. off Prescott Highway, 800/684-7583, were constructed between 1914 and 1925 and are listed on the National Register of Historic Places. Another historic property, the **Rancho Casitas Guest Ranch**, 56500 Rancho Casitas Rd., 520/684-2628, boasts breathtaking views from its Spanish-style casitas, which have fully equipped kitchens and fireplaces. Rates range from $400 to $525 per week without meals.

Merv Griffin's Wickenburg Inn & Dude Ranch, 34801 Hwy. 89, 800/942-5368, caters to both families and city slickers with cattle drives, all-day horseback rides, and tennis lessons. Children will be entertained by an arts and crafts studio, nature museum, and kids' pool with a sandy beach. Open year round, Merv's rates start at $210 for a double, including all meals and horseback riding.

Rancho de los Caballeros, 1551 S. Vulture Mine Rd., 520/684-5484, is a 20,000-acre historic guest ranch and golf club offering tennis, trap and skeet shooting, Western cookouts, and a kid's program. Rates start at $266 per double. Most guest ranches are closed during the summer.

Other Wickenburg options include the **Sombrero Ranch B&B**, 31910 W. Braillar Rd., 520/684-0222, dating from 1937, which has a commanding view of the town and the surrounding countryside. Rates start at $75. The downtown **Best Western Rancho Grande**, 293 E. Wickenburg Way, 800/854-7235, has a variety of rooms, including six family suites, so ask for a

---

SIGHTS
- **A** Jerome State Historic Park
- **B** Phippen Museum of Western Art
- **C** Robson's Arizona Mining World
- **D** Tuzigoot National Monument

FOOD
- **E** English Kitchen
- **E** House of Joy

LODGING
- **E** Ghost City Inn
- **E** Inn at Jerome
- **F** Rocamadour B&B
- **E** Surgeon's House

CAMPING
- **G** Dead Horse Ranch State Park
- **H** Prescott National Forest
- **I** Willow Lake RV & Camping

Note: Items with the same letter are located in the same place.

description. Rates range from $59 to $100. The **Super 8**, 975 N. Tegner, 520/684-0808, won a national design award for its western theme.

Prescott offers several historic inns. **Hassayampa Inn**, 122 E. Gurley, 800/322-1927, was built as a luxury hotel in 1927 and is listed on the National Register of Historic Places. Rooms have their original furnishings or antiques, and rates range from $99 to $175 for suites. **Hotel Vendome**, 230 S. Cortez, 800/967-4637, was built in 1917 and has its own resident ghost. Rates, including continental breakfast, start at $69.

Rocamadour B&B, 3386 N. Hwy. 89, 520/771-1933, is located in the scenic Granite Dells north of town. Rock lovers can stay in a cottage built into the boulders with a huge hot tub on the deck. Rates from $85 to $125 include a full breakfast.

Two B&Bs along Jerome's main street are filled with antiques and have fabulous views. **Ghost City Inn**, 541 N. Main St., 888/64-GHOST, and the **Inn at Jerome**, 309 Main St., 800/634-5094, have rooms ranging from $70 to $95. The most interesting place in town is the **Surgeon's House**, 800/639-1452, built in 1917 as the home of Jerome's resident surgeon. You can stay in the chauffeur's quarters or in the main house; rooms are $85 to $95, and suites are $125.

CAMPING

In Wickenburg, **Desert Cypress RV Park**, 610 Jack Burden Rd., 520/684-2153, has RV sites with a pool and showers for $15 per night. At **Horspitality RV Park**, 51802 Hwy. 60, 520/684-2519, you can park your rig and your horse. In addition to its boarding stables, the park also has showers, snack bar, and a rec room with activities.

There are almost 20 campgrounds in the **Prescott National Forest**, 520/455-1762, from Granite Mountain Wilderness to Lynx Lake. Call the Forest Service office for maps and details. **Willow Lake RV & Camping** is near Prescott, 1617 Heritage Park Rd., 520/445-6311. Just past Jerome is the scenic **Dead Horse Ranch State Park**, 675 Dead Horse Ranch Rd., Cottonwood, 520/634-5283, with developed campsites and RV hookups. The park offers hiking trails and fishing.

16
MOGOLLON RIM

The Mogollon Escarpment runs diagonally across Arizona from New Mexico to Lake Mead. But it is the 42-mile stretch between Arizona Routes 87 and 260 that offers some of the longest, most dramatic panoramas in the entire state, with some sections rising up to 2,000 feet above the Tonto Basin.

In 1872, General George Crook decided to cut a wagon road along the crest of the rim to connect Fort Apache, Camp Verde, and Whipple Barracks at Prescott. Today this route is your passage to outstanding fishing, hiking, and a variety of popular outdoor activities. Western author Zane Grey immortalized the area with more than 50 books set in what he called the Tonto Rim.

The Apaches and settlers had numerous conflicts until the land was settled in the 1880s. One of the bloodiest battles occurred nearby, over several years—not between cowboys and Indians, but between cattle and sheep ranchers. It didn't end until the turn of the century, after nearly 30 men had been killed and one family was virtually wiped out. Payson's annual "World's Oldest Continuous Rodeo" has been held each year during the second week of August for more than 115 years. It's a great way to glimpse the importance of the local ranching heritage.

As if the scenery could get any better, the drive out of the forested rim to the desert along the Apache Trail will leave you breathless. President Theodore Roosevelt described the road as "one of the most spectacular best-worth-seeing sights of the world." You'll maneuver hairpin turns that twist like

MOGOLLON RIM REGION

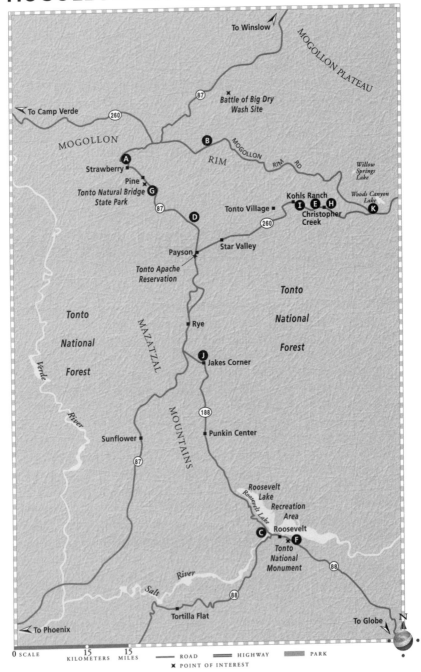

To Winslow

MOGOLLON PLATEAU

87

× Battle of Big Dry
Wash Site

To Camp Verde

260

MOGOLLON

B

MOGOLLON RIM RD

RIM

Willow
Springs
Lake

A

Strawberry

Pine

Tonto Natural Bridge
State Park

G

×

87

Kohls Ranch

Woods Canyon
Lake

Tonto Village

I E H

K

D

Christopher
Creek

260

Payson

Star Valley

Tonto Apache
Reservation

Tonto

National

Tonto

National

Forest

Forest

Rye

MAZATZAL

Jakes Corner

J

188

MOUNTAINS

Verde

Sunflower

87

Punkin Center

River

Roosevelt
Lake
Recreation
Area

Roosevelt Lake

Roosevelt

C F

Tonto
National
Monument

88

River

88

Salt

Tortilla Flat

To Phoenix

N

To Globe

SCALE
0   15   15
KILOMETERS MILES

ROAD   HIGHWAY   PARK

× POINT OF INTEREST

a snake, climb ridges, then plunge back down. You can fish next to sheer cliff walls and camp on the shoreline at the bottom of the canyon. From the Mogollon Rim to the Apache Trail, this part of the state is unparalleled in scenic views and outdoor opportunities.

A PERFECT DAY ON THE MOGOLLON RIM

Put on some sturdy shoes, pack a water bottle and a snack, and hike the trail to explore the Tonto Natural Bridge. If you feel surefooted enough, climb over the rocks and relax under the bridge. Walk along the creek and be sure to hike out on the other trail. Don't forget to look at the historic photos that hang in the old lodge. Drive north to Forest Road 300 and take the Mogollon Rim Road to Woods Canyon Lake. Bring a picnic lunch and your camera. You can see the Battleground Monument, where a U.S. Cavalry and Apache battle took place, an old tombstone from 1887, and Hi-View Point, the most photographed scenic overlook on the Rim, where you might want to relax and watch the sunset.

SIGHTSEEING HIGHLIGHTS

★★★★ TONTO NATIONAL MONUMENT
Highway 88, Roosevelt; 520/467-2241
The prehistoric Salado people built adobe structures in the shelter of these caves more than 750 years ago. These hunters and farmers diverted water from the Salt River to irrigate their crops. No one

SIGHTS
- **A** Fossil Creek
- **B** Mogollon Rim Road
- **C** Roosevelt Dam, Lake and Visitor Center
- **D** Shoofly Ruins
- **E** Tonto Creek Fish Hatchery
- **F** Tonto National Monument
- **G** Tonto Natural Bridge State Park

FOOD
- **H** Creekside Steakhouse and Tavern
- **I** Kohl's Ranch Lodge
- **A** Strawberry Lodge

LODGING
- **H** Christopher Creek Lodge
- **I** Kohl's Ranch Resort
- **A** Strawberry Lodge

CAMPING
- **H** Christopher Creek
- **J** Jakes Corner RV Park
- **G** Lake Roosevelt's Cholla and Windy Hill Recreational Sites
- **K** Wood's Canyon Lake, Aspen and Spillway Campgrounds

Note: Items with the same letter are located in the same place.

knows why they abandoned the dwellings around A.D. 1450. Visitors today can hike up a steep half-mile trail to the Lower Ruin and explore the old rooms. Ranger-led hikes will take you to the more complex 40-room Upper Ruin. The views of Roosevelt Lake are stunning, and interpretive signs explain Sonoran Desert plant and animal life along the steep trail to the Ruins. The visitor center has displays and an audiovisual program on the culture and crafts of the Salado people. If you have kids, ask for the Junior Park Ranger booklet.

Details: *Visitor center and Lower Ruin open daily 8–5. Three-hour Upper Ruins tour by advanced reservations only. During summer, plan hikes in early morning. (1–3 hours)*

★★★★ TONTO NATURAL BRIDGE STATE PARK
Highway 87, 15 miles north of Payson; 520/476-4202

This, the largest travertine bridge in the world, reaches 183 feet high and spans 150 feet wide. After a rigorous hike down a series of stone-cut steps, climb over large, sometimes slippery boulders to cool off under the spray of water from above. Several clear cold-water pools are popular summer swimming spots. The bridge was discovered in 1877 by Dan McGowen, when he was being chased by Apaches.

The historic park lodge, built in 1927 by McGowen's nephew, has been restored and now houses park offices. In it you can see historic photos and original furnishings, and enjoy a nice gift shop. Be sure to wear sturdy tennis shoes or boots.

Details: *Open daily Apr–Oct 8–5, Nov–Mar 9–6. $5 per vehicle. (1–3 hours)*

★★★ MOGOLLON RIM ROAD
30 miles north of Payson on Highway 87 (Forest Road 300)

This 45-mile, two-lane gravel road is part of the old wagon trail built by General Crook in 1872. The **General George Crook National Recreation Trail** hugs the edge of the Mogollon Rim and provides spectacular views of the forests and valley below. You can picnic, hike, and camp among the towering pines and spruce accented by fields of lush fern and wildflowers. You'll likely see elk and deer—and maybe an occasional bear or mountain lion. Secluded mountain streams and lakes provide summer fishing. Check with the Payson Ranger District, 520/474-7900, for maps and details. The road is well maintained during summer, and you won't need four-wheel drive, but always ask about road conditions in case of rain or snow. It's not maintained in winter.

Details: (2–4 hours)

★★★ ROOSEVELT DAM
**Lake and Visitor Center, Highway 88, Roosevelt
520/467-3200**

Teddy Roosevelt was so enamored of the landscape in this part of Arizona that this 23-mile-long lake was named after him at its development in 1911. Roosevelt is the largest masonry dam of its type in the world, and all the necessary construction materials were hauled by wagon over the Apache Trail. Spanning 1,080 feet across the lake, the bridge is the longest two-lane, single span, steel-arch bridge in North America. The lake has 128 miles of shoreline for camping, swimming, fishing, and hiking. You'll find boat, Jet Ski, and water-ski rentals at the Roosevelt Lake Marina, 520/476-2245. The visitor center, 520/467-3200, is open daily from 7:45 to 4:30 and presents exhibits on the dam's construction and information about the importance of water.

★★ FOSSIL CREEK
Off Highway 87, Strawberry

If you like rockhounding or exploring remote locales, take a drive along Fossil Creek Road, a two-lane dirt road carved into the side of a steep mountain. Just don't look down! The road is well-maintained, but don't try it after a rain. At the bottom of this spectacular canyon is Fossil Creek, so named because of the fossils embedded in rocks along the creek. The stream is clear and cold, and if you hike along the creek you'll find a bigger pool great for a summer dip, complete with an old-fashioned rope swing. The biggest surprise of this pristine remote wilderness is the **Verde Hot Springs**, about a mile upstream from the point where Fossil Creek and the Verde River converge. It was originally the site of an exclusive 1920s resort, rumored to be a popular party spot during Prohibition. It burned down in 1962, leaving two natural hot tubs, one in a tiny stone building and one in the open air.

Details: Take Fossil Creek Road at Arizona's oldest school building, the Little Red Schoolhouse, in Strawberry. The pavements ends a few miles out of town. The dirt road eventually ties into paved FS 9. Turn east and you'll loop back to Strawberry. (half to full day)

★★ MUSEUM OF THE FOREST
700 Green Valley Parkway, Payson; 520/474-3483
A Zane Grey exhibit in this small museum includes old photos, posters of movies based on his books, and displays of his writing. You'll also find miniature farm equipment and an 1800s sawmill model.
Details: Open Wed–Sun noon–4. $1 admission. (30 minutes)

★★ TONTO CREEK FISH HATCHERY
Highway 260, 17 miles east of Payson; 520/478-4200
The hatchery grows trout to stock Arizona lakes and streams. You'll see them at all stages of growth. You can start a feeding frenzy by tossing in "trout food" from nearby vending machines. The accompanying visitor center presents exhibits on how fish are grown and information on the state's water recreation areas. This is a fun stop for kids and adults.
Details: Open daily 8–4. Free. (1 hour)

★ SHOOFLY RUINS
Highway 87, Payson
The Shoofly Village was occupied about 1,000 years ago, and all that remains today are the rock foundations of the 87-room structure. You can hike around the area and walk an interpretive trail explaining the site.
Details: Two miles north of Payson on Houston Mesa Road. Free. (30 minutes)

★ ZANE GREY MUSEUM
408 W. Main, Payson; 520/474-6243
If you're a fan of Western author Zane Grey, stop by this small museum. It contains information about Grey's life as well as collector editions of his (and others') Western books. Grey lived in a log cabin north of town when he wrote many of his famous novels. A few years ago, a devastating forest fire burned the cabin and its contents to the ground.
Details: Thu–Tue 10–5. Free. (30 minutes)

FITNESS AND RECREATION
Three national forests—Coconino, Tonto, and Apache-Sitgreaves—converge in the Mogollon Rim wilderness. Contact each national forest for lake and trail maps.

Several canyons north of the rim have been dammed to create fishing lakes. **Woods Canyon Lake** and **Willow Springs** are popular fishing spots with easy access, as are **Tonto Creek** and **Christopher Creek**, all of which are stocked with trout. The more remote **Chevlon Creek** and **Canyon Creek** allow lure and fly fishing only. More than six designated wilderness areas offer horseback riding, cross-country skiing, and mountain biking and hiking trails. **Horton Springs**, the headwaters of Horton Creek, is a popular hike. The trailhead is north of Kohl's Ranch at Upper Tonto Creek Campground.

For horseback riding, contact Don Donnelly Stables, 10 miles east of Payson on AZ 260, 520/478-4701, or O.K. Stables, 520/476-4303, on Highway 87 in Pine. The historic Strawberry Equestrian Park, 520/476-4363, also offers horseback rides. Rates start around $20 per hour. Or rent cross-country skis at **Forest Lakes Touring Center and Cabins**, 36 miles east of Payson on AZ 260, 520/535-4701. Maps and weather information are available from the Payson Ranger Station, 1009 E. Highway 20, 520/474-7900.

FOOD

You'll find lots of hardy restaurant choices in Rim Country. **Creekside Steakhouse and Tavern**, on Highway 260 in Christopher Creek, 520/478-4557, has a classic cowboy look. The log building nestled among the pines is a popular stop for breakfast, lunch, or dinner. Another reminder of the Old West is the dining room at **Kohl's Ranch Lodge**, on Highway 260, 800/331-5645, serving everything from burgers to seafood. If you're in Strawberry on Highway 87, eat at the **Strawberry Lodge**, 520/476-3333, a fixture for years. Try their homemade pies.

In Payson, the **Oaks Restaurant & Lounge**, 302 W. Main, 520/474-1929, is a nice place to dine. For Mexican food, **La Casa Pequena**, 911 S. Beeline Hwy. 520/474-6329, is good. If you're into browsing for antiques and crafts, have lunch at the **Heritage House Garden Tea Room**, 202 W. Main, 520/474-5501. It's set in a remodeled house and offers lots to look at. Be sure and sample one of the yummy deserts. There are also several chain and fast-food choices in Payson. If you want to belly up to an authentic Old West cowboy bar, stop by the **Oxbow Inn**, 607 W. Main, 520/474-8585, in Payson.

LODGING

The rim has several mountain retreats. **Kohl's Ranch Resort**, Highway 260, 17 miles east of Payson, 800/331-5645, was built over 50 years ago and was recently remodeled. Located on the banks of Christopher Creek, it's popular

PAYSON

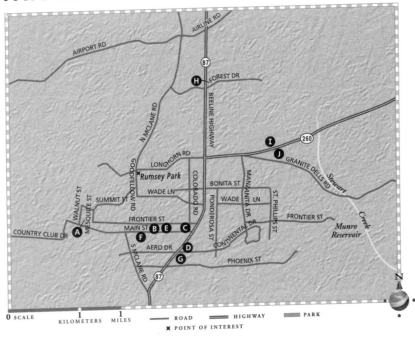

SIGHTS
- **A** Museum of the Forest
- **B** Zane Grey Museum

FOOD
- **C** Heritage House Garden Tea Room
- **D** La Casa Pequera
- **E** Oaks Restaurant & Lounge
- **F** Oxbow Inn

LODGING
- **G** Best Western Paysonglo Lodge
- **H** Inn of Payson
- **I** Majestic Mountain Inn
- **J** Payson Pueblo Inn

with Phoenix residents looking to escape the summer heat. Book reservations early. Peak rates for its rooms and cabins range from $95 to $205. Not far away, another five miles east on Highway 260, is the rustic **Christopher Creek Lodge**, 520/478-4300, in a charming location. Rates are $50 to $90. **Strawberry Lodge,** Hwy. 87 and Fossil Creek Rd., Strawberry, 520/476-3333, is an old but interesting mountain lodge.

Payson contains several good motels. **Best Western Paysonglo Lodge**, 1005 S. Beeline Hwy., 800/772-9766, is located near the Mazatzal Casino. **Payson Pueblo Inn**, 800/888-9828, and **Majestic Mountain Inn**, 800/408-2442, have nice rooms but neither has a pool. The **Inn of Payson**, 801 N. Beeline Hwy., 800/247-9477, with a restaurant and heated pool, was recently remodeled. These motel rooms range from $60 to $125.

CAMPING

The campgrounds along Highway 260 and the Mogollon Rim are popular summer sites. **Aspen** and **Spillway** have camping and RV sites near Wood's Canyon Lake. A grocery store and boat rentals are nearby. You'll often spot a deer or elk near your camp. **Christopher Creek** is another scenic spot. To get a space during summer, arrive by Thursday afternoon or early Friday morning. Reserve at 800/280-2267.

You can purchase detailed maps of national forests from each national forest headquarters or by contacting USDA Forest Service, Public Affairs Office, 517 Gold Avenue S.W., Albuquerque, NM 87102, 505/842-3292.

Near Roosevelt Lake is **Jakes Corner RV Park**, three miles south of Highway 87 on AZ 188, 520/474-4802. The **Cholla** and **Windy Hill Recreational Sites**, near Roosevelt Lake, are the largest solar-powered facilities in the world. Amenities include showers, kids' playgrounds, and a fabulous 360-degree view.

Apache Trail

The stories and legends surrounding the Apache Trail are as rich and varied as the magnificent scenery along the twisted, rugged road. The jagged ridges and towering cliffs are the result of violent volcanic eruptions spitting fire and chunky lava more than 20 million years ago. During the 1800s this was a raiding route for the Apache, and by the mid-nineteenth century came the legends of fabulous gold and silver mines that still persist today. From 1903 to 1905, the Apache Trail was carved out of the Superstition Wilderness to link the Phoenix area with Roosevelt Dam.

After crossing Roosevelt Dam and winding your way through a rocky canyon, you'll come to **Apache Lake**, set amid colorful sheer cliffs. It's popular for fishing, boating, and camping along the shoreline. The Apache Lake Marina, AZ 88, 520/467-2511, offers a motel, RV park, groceries, boat rentals, and fishing supplies. Next you'll cross the old road camp **Tortilla Flat**, 602/377-5638, which has an Old West restaurant, saloon, and general store that are open daily. Try some prickly pear ice cream. **Tortilla Flat Campground**, two miles from Canyon Lake Marina, 800/280-CAMP, has fabulous views with RV and campsites. Not far away is **Canyon Lake**.

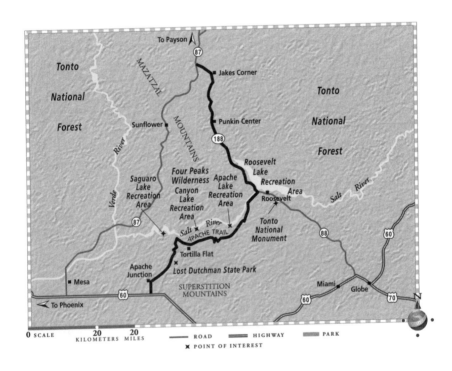

The most dangerous part of this journey is keeping your eyes on the road as it twists and turns while you're trying to look around at the spectacular landscape. The lake water below often takes on a deep emerald color, contrasted by the pinks and reds of the contorted canyon. Along the way, you'll find a marina, swimming beaches, boat launch, hiking trails, and campsites. Near Canyon Lake Marina you can take a 90-minute cruise around the shoreline on the reproduction paddlewheel **Dolly II** or a popular two-hour sunset dinner cruise. Call 480/827-9144 for further information. Rates range from $8 to $25.

As you traverse down the Apache Trail, you'll see the 7,645-foot **Four Peaks** in the distance. **Weaver's Needle Vista** provides a dramatic view of the stone spire that appears through a notch in the Superstitions. Supposedly Jacob Waltz, the old Dutchman who died without telling anyone the exact location of his fabled Lost Dutchman Mine, claimed it was in the shadow of the needle. Nearby, at the 300-acre **Lost Dutchman State Park**, 6109 N. Apache Trail, 480/982-4485, you'll see stands of saguaro cactus lining the Apache Trail. A native plant trail features mesquite, paloverde, ironwood, cholla, and prickly pear. There are campsites and picnic ramadas. Park entrance is $3 per vehicle, and camping is $8.

The **Goldfield Ghost Town**, four miles south of Apache Junction on AZ 88, 480/983-0333, is a fun stop for kids and adults. The original campsite was established in 1892 when gold was discovered nearby. You can tour an underground mine, shop, and ride the only narrow-gauge railroad train in the state. The ghost town is open daily 10 to 6, with fees for some exhibits and rides. The **Superstition Mountain/Lost Dutchman Museum**, 2151 W. Warner Rd., Apache Junction, 480/983-4888, has interesting geology and local history exhibits.

Apache Trail Tours, 480/982-7661, gives several Superstitions driving tours, from $50 to $100 per person, and hiking trips at $10 per person per hour. Superstition Riding Stables, 480/982-6353, offers one- to four-hour drives as well as overnight pack trips, picnics, and hayrides. OK Corral Horse Rentals, 480/982-4040, has one-hour rides for $17. For a truly spectacular view, Heliservices, at Goldfield Ghost Town, 480/830-9410, will give you a 12-minute helicopter tour for $39 or a 36-minute flight for $105. The Apache Trail ends at the town of Apache Junction.

To stay at the base of the Superstitions, consider **Gold Canyon Resort**, 6100 Kings Ranch, 800/624-6445, which has impressive mountain views and a top 18-hole golf course. This is a true resort setting with pool, spa, tennis courts, and two fine restaurants. Rates range from $150 to $230. Nearby is an older Spanish-style resort, the **Superstition Grand Hotel**, 201 W. Apache Trail, Apache Junction, 480/982-3500, that has hosted Elvis, Audie Murphy, and Ronald

Reagan. Kitchenettes and family units range from $95 to $110. The Western-style **Grand Steakhouse** serves breakfast, lunch, and dinner, with rates a more modest $65 to $75. Contact the Apache Junction Chamber of Commerce, 602/982-3141, for additional information.

APPENDIX

Consider this appendix your travel tool box. Use it along with the material in the Planning Your Trip chapter to craft the trip you want. Here are the tools you'll find inside:

Planning Map. Make copies of this map and plot out various trip possibilities. Once you've decided on your route, you can write it on the original map and refer to it as you're traveling.

Mileage Chart. This chart shows the driving distances (in miles) between various destinations throughout the state. Use it in conjunction with the Planning Map.

Special Interest Tours. If you'd like to plan a trip around a certain theme—such as nature, sports, or art—one of these tours may work for you.

Calendar of Events. Here you'll find a month-by-month listing of major area events.

Resources. This guide lists various regional chambers of commerce and visitors bureaus, state offices, bed-and-breakfast registries, and other useful sources of information.

PLANNING MAP: Arizona

ARIZONA
1. Phoenix
2. Sedona and Oak Creek Canyon
3. Gateway to the Grand Canyon
4. Grand Canyon
5. Arizona Canyonlands
6. Indian Country
7. White Mountains and Apache Country
8. Mining Middle Country
9. Cowboy Country
10. Southeastern Arizona
11. Southern Lands
12. Tucson
13. Southwest Corner: Yuma and Beyond
14. Arizona's West Coast
15. Central Arizona
16. Mogollon Rim

You have permission to photocopy this map.

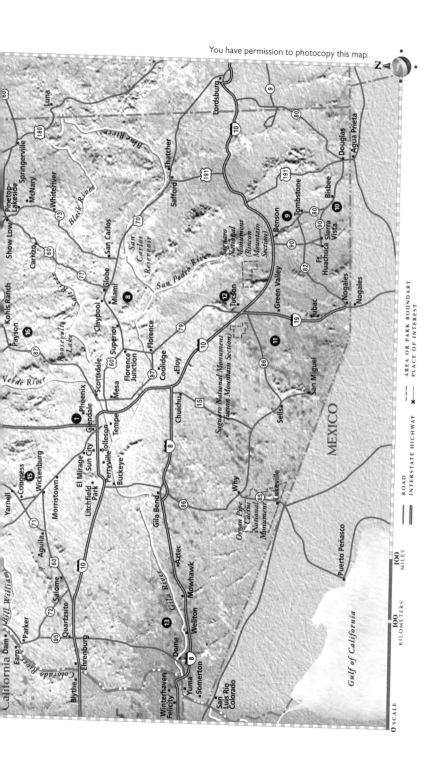

N

ROAD

INTERSTATE HIGHWAY

– – – AREA OR PARK BOUNDARY

★ PLACE OF INTEREST

0 SCALE

100
MILES

100
KILOMETERS

MEXICO

Gulf of California

California Dam ▪ Bill William

Colorado River

Earp▪ ▪Parker

Blythe▪

Ehrenburg▪

Quartzsite▪

Salone▪ 72

60

Aguila▪

Yarnell▪

Congress▪ 15

Wickenburg▪

Morristown▪

Litchfield
Park▪

El Mirage▪

Sun City▪

Perryville▪

Toleson▪

Buckeye▪

Gila Bend▪

86

Aztec▪

Mowhawk▪

Wellton▪

Dome▪ 13

8

Winterhaven
Felicity▪

Yuma▪

Somerton▪

San Luis Rio
Colorado

Luna▪

180

Springerville▪

Pinetop-
Lakeside

Show Low▪

McNary▪

Whiteriver▪

73

Carrizo▪ 60

Kohls Ranch▪

Payson▪ 16

87

Verde River

Roosevelt
Lake

77

San Carlos▪

Globe▪

Miami▪ 8

Claypool▪

Superior▪

60

Scottsdale▪

Mesa▪

Tempe▪

Phoenix▪ 1

Glendale▪

Florence
Junction▪

Coolidge▪

87

8

Chuichu▪

15

Why▪

Organ Pipe
Cactus
National
Monument

Lukeville▪ 85

Sells▪

San Miguel▪

86

Puerto Peñasco▪

Black River

Thatcher▪

Safford▪

191

San Pedro River

70

San
Carlos
Reservoir

Florence▪

79

Eloy▪

10

Saguaro National Monument
(Tucson Mountain Section)

Tucson▪ 12

11

Green Valley▪

Tubac▪

19

Nogales▪

Nogales▪

Lordsburg▪

9

80

10

470

Douglas▪

Agua Prieta▪

Bisbee▪ 10

Tombstone▪ 80

191

Benson▪ 9

Ft.
Huachuca▪

Sierra
Vista▪ 90

90

82

Saguaro
National
Monument
(Rincon
Mountain
Section)

ARIZONA MILEAGE CHART

	Bisbee	Flagstaff	Globe	Grand Canyon	Kingman	Nogales	Page	Payson	Phoenix	Prescott	Sedona	Show Low	Tombstone	Tuba City	Tucson
Flagstaff	351														
Globe	200	173													
Grand Canyon	431	81	254												
Kingman	391	143	273	170											
Nogales	89	320	169	401	360										
Page	487	136	309	137	279	456									
Payson	280	91	82	172	234	247	227								
Phoenix	205	146	87	226	186	175	282	93							
Prescott	307	87	189	126	144	276	228	190	102						
Sedona	325	28	142	108	171	294	164	86	119	60					
Show Low	287	139	87	220	282	256	275	90	174	228	175				
Tombstone	24	327	176	408	367	71	463	266	181	283	301	263			
Tuba City	430	79	254	79	222	399	77	170	225	161	107	218	406		
Tucson	94	257	106	338	297	63	393	183	111	213	230	193	70	336	
Yuma	334	307	271	316	216	303	446	277	184	218	288	348	310	380	240

SPECIAL INTEREST TOURS

With *Arizona Travel•Smart* you can plan a trip of any length—a one-day excursion, a getaway weekend, or a three-week vacation—around any special interest. To get you started, the following pages contain eight tours geared toward a variety of interests. For more information, refer to the chapters listed—chapter names are bolded and chapter numbers appear inside black bullets. You can follow a suggested itinerary in its entirety, or shorten, lengthen, or combine parts of each, depending on your starting and ending points.

Discuss alternative routes and schedules with your travel companions—it's a great way to have fun, even before you leave home. And remember: Don't hesitate to change your itinerary once you're on the road. Careful study and planning ahead of time will help you make informed decisions as you go, but spontaneity is the extra ingredient that will make your trip memorable.

NATURAL WONDERS TOUR

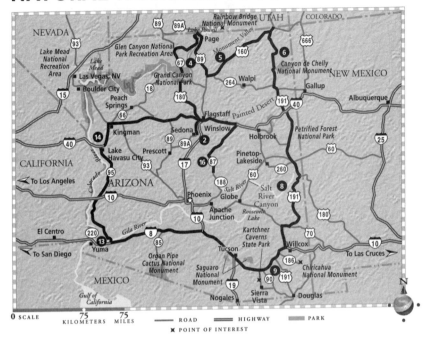

Arizona boasts some of the most scenic natural wonders in the world. Bring plenty of film for this spectacular tour.

❷ Sedona
❹ Grand Canyon
❺ Canyonlands (Rainbow National Monument)
❻ Indian Country (Canyon de Chelly, Monument Valley, Petrified Forest National Park)
❽ Mining Middle (Salt River Canyon)
❾ Cowboy Country (Chiricahua "Wonderland of Rocks," Kartchner Caverns)
⓭ Southwest Corner (Sand Dunes of the Colorado River)
⓮ West Coast (Havasu Canyon)
⓰ Mogollon Rim (Apache Trail)

Time needed: 2–3 weeks

BIRDING TOUR

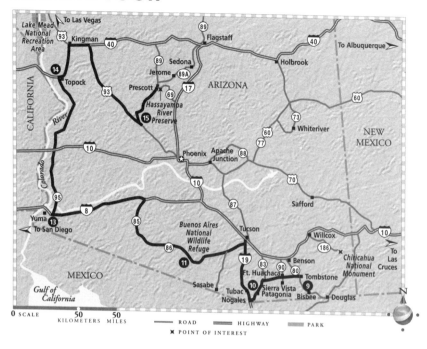

Arizona is a top spot for birding. You might see the rare elegant trogon or the Mexican spotted owl on this tour, along with many species of hummingbirds and flycatchers.

- **❾ Cowboy Country** (Cave Creek Canyon)
- **❿ Southeastern Arizona** (Garden Canyon, Patagonia-Sonoita Creek Preserve, Ramsey Canyon Preserve, San Pedro Riparian Area)
- **⓫ Southern Lands** (Buenos Aires National Wildlife Refuge, Madera Canyon)
- **⓭ Southwest Corner** (wildlife refuges)
- **⓮ West Coast** (Topock Gorge)
- **⓯ Central Arizona** (Hassayampa River Preserve)

Time needed: 1–2 weeks

ARCHAEOLOGICAL SITE TOUR

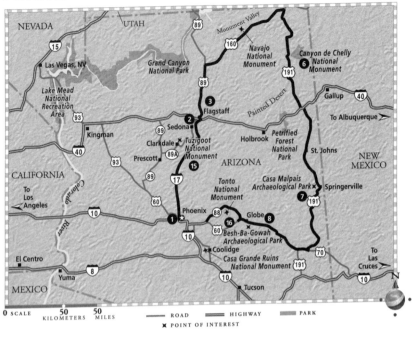

Centuries-old cliff dwellings offer a glimpse into the past. Several sites let you participate in ongoing excavations.

❶ **Phoenix** (Pueblo Grande Museum)
❷ **Sedona** (Montezuma Castle National Monument)
❸ **Flagstaff** (Walnut Canyon National Monument, Wupatki National Monument)
❻ **Indian Country** (Canyon de Chelly, Navajo National Monument)
❼ **White Mountains** (Casa Malpais Archaeological Park, Raven Site Ruin)
❽ **Mining Middle** (Besh-Ba Gowah Archaeological Park, Casa Grande Ruins National Monument)
⓯ **Central Arizona** (Tuzigoot National Monument)
⓰ **Mogollon Rim** (Tonto National Monument)

Time needed: 7–10 days

SKYWATCHING AND STAR-GAZING TOUR

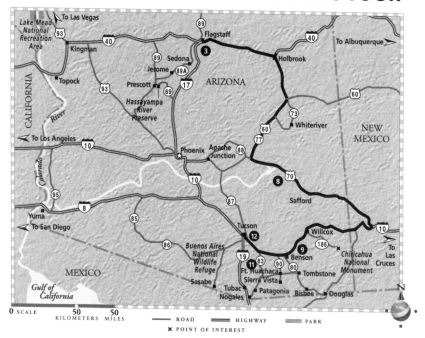

The world's largest telescope, the telescope that discovered Pluto, and others let you gaze into the cloudless desert skies.

❸ **Flagstaff** (Lowell Observatory)
❽ **Mining Middle** (Mount Graham Observatory, Discovery Park)
❾ **Cowboy Country** (Skywatcher's Inn)
⓫ **Southern Lands** (Kitt Peak Observatory, Fred L. Whipple Observatory)
⓬ **Tucson** (Flandrau Science Center and Planetarium)

Time needed: 1 week

ECO-EDUCATION TOUR

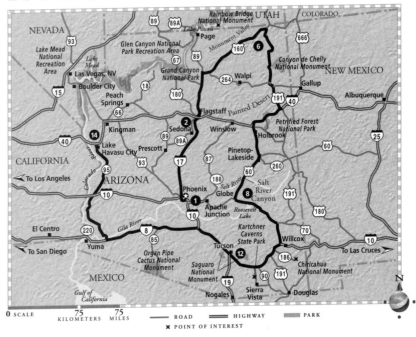

Learn more about the ecology of the Southwest—and enjoy stunning scenery in the process.

❶ **Phoenix** (Desert Botanical Garden)
❷ **Sedona** (Red Rock State Park)
❻ **Indian Country** (Hopiland)
❽ **Mining Middle** (Biosphere 2, Boyce Thompson Arboretum)
⓬ **Tucson** (Arizona-Sonoran Desert Museum, Organ Pipe Cactus National Monument, Saguaro National Park)
⓮ **West Coast** (Hoover Dam Tour)

Time needed: 1–2 weeks

BEST OF THE OLD WEST TOUR

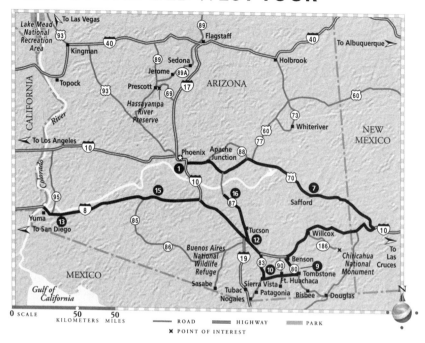

Saddle up, pardner! Arizona is Cowboy Country.

❶ **Phoenix** (Rawhide)
❼ **White Mountains** (Cattle drive at Sprucedale Ranch, Fort Apache Historic Park)
❾ **Cowboy Country** (Tombstone)
❿ **Southeastern Arizona** (Fort Huachuca Museum)
⓬ **Tucson** (Old Tucson Studios)
⓭ **Southwest Corner** (Yuma Territorial Prison State Park)
⓯ **Central Arizona** (rodeos, Vulture Gold Mine Tour)
⓰ **Mogollon Rim** (Goldfield Ghost Town, rodeos)

Time needed: 1–2 weeks

FAMILY FUN TOUR

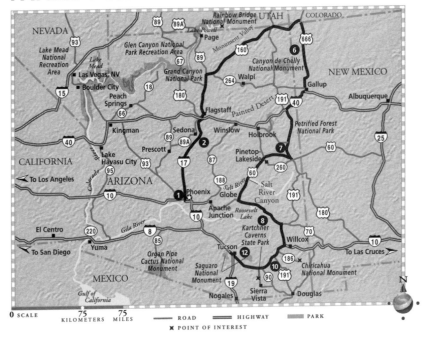

In both summer and winter, you'll find fun for all ages throughout the state.

❶ **Phoenix** (Arizona Science Center)
❷ **Sedona** (swimming at Slide Rock State Park, Verde Canyon Railway)
❻ **Indian Country** (Rock Art Canyon Ranch)
❼ **White Mountains** (skiing at Sunrise Park Resort)
❽ **Mining Middle** (Gila River float trip)
❿ **Southeastern Arizona** (Copper Queen Mine Tour)
⓬ **Tucson** (Sabino Canyon tram ride, Tucson Children's Museum)

Time needed: 7–10 days

ART AND CULTURE TOUR

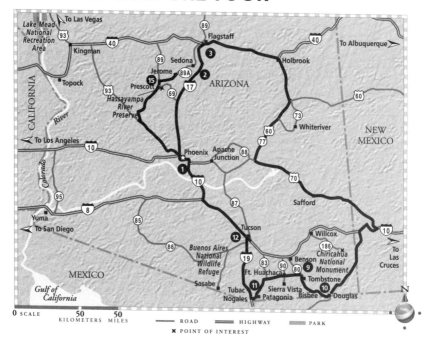

Arizona's cultural offerings are as diverse as its scenic beauty.

❶ Phoenix (Phoenix Art Museum, Heard Museum, Scottsdale Art Walk, Taliesin West)

❷ Sedona

❸ Flagstaff (Museum of Northern Arizona)

❾ Cowboy Country (Amerind Foundation Museum)

❿ Southeastern Arizona (Bisbee)

⓫ Southern Lands (Tubac)

⓬ Tucson (Center for Creative Photography, Tucson Museum of Art, historic walking tours)

⓯ Central Arizona (Desert Caballeros Western Museum, Jerome)

Time needed: 1–2 weeks

CALENDAR OF EVENTS

January

Fiesta Bowl Parade, Phoenix: More than 16 million television viewers watch this parade down Central Avenue, which is lined with over 300,000 spectators.

Fiesta Bowl Game, Tempe: One of the top college bowl games in the country, played in Sun Devil Stadium at Arizona State University

Wings Over Willcox, Willcox: Bird-watchers converge for this sandhill crane celebration, which includes guided tours, a "hawk stalk," and excursions.

Barrett-Jackson Auction, Scottsdale: More than 900 classic and collectible automobiles with a combined value of more than $100 million go on the auction block, luring bidders and spectators from around the globe.

Phoenix Open Golf Tournament, Scottsdale: Arizona's largest spectator event; held at the Tournament Players Club

Quartzsite Main Event, Quartzsite: From mid-January to mid-February, dealers sell gems, minerals, jewelry, and fossils. Festivities include camel and ostrich races.

Parada del Sol, Scottsdale: "The West's Most Western Town" hosts the world's longest horse-drawn parade. The event includes southwestern food, gunfights, western dances, and a rodeo.

February

Winterfest, Flagstaff: Sled-dog races, stargazing at Lowell Observatory, snow games, Nordic and alpine skiing, concerts, arts and crafts, and the Frozen Buns Fun Run

Renaissance Festival, Apache Junction: Hundreds of costumed participants re-create the atmosphere of a sixteenth-century "European Market Faire" with games, entertainment, food, and jousting.

Gem & Mineral Show, Tucson: The world's largest mineral, gem, lapidary, fossil, and rock show

Gold Rush Days, Wickenburg: Gold panning, mucking, and drilling contests, a rodeo, parade, and arts and crafts

O'odham Tash, Casa Grande: Indian ceremonial dances, a powwow, all-Indian rodeo, chicken-scratch dances, and Native American arts and crafts

Arabian Horse Show, Scottsdale: Two thousand horses from all over the world compete here.

La Fiesta De Los Vaqueros, Tucson: This outdoor PRCA rodeo features the world's longest non-motorized parade.

Lost Dutchman Days, Apache Junction: Commemorates the Legend of the Lost Dutchman Mine and area history. Activities include a rodeo, parade, entertainment, gold panning, and a modern-day gold rush.

March

Heard Museum Guild Indian Fair and Market, Phoenix: More than 300 juried Native American artists sell fine art and crafts. You can also enjoy a variety of Native American music, dance, and foods and watch the championship Hoop Dance contest.

International Film Festival, Sedona: International independent films, emerging Asian cinema, and panel discussions with leading film professionals

Indy Racing League 200, Phoenix: Headliners like Mario Andretti, Al Unser Jr., Rick Mears, and Danny Sullivan test the world's fastest one-mile oval at speeds of more than 170 miles per hour.

Ostrich Festival, Chandler: Ostrich racing is the highlight. Other events include live entertainment, a parade, collectibles and auto shows, and a petting zoo.

Civil War Battle Re-enactment, Picacho Peak: Costumed soldiers re-enact Arizona's only Civil War battle. Period demonstrations include candlemaking, sewing, and cooking.

Spring Festival of the Arts, Tempe: More than 450 artists, traditional and ethnic foods, entertainment, and a special area for children

April

The Tradition at Desert Mountain, Scottsdale: One of four major championships on the Senior PGA tour

Festival of the Southwest, Sierra Vista: This arts-and-crafts and music festival includes a popular marathon across the Mule Mountains and the San Pedro Valley.

Waila Festival, Tucson: Waila is the social dance music of the Tohono O'odham Indian nation. Artisans sell their wares, and outdoor booths offer ethnic foods including squash and cheese, popovers, and tepary beans.

International Mariachi Conference, Tucson: Performances, music and dance workshops, a parade, and art exhibit

Route 66 Fun Run Weekend, Seligman to Topock: Car rally, car show 'n' shine, street dance, Miss Route 66 Pageant, and '50s-style dinner-dance

Country Thunder USA, Queen Creek: Outdoor festival featuring more than 20 major country recording stars like LeAnn Rimes, Clint Black, and Chris LeDoux. You'll find lots of food, arts and crafts, and plenty of campsites.

May

Tucson Folk Festival, Tucson: Folk performances, workshops, gospel programs, and a children's show

Lake Havasu Striper Derby, Lake Havasu City: The largest two-person tournament of its kind in the West, with $50,000 in prizes

Paseo de Casas, Jerome: Tour homes and historic buildings, from turn-of-the-century Victorians to renovated miner shacks.

George Phippen Memorial Day Western Art Show and Sale, Prescott: This juried outdoor western art show and sale features 125 artists, a popular "Quick Draw," and an auction.

Wyatt Earp Days, Tombstone: Crowds line the dirt streets to see gunfights, saloon girls, and a parade. There's lots of music and a chili cook-off.

Herb Festival at Boyce Thompson Arboretum, Superior: Tour the herb gardens, sample herb oils and vinegar, and learn how to grow and harvest your own herbs.

Bill Williams Rendezvous, Williams: This fun event commemorates the Mountain Men's annual trek to town and features black-powder shoots, frontier crafts and workshops, barn dances, a shoot-out, stage shows, and pig races.

Cinco de Mayo Celebrations, various locations. Communities throughout the state celebrate Cinco de Mayo (May 5) with festivals and fairs.

June

National Trails Day Celebration, Show Low: Guided hikes, guided mountain biking, horseback riding, and live entertainment

Folk Arts Fair, Prescott: The Sharlot Hall Museum hosts demonstrations of traditional arts such as quilting, woodcarving, spinning, weaving and candle-making. There are games, hands-on crafts, food, and music.

Old West Celebration and Bucket of Blood Races, Holbrook: Races include a 10K and two-mile fun run and a 20-mile bike ride from the Petrified Forest National Park. Other highlights are arts and crafts, food, music, and a Route 66 car and truck show.

Territorial Days, Prescott: Arts and crafts, food, games for the kids, old-time photos, and entertainment

Cowboy Golf on the Range, Springerville/Eager/Greer: Golf is played on horseback on the open range. Other highlights are a steak fry, the Ben Johnson Memorial Charity Golf Tournament, and a western art show and sale.

Astronomy Festival, Sedona: Red Rock State Park hosts lectures, workshops, viewing, and astrophotography with shared telescopes. The giant Astro-Platform, the new solar telescope, is also available.

July

Frontier Days and World's Oldest Rodeo, Prescott: A rodeo, parade, fireworks, entertainment, softball tournament, carnival, and Old West melodramas

Railhead Cowboy Shooting Competition and Encampment, Williams: Competitors dressed in 1880s costumes use period reproduction or vintage guns. "Settler's Row" features merchants in period clothing.

Native American Dances, Holbrook: From July 1 to mid-August, you can watch and learn a variety of authentic Native American dances.

Jazz Rhythm & Blues Festival, Flagstaff: Local, regional, and national jazz artists perform.

Pioneer Days, St. Johns: For the 119th year, this festival features old-time storytelling, a musical pageant, dances, a campfire circle, and two rodeos.

Native American Art Festival & Indian Market, Pinetop/Lakeside: Native American arts and crafts; performances by dancers, storytellers, and musicians representing Navajo, Hopi, Apache, Zuni and other tribes

August

Vigilante Days, Tombstone: Cowboy shootouts, mock hangings, saloon girls, country music, and a chili cook-off

Southwest Wings Birding Festival, Sierra Vista: Sierra Vista is the hummingbird capital of the United States. Activities include field trips, lectures, Bat Stalks, Owl Prowls, displays, and crafts.

Cowboy Poets Gathering, Prescott: Working cowboys gather to recite poetry and sing. Sessions include old-time singing, songwriting, cowboy yodeling, and traditional and contemporary cowboy poetry.

White Mountain Bluegrass Music Festival, Pinetop/Lakeside: Top bluegrass bands from the Southwest, gospel music, and jam sessions

World's Oldest Continuous Rodeo, Payson: Bull riding, calf roping, barrel racing, arts, crafts, and food

Fiesta De San Agustin, Tucson: The city's oldest festival honors Tucson's patron saint and the founding of the Presidio of Tucson in 1775.

September

Navajo Nation Fair, Window Rock: The largest Indian fair in the world features arts and crafts, exhibits, horse racing, rodeo, traditional song and dance, a fry-bread contest, and an exciting powwow.

White Mountain Apache Tribal Fair and Rodeo, Whiteriver: All-Indian rodeo with concerts, a parade, carnival exhibits, and a Crown-Dance competition

Chamber Music Festival, Grand Canyon: Evening concerts feature musicians from around the country—from jazz to classical

Harvesting of the Vine Festival, Elgin: Wine samples, seminars, and lots of music and dancing

Fall Festival, Pinetop/Lakeside: "Run to the Pines" car show, dog show, antiques, parade, fair, 10K race, fishing derby, music, and arts and crafts

State Championship Old Time Fiddler's Contest, Payson: Fiddlers compete for the title of State Champion and the right to go to the National Championship. The festival includes storytellers, an old-time dress contest, cloggers, and food and craft booths.

Jazz on the Rocks, Sedona: Performances and jam sessions

October

Rex Allen Days, Willcox: Cowboy movie star and singer Rex Allen is honored by his hometown with a parade, golf tournament, PRCA rodeo, concerts, cowboy dances, and an art show and sale.

Rodeo Showdown, Phoenix: Top rodeo athletes compete in this PRCA-sanctioned event. Top country entertainment, shopping, and great food are other highlights.

London Bridge Days, Lake Havasu City: Events include an English costume contest, music, a parade, and the English "Quit Rent Ceremony" as the city commemorates the moving of the bridge from the Thames River in London to the Colorado River.

La Fiesta De Los Chiles, Tucson: You can taste chile dishes from around the world and can purchase fresh chiles, ristras, and ornamental and edible chile plants.

Apache Jii Day, Globe: The famous Apache Crown Dancers delight crowds, who also enjoy Native American food, arts, crafts, and a fashion show.

Dia de Los Muertos Festival, Phoenix: The Day of the Dead is a traditional Mexican holiday for honoring ancestors. Activities at the Phoenix Heard Museum's festival feature arts, crafts, a mercado, music, dance, and food.

November

Thunderbird Balloon Classic, Scottsdale: More than 150 colorful hot-air balloons fill the skies during two days of air shows, crafts, and entertainment.

Fountain Festival of Arts & Crafts, Fountain Hills: More than 400 artists compete for cash awards and ribbons.

El Tour de Tucson, Tucson: At 110 miles, this is the largest perimeter bicycling event in the United States. There are also 75-, 50-, and 25-mile categories.

December

Fall Festival of the Arts, Tempe: More than 500 artists and craftspeople, ethnic and traditional food, entertainment, and Kidspace, a popular children's area

Festival of Lights Boat Parade, Lake Powell: Boats decorated as "floating Christmas trees" glide across Lake Powell. Day festivities include food and music.

Indian Market, Phoenix: Seven hundred Native American artisans from 70 tribes sell their wares at South Mountain Park Activity Center. Festivities include tribal singers, dancers, and cuisine, including fry bread and chili.

Football Bowl Game, Tucson: America's newest post-season collegiate bowl game includes the Copper Bowl, a million-dollar hole-in-one shoot-out, golf and tennis tournaments, a parade, and a pep rally.

Red Rock Fantasy of Lights, Sedona: More than one million lights shine in 60 displays at Los Abrigados Resort. Crowds also enjoy horse-drawn surrey rides, caroling, craft-making, guided tours, and a visit from Santa.

New Year's Eve Block Party, Tempe: Tempe officially welcomes the two Fiesta Bowl teams at this giant party that features food, rides, fireworks, music, and a pep rally with marching bands and cheerleading squads.

RESOURCES

Arizona Office of Tourism, 2702 North Third Street, Suite 4015, Phoenix, AZ 85004; 888/520-3444; www.arizonaguide.com

Arizona Association of Bed & Breakfasts, P.O. Box 36656, Tucson, AZ 85740; 520/887-4247

Arizona Dude Ranch Association, 34901 North Highway 89, Wickenburg, AZ 85390; 520/684-7811

Arizona Nature Conservancy, 300 East University Boulevard, Suite 230, Tucson, AZ 85705-7899; 520/622-3861

Arizona State Parks, 1300 West Washington, Phoenix, AZ 85004; 602/542-4174; www.pr.state.as.us

Bureau of Land Management, 222 North Central Avenue, Phoenix, AZ 85004-2203; 602/417-9422

Campsite Information, 800/280-CAMP

Flagstaff Convention and Visitors Bureau, 211 West Aspen Avenue, Flagstaff, AZ 86001; 520/779-7611

Globe/Miami Chamber of Commerce, 1360 North Broad Street, Globe, AZ 85501; 800/804-5623

Grand Canyon Chamber of Commerce, P.O. Box 3007, Grand Canyon, AZ 86023; 520/638-2901

Hopi Office of Public Relations, P.O. Box 123, Kykotsmovi, AZ 86039; 520/734-2441

Lake Havasu City Visitor and Convention Bureau, 1930 Mesquite Avenue #3, Lake Havasu City, AZ 86403; 800/242-8278

National Forest Service, for maps and brochures of each area:
Apache-Sitgreaves, 520/333-4301
Coconino, 520/527-3600
Coronado, 520/670-4552
Kaibab, 520/635-2681
Prescott, 520/445-1762
Tonto, 602/225-5200

National Park Service, 3115 North Third Avenue #101, Phoenix, AZ 85013; 602/640-5250

Navajo Nation Tourism Department, P.O. Box 663, Window Rock, AZ 85615; 520/871-6659

Page/Lake Powell Chamber of Commerce, 106 South Lake Powell Boulevard, Page, AZ 86040; 520/645-2741

Payson Chamber of Commerce, 100 West Main Street, P.O. Box 1380, Payson, AZ 85547; 800/6-PAYSON

Phoenix Convention and Visitors Bureau, 400 East Van Buren, Suite 600, Phoenix, AZ 85004; 602/254-6500

Pinetop/Lakeside Chamber of Commerce, 592 West White Mountain Boulevard, Lakeside, AZ 85929; 520/367-4290.

Prescott Chamber of Commerce, 117 West Goodwin, Prescott, AZ 86302; 800/266-7534

Scottsdale Chamber of Commerce, 7343 Scottsdale Mall, Scottsdale, AZ 85251; 800/877-1117

Sedona/Oak Creek Canyon Chamber of Commerce, P.O. Box 478, Sedona, AZ 86336; 800/288-7336

Tombstone Chamber of Commerce and Visitor Center, P.O. Box 995, Tombstone, AZ 85638; 520/457-9317

Tucson Convention and Visitors Bureau, 130 South Scott Avenue, Tucson, AZ 85701; 800/638-8350

Wickenburg Chamber of Commerce, 215 North Frontier Street, Wickenburg, AZ 85358; 800/WICKCHAMBER

Yuma Convention Bureau and Chamber of Commerce, 488 South Maiden Lane, Yuma, AZ 85366; 800/293-0071

INDEX

Map Index

You'll Feel like a Local When You Travel with Guides from John Muir Publications

CITY·SMART™ GUIDEBOOKS

Pick one for your favorite city: *Albuquerque, Anchorage, Austin, Calgary, Charlotte, Chicago, Cincinnati, Cleveland, Denver, Indianapolis, Kansas City, Memphis, Milwaukee, Minneapolis/St. Paul, Nashville, Pittsburgh, Portland, Richmond, Salt Lake City, San Antonio, St. Louis, Tampa/ St. Petersburg, Tucson*

Guides for kids 6 to 10 years old about what to do, where to go, and how to have fun in: *Atlanta, Austin, Boston, Chicago, Cleveland, Denver, Indianapolis, Kansas City, Miami, Milwaukee, Minneapolis/St. Paul, Nashville, Portland, San Francisco, Seattle, Washington D.C.*

TRAVEL✦SMART®

Trip planners with select recommendations to: *Alaska, American Southwest, Carolinas, Colorado, Deep South, Eastern Canada, Florida Gulf Coast, Hawaii, Illinois/Indiana, Kentucky/Tennessee, Maryland/Delaware, Michigan, Minnesota/Wisconsin, Montana/Wyoming/Idaho, New England, New Mexico, New York State, Northern California, Ohio, Pacific Northwest, Pennsylvania/New Jersey, South Florida and the Keys, Southern California, Texas, Utah, Virginias, Western Canada*

Rick Steves' GUIDES

See *Europe Through the Back Door* and take along guides to: *France, Belgium & the Netherlands; Germany, Austria & Switzerland; Great Britain & Ireland; Italy; Russia & the Baltics; Scandinavia; Spain & Portugal; London; Paris;* or the Best of Europe

ADVENTURES IN NATURE

Plan your next adventure in: *Alaska, Belize, Caribbean, Costa Rica, Guatemala, Honduras, Mexico*

JMP travel guides are available at your favorite bookstores. For a FREE catalog or to place a mail order, call: 800-888-7504.

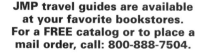
John Muir Publications ✦ P.O. Box 613 ✦ Santa Fe, NM 87504

TAMARA HAWKINSON

ABOUT THE AUTHOR

Tamara Logsdon Hawkinson grew up in the small mountain community of Payson, Arizona. She counts among her friends many of the old ranching families who settled the rough area.

Tamara, her husband, Jim, and their three children now live in Scottsdale, Arizona. Her historical and travel articles have been published in magazines and newspapers throughout the West. Tamara is a frequent contributor to *Persimmon Hill*, published by the National Cowboy Hall of Fame, and her articles have won numerous awards. She is a member of Western Writers of America, Women Writing the West, and Arizona Press Women.